SELLING AND DESIGNING
PARTY FLOWERS

Selling and Designing Party Flowers

teleflora®

Selling and Designing Party Flowers

Second Edition

© Copyright 1993
by Teleflora
Paragould, Arkansas

First edition published 1992

Library of Congress Catalog Card Number: 93-83788
International Standard Book Number: 1-56963-009-7

Printed by:
Teleflora
Leachville, Arkansas

Other textbooks in Teleflora's Encycloflora™ series:

Purchasing and Handling Fresh Flowers and Foliage

Basic Floral Design

Green and Blooming Plants

Retail Flower Shop Operation

Visual Merchandising for the Retail Florist

Marketing and Promoting Floral Products

Floral Design for the Holidays

Designing with Balloons and Flowers

Selling and Designing Wedding Flowers

Selling and Designing Sympathy Flowers

Advanced Floral Design

Acknowledgments

*T*eleflora gives special thanks to the individuals who participated in the creation and development of this comprehensive floral training manual.

Frances Porterfield, AAF	Topeka, KS
Terry Lanker, M.Ed.	Wooster, OH
Richard Paul Salvaggio, AIFD, AAF, PFCI	Los Angeles, CA
Chuck Greif, AIFD	Stamford, CT
Nancy Kitchen, AIFD	Rahway, NJ
Holly Money-Collins, AIFD	San Francisco, CA
Dianne Noland, M.S.	Urbana, IL
Frankie Shelton, AIFD, AAF, PFCI	Houston, TX
Fay Weinstein, AIFD	Hillsdale, NJ
Gary Wells, AIFD	Kentwood, MI

Please note that Redbook Florist Services has been acquired by Teleflora effective June 9, 1997. All references made in this publication to Redbook and Redbook Florist Services are transferred to Teleflora.

Contents

CONTENTS

ix

Appendices

Preface

Selling and Designing Party Flowers has been prepared for the individual who seeks knowledge and professionalism in the floral industry as specifically related to party work.

The book is a pool of comprehensive information regarding planning, organizing, managing, and designing floral decorations for parties and special occasions. The marketing and promotion of party services, the development of party themes, and the use of party props are discussed in detail. Instructions for creating unique party decorations for indoor and outdoor events are also included, along with ideas for one-of-a-kind table settings. A special chapter on balloon decorations also provides step-by-step procedures for creating large balloon structures.

Many of the methods, ideas, and conclusions presented in this book were drawn from the combined professional and personal experiences of a select group of retail florists and floral industry professionals. Information drawn from other sources has been noted.

Selling and Designing Party Flowers has been written for use as a reference and training manual and will prove valuable to professionals at all levels of expertise and in many branches of the floral industry. The concise text contains suggestions for improving party sales and specific instructions for creating both common and unique party floral designs. Illustrations for the design techniques described are also included.

Lıst of Illustrations

List of Illustrations

List of Illustrations

List of Illustrations

List of Tables

Introduction

The party business is an ever-expanding source of revenue for retail florists. The number of special events and social occasions requiring floral decorations seems to be continually on the rise. Undoubtedly, there are some areas, particularly large cities, where party work is more heavily concentrated. Parties in these areas are frequently large-scale events. However, in towns of every size, there are corporate banquets, mayoral dinner parties, golden anniversaries, and other special functions that call for creative and decorative floral touches.

Party flowers can be as simple as a single mass arrangement in the foyer of a home or as elaborate as an outdoor affair with extensive tent decorations and pool floats at a country club. The florist may simply design and deliver the decorations or may be highly involved in planning and setting up the details of the event including color schemes, floor plans, menus, table types, invitations, and entertainment, as well as floral and other decorations.

In order to establish a strong party business, the florist must market his or her services to the appropriate clientele. Awareness of the social, political, corporate, and community functions in a specific area is a key to targeting promotional efforts aimed at increasing a shop's party business. Traditional promotional efforts, such as radio and Yellow Pages advertising, are less effective than direct marketing approaches aimed at selected groups.

Once the florist has reached the client through promotional efforts, he must be able to sell the products and services of the floral shop convincingly and profitably. Numerous consultations may be necessary to determine the client's needs and the appropriate decorations to fit the party site and theme. A diverse range of innovative design ideas should be offered in order to give the customer a choice.

Many floral shops have branched out into the party business to offer a myriad of specialty products in addition to flowers. Linens are one product line that many party floral shops now offer. Prop rentals, including candelabras, champagne fountains, statues, tents, and even tables and chairs, are frequently offered by some large-scale party florists. Customized paper products, including printed invitations, maps, napkins, and matches, are commonly offered by party florists. Special party favors for guests to take home are also sold as add-ons to the flower order. A tremendous amount of planning and organization must be devoted to party preparation. Flowers must be ordered; props must be cleaned, serviced or constructed; work schedules must be coordinated; and ultimately the decorations must be designed and installed in an efficient and professional manner. Visiting the party site in advance will help the florist plan for unexpected problems or challenges. Working with the facility manager, caterer, or party planner is essential to a well organized installation, as well as teardown.

Theme parties are becoming increasingly popular. Florists are often asked to design decorations to suit specific themes based on holidays, seasons, geographic regions, countries, movies, or other carefully selected and highly original titles. Some themes dictate elegant or romantic decorations, while others inspire flowers which are playful and fun. Successful party florists must be adept at creating floral decorations that reflect the desired mood and atmosphere regardless of the party theme.

Decoration choices for parties run the gamut from standard centerpieces to complete table settings to stage and dance floor accents to special ceiling treatments and even elaborate chandelier enhancements. For outdoor parties, decorations may include tent, pool, and gazebo accents, as well as temporary "gardens" created out-of-season, using fresh cut flowers in concealed containers.

Balloons are popular atmosphere-enhancers for indoor or outdoor use. Arches, columns, figures, and other structures made of balloons can fill a space quickly and less expensively than flowers. When combined with flowers, however, the use of balloons is doubly effective. Blooming and foliage plants are another excellent option for filling space at low cost. Plants, which are typically rented rather than sold to the client, can be used individually, or in clusters, islands or hedges to provide a spot of color, a neutral backdrop, a directional pathway, or a frame for a focal point within the party setting.

Introduction

Parties require a great investment of time and energy by the florist to ensure the professionalism of each job. Florists who desire to enter or expand this special floral market must be committed to, and derive satisfaction from, dealing with party clients of all kinds. Every party is unique and the florist must strive to create decorations that are well suited to the occasion in order to ensure that even the simplest of parties is an *event*.

Marketing and Promotion

*P*arty work or special event services can be very challenging and stimulating for florists. The events, whether anniversary or birthday parties, banquets, bar mitzvahs, conventions, or receptions, are happy, fun occasions. Many interesting people will be encountered, providing an opportunity to showcase the florist's talents to a wide variety of individuals. Professional growth and satisfaction often result from the successful creation of floral decorations with original themes for a variety of events.

Marketing party work services is essential for florists to be successful in such a venture. Florists must assess the market needs, the employee talent available, and the pros and cons of party work. Determining the kind of parties to target is also important. In this chapter, ideas for advertising and promoting a florist as someone who specializes in planning parties and special events are detailed.

Assess the Market

Is there an untapped potential for the florist's services as a party planner? The potential for party work can be assessed by discussing the idea with other professionals, such as caterers; restaurant managers; event managers for hotels, country clubs, civic centers, and reception halls; and event planners for convention centers. The number of parties or banquets that are currently being planned in the area and the revenue potential should be determined. It should also be determined which florists are currently involved in party work. Finding out who their customers are, if they are pleased with the florist's services, and how loyal they are to a potential florist would also be beneficial.

To assist in evaluating the market potential, the motels, hotels, convention centers, community or civic centers, country clubs,

5

churches, or halls and current event activities should be listed in a chart similar to the one below.

	Location	Estimated # Events/Week	Avg. $/Event	% of Events Expect to Attract
		Market Potential Chart		
1.				
2.				
3.				
4.				
5.				

From these estimates, the revenue potential can be determined. A targeted client base should also be determined and strategies devised to attract the potential customers. Brainstorming with employees for other potential party work sources can be beneficial.

Pros and Cons of Party Work

Before beginning a large scale venture into party work, both the potential and the pitfalls of party work should be considered. A non-exhaustive discussion of the positive and negatives of professional party planning and implementation follows.

Positive Aspects of Party Work

• Party work provides florists with the opportunity to be creative and innovative.

• Party events are happy, upbeat occasions, which are usually held in attractive, possibly elegant, settings.

• Party services allow florists to display their skills to a large number or varied groups of people at one time.

• Party work often results in referrals and new clients.

• The potential for financial gain from party work is a positive factor.

Notes

- In regard to party design work, parties may feature large, creative, or artistic pieces, as well as incorporating special props and effects.

- Party work provides florists with the challenge and opportunity of creating an illusion, an overall theme, or a memory picture.

- Large events often enable florists to purchase in bulk and to receive price breaks.

- Party work often results in tremendous professional satisfaction when an event is successfully completed.

Negative Aspects of Party Work

- Party work demands a continually high level of creativity.

- Clients are often very demanding.

- Party work often requires fast-paced work and long hours, especially on weekends.

- A significant investment of time, effort, and resources must be made, possibly for an insufficient return.

- In some cases, there may be non-payment or delinquent payment for services rendered.

- Design work may be repetitive, and a lack of design space may be an inconvenience when designing numbers of centerpieces.

- Flower substitution when ordering can cause design challenges.

- Props for party work may be complicated and/or time consuming to construct. Lack of storage for props can be a problem, and the cost of acquiring storage space may be expensive.

- Delivery mishaps are a possibility.

- Setting up party work can be hectic and rushed, due to the lateness of prior events.

- "Burn out" sometimes occurs among staff when too many events are scheduled too close together.

Employee Talent Assessment

If party work is going to be emphasized in a shop, the florist has to critically and objectively analyze the skill strengths and weaknesses of the shop personnel, including the owner and manager, as well as shop employees. The staff's qualifications in the following areas should be considered.

- Floral experience of 5 years or more

- Party work experience

- A flair for party design

- Willingness to work on weekends

- Design style expertise

- "Big picture" people versus "detail" people

The shop's style, whether it is middle market or high end, must be determined based on the design style or expertise and training of the staff. This key fact will assist in identifying the target market.

The talents required to stage memorable parties include planning and selling skills, designing and buying skills, organizational expertise, scheduling and staffing skills, and a high level of creativity, as well as practicality and common sense. One person, such as the owner or manager, may possess all of these skills; however, these specific areas may also be divided among several key people who function as a team. Several people may have expertise in the same area and can be utilized alternately, depending upon the work load. Key shop personnel who could fill the skill areas required for successful parties should be charted on a party work personnel worksheet, such as the one in Appendix A. Management can provide for training by targeting a promising, yet inexperienced employee to learn the skill by accompanying an experienced employee through the day. For example, the novice could be introduced to the selling process by witnessing the successful selling technique of the employee who is most skilled in that area.

Marketing Ideas

After assessing the party work market and the employees' party work skills, the decision should be made about which market to target and how to begin attracting that clientele. Depending upon the potential in the area, many strategies, ranging from simple to elaborate, can be utilized to attract party work customers.

Referrals

Word of mouth is the most valuable advertising vehicle for party work. A satisfied customer and his guests, who are also potential party givers, are a valuable resource in obtaining additional work for special events and parties.

For a big party that other party-givers are likely to attend, pieces should be designed for maximum impact. A large focal point piece should be designed and carried through on a smaller scale in the centerpieces. Making a big statement and designing memorable, exciting settings assists greatly in securing favorable referrals.

Excellent service should be emphasized during the consultation and in the weeks prior to each event. Accessibility to the client for questions is very reassuring; therefore, a professional and friendly demeanor should be maintained. Through professional communication and service, a rapport can be developed with each client.

A follow-up call should be made to the client to express appreciation for his patronage and to ask for a referral. Following is a sample conversation that could be used when calling a client.

"Hi! This is Floral Fantastics! We loved doing your party and want to thank you for the business. Did everything go well?"

Through positive wording and an upbeat manner, individuals can be led to respond positively.

In closing, a referral can be requested in the following manner.

"Oh, I'm so glad that everything went well and that you were pleased. I am trying to build my clientele. Please tell others about us and our party work services. Thanks again."

Printed Materials

The shop's party work expertise should be marketed in print. Business cards and brochures promoting the shop's party work services can be very beneficial.

Business Cards

Business cards that highlight the party work side of the business can be printed. The target market should be considered when designing such cards. For understated elegance, a white embossed business card with an antiqued ribbon accent might be chosen. *(Figure 1.1a)* For an elegant look, a business card of hand-torn parchment would be ideal. *(Figure 1.1b)* For an all occasion, middle market style of party business card, there are several options. *(Figure 1.1c)*

Brochures

A brochure can provide a detailed description of a florist's party work services. The full range of a shop's party services, as well as any unique specialties, can be included. *(Figure 1.2)*

Professional ads that are effective and eye-catching should be carefully examined and adapted for a party work brochure. Various formats and/or folds can be experimented with to determine the most appropriate design. A simple format could be a single fold vertical or horizontal format. *(Figure 1.3a on page 11)* However, to add more text and photos to the brochure, two or three folds can also be used. *(Figure 1.3b on page 11)* A diagonal fold or triangular fold brochure can attract a great deal of attention. *(Figures 1.3c and 1.3d on page 11)*

The style of brochure chosen should represent the shop's image. A single color or color combination should be chosen to enhance the brochure's appearance and to draw attention to the text. An eye-catching format for the front page of the brochure is

Figure 1.1a   Example of a Business Card

Figure 1.1b   Example of a Business Card

Figure 1.1c   Example of a Business Card

Floral Fantastics
Party Services

Services Available

• Planning/Consultations
• Delivery
• Setup

Types of Rental Items

• Props
• Candelabra
• Columns
• **and much, much more!**

Figure 1.2   Example of Wording for Brochure

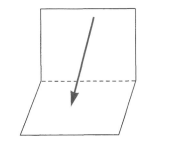

Figure 1.3a Sample Brochure Formats
- Single Fold

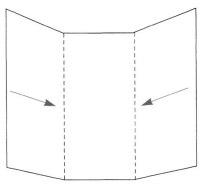

Figure 1.3b Sample Brochure Formats
- Double Fold

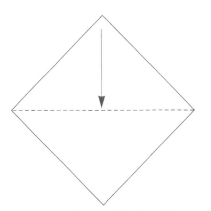

Figure 1.3c Sample Brochure Formats
- Diagonal Fold

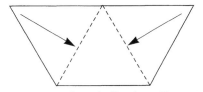

Figure 1.3d Sample Brochure Formats
- Triangular Fold

the spiral. *(Figure 1.3e on page 12)* The brochure can be as elaborate as the budget allows. Photos and drawings can be added to help the clients visualize the services provided.

Once party work materials are printed, they should be widely distributed to potential customers. Brochures and business cards can also be mailed as direct mail pieces, enclosed with monthly statements, included with a delivered floral item, handed out to walk-in customers, and prominently displayed on the display counter with a sign encouraging customers to take one.

Phone Numbers

The shop's party services can be highlighted with a "party" phone number. Following are examples of fun phone numbers.

XXP-ARTY
GO PARTY
HAVE FUN
FUN-TIME
XXX-XFUN
XXX-4FUN

An initial advertising campaign could involve radio ads featuring the phone number against the background sounds of a great party complete with noisemakers, clinking champagne glasses, or children's laughing voices. The ads should target the appropriate audience or there should be several ads, each focusing on a slightly different type of audience or party service.

Yellow Pages

The party phone number should prominently appear in the Yellow Pages, as well as in all of the shop's advertisements in the phone directory. A catchy phone number will be more easily remembered and used than a regular number. Drawings or photos of party designs can also be featured in the Yellow Pages. Likewise, event and party planning should be highlighted in the text of the advertisement.

Window Display

A party window display can be used to call attention to the shop's party work expertise. The window display can show examples of the creativity of a shop's designers. Examples of small, medium, and large-scale events should also be provided.

For a small "Sweet 16" party, the window display might feature a small round table with a balloon design as a centerpiece. Pink colors with lots of ribbon and three heart-shaped balloons would be especially appropriate. Small bouquets of flowers with trailing ribbons can be tied to the back of each chair. *(Figure 1.4)*

For a medium-scale display that is somewhat more elaborate, a 50th anniversary theme might be chosen. *(Figure 1.5)* The theme should be carried out in golds, yellows, and whites. A large round table covered with a white tablecloth could be set up and covered with a square gold tablecloth or gold mylar. To symbolize wedding bands, two round wreath rings or hula-hoops can be covered with gold metallic foil or mylar. The two rings can be attached to a two-tier floral centerpiece of yellow lilies, white open roses, and trailing greenery, such as sprengeri fern. If the table is large enough, a punch bowl and cups, and possibly even a mock cake with yellow, gold, and white floral decorations, can be displayed. Spotlights can be used to effectively accent the golds.

For a large-scale window display, a tropical paradise theme can be chosen. *(Figure 1.6)* A setting of three palm trees with a small pool at the base could be constructed and arrangements of tropical flowers placed near the edge of the pool. Using a patio table with an umbrella, a floral centerpiece can be created with a foliage garland loosely wrapped around the umbrella pole connecting it to the second design attached at the top. Bright, tropical flowers and foliage should be selected for the arrangements, and colorful tableware and beach towels could be used as props. Sand on the floor is an option. Leis and business cards could be handed out to walk-in customers in conjunction with the window display. This theme could also be repeated at an actual event held at a country club, convention center, or wedding hall.

A shop's party work business cards or brochures should be prominently displayed near window displays. Signage with messages, such as "The Fun Florist Can Create Your Moment," or "Party Work Specialists," can also be used to convey the availability of party services.

In-Store Displays

The attention of prospective clients can be captured with a creative, fun in-store party display. A small area, such as a corner, a shelving unit, or a table, should be selected to introduce clever party decorations or theme ideas. The display should be changed frequently to promote new interest.

Figure 1.3e   Sample Brochure Format

Figure 1.4   Window Display for "Sweet 16" Party

Figure 1.5   Window Display for 50th Wedding Anniversary

Figure 1.6   Window Display for Tropical Paradise Theme

Notes

Bright, eye-catching signs can be used to direct attention to in-store displays. Signs, such as the examples listed here, should enhance in-store displays.

Let's Party!!
Party Idea of the Month
Enhance Your Entertaining with Ender's Florist's Ideas!
Flowers and Fun!
Featuring our Party Work Service

Employees should be asked to contribute ideas for fun and timely party themes for displays. A schedule and budget for the displays could be devised and employees assigned responsibility for specific displays and/or months.

Following are ideas for party displays that would be appropriate throughout the year.

New Year	House Warming
Chinese New Year	Big Promotion
Spring Fling	Kids Away for Summer Camp
Circus Days	Dancin' and Romancin'
Bridal Shower	Football Frenzy
Prom Time	Cocktail Hour
Graduation	Anything Goes
New Driver's License	Fall Frolic
Summer Barbecue	The Witching Hour
Birthday Bash	Kris Kringle

The display ideas and implementation should be kept simple and creative. With varied and constantly changing in-store displays, interest in party services will be created.

Special In-Store Events

Excitement about the professional party services that a florist supplies can be created through special in-store events. In-store events allow florists to use visual aids to display their work.

Open House

A special open house during which customers can view the professional and varied types of party and event planning offered in a shop could be held. A time that will not be extremely busy with holiday or wedding work should be chosen. Special engraved invitations should be sent to both current and potential customers, as well as business contacts in related areas, such as catering managers, convention center managers, and event planners for civic centers and halls.

A fun atmosphere with an attention-getting entryway, such as a trellised garden walk or a forest lit with sparkling white lights, should be created. The shop itself could be decorated with a variety of party ideas. An appropriate traffic flow route should be established from one party table or scene to the next. If the overall space is large enough, the guests could be allowed to mingle freely from table to table and area to area.

The number of themes or ideas to be portrayed should be determined and carried out effectively. A good variety will showcase the shop's creativity and flexibility. A futuristic theme, a jazz theme, a garden tea party, and a sports theme would provide variety and ideas for guests.

Providing a party favor with an attached business card or brochure for each guest is a good idea. Of course, beverage and hors d'oeuvre tables can be attractively and creatively decorated to provide guests with ideas, as well as refreshments.

Other examples of the shop's party expertise could be featured through visual media, such as the shop's party portfolio, slides, or an endless loop video. Slides, photos, and videos of the highest quality should always be shown. Visual media of poorer quality will reflect unfavorably on the florist's professionalism and quality of service.

Decorating the Delivery Vehicle

The delivery vehicle is a very visible marketing tool. It should be used to promote the party work services to the public.

The shop logo on the vehicle can be embellished to call attention to the shop's party services. An additional line could be painted on the vehicle, such as

For tons of fun at your next party, call us!

or

For that perfect event, it's Floral Fantastics!

Depending upon the target audience, the logo could have other features added to it to proclaim that this shop is a party work florist. Ideas include streamers, confetti, and noisemakers, or an

Notes

elegant floral design next to a candelabra. Decals or painted additions can easily be added. Magnetic decals or signs are also very flexible and can easily be added or removed as needed.

For a bold, more eye-catching approach, a three-dimensional flower entwined with streamers can be added to the top of the vehicle. These figures can be custom made out of fiberglass by sign-making companies who specialize in forming and attaching advertising items to vehicles. Other ideas include a floral candelabra and flowers and balloons.

Benefits and Galas

Florists who do party work may find that the business created by designing beautiful pieces for benefits or galas is well worth the time and expense. Often, the agreement will be to provide floral pieces in exchange for the exposure and the free advertising in the program. When participating in such an event, a florist should be sure that no other florist is providing floral pieces for the event or the effect will be diluted. Some florists contribute their time and design expertise only (the flowers are provided) for one big party each year.

Other galas in which to consider involvement are auctions, such as a Festival of Trees. Florists and others decorate a Christmas tree to auction for raising funds for worthwhile events or charities. Showcases of homes, museums, or artwork are other worthwhile events to build clientele. Although these events are not parties, these galas or showcases are events that are often attended by individuals who frequently give parties. Participation in these happenings helps in gaining name recognition for the florist and helps build a good networking with other professionals.

The benefits of the florist's involvement in any benefit, gala, or showcase should be weighed to determine if the proper audience will be reached by participating in the event. The expected numbers of people; the organization(s) involved; the type of advertising; the success of past events, if they have been held before; and the details of the event, such as setup, access time, duration, and take-down, should be identified before a florist agrees to participate in such an event.

Networking

Networking with other allied professionals in the party field is valuable for building additional business. Florists should court business people, such as caterers; hotel and site event planners;

managers at restaurants, halls, or convention centers; and party supply people, to encourage them to help sell parties. Florists can personally visit the site to discuss the shop's party expertise. The following day, a floral design could be sent to provide a sample of the shop's work. On a follow-up visit, a commission should be negotiated and the shop's business cards placed in a prominent place at the site. Correspondence may also be sent, including the shop's brochure and business cards. The value of networking should never be underestimated. Building good contacts and rapport with others in the party planning field can prove to be profitable.

Party work can be a creative, successful, and profitable venture if planning and marketing are emphasized. Market needs, revenue potential, and available employee talents are all important considerations, as are the potential benefits versus the pitfalls of the party work business. There are many ways to market and promote a shop's party work expertise. Florists who implement the strategies described in this chapter will be well on their way to successful party business.

Notes, Photographs, Sketches, etc.

Notes, Photographs, Sketches, etc.

Marketing and Promotion

Notes, Photographs, Sketches, etc.

Selling

*T*he process of selling party flowers is similar to selling flowers for weddings. Consultations are needed to determine the customer's needs and preferences. Site visitation may also be necessary to determine appropriate decoration styles and colors. Proposals and contracts are required to ensure agreement on the goods and services to be provided and the prices and payment policies expected. Add-on sales, such as printed napkins and invitations, are suggested where appropriate to increase profits.

Although the selling process is similar, party clients have somewhat different floral needs than wedding clients. Party clients typically fall into one of two categories: corporate or social. Corporate clients include the wide range of large and small businesses that require decorations for luncheons, banquets, conventions, annual stockholders meetings, company picnics, and other business events. Social clients include private individuals, as well as social organizations, who are planning dinner dances, anniversary parties, fund-raisers, or other social gatherings. The needs of each of these types of clients varies considerably with the type, size, and budget of the party being planned.

This chapter provides information on selling parties of all sizes to clients of all kinds. The consultation process is discussed in detail, as well as important issues regarding proposals and contracts. Recommended add-on sales items that are appropriate for sale by retail florists are described to assist florists in maximizing party profits. A sample party planner is provided in Appendix A for use in working with clients to plan the ultimate party setting.

Consultation

The party consultation is the heart of the selling process. It is important for the florist to make appointments for party consultations and to set aside the time required to discuss the client's needs. The consultation area must be located in a part of the shop that is conducive to private conversation. An organized order form or party planner should be used to record the details of the event. Open communication is a necessity, and the skilled party consultant will lead the client through a logical sequence of discussion points.

Making Appointments

Appointments should be made for consultations with party clients. Whether a client inquires in person or over the telephone, only basic party information should be discussed until the party consultant can devote his undivided attention to the customer. At the time an inquiry is made about party flowers, the florist should first check his calendar of upcoming events and make sure the date is open. It may be necessary for the florist to ask preliminary questions regarding the scale of the party in order to determine if he can commit to an event on a date when other parties or weddings are scheduled.

When setting up the consultation appointment, a minimum of one hour should be allotted. Many florists prefer to set appointments for late afternoon or evening hours when the shop is quieter. A follow-up phone call or postcard is useful to remind the client of the appointment date and time. The customer should be asked to bring any available sample items that will help establish the look of the party. Invitations, linens, and floor plans are examples of items that often prove useful. Basic information about the party, including the location, theme, color scheme, formality, and number of guests, should be asked at the time the appointment is made so that the florist may prepare some general ideas in advance. Prior to the consultation appointment, the florist should refer to the site file (see Chapter 3) to determine specific requirements of the party facility. A visit to the location to conduct a site analysis (see Chapter 3) might also be necessary to be adequately prepared for the consultation.

Consultation Area

In most floral shops, party consultations are conducted in the same area as wedding consultations. Ultimately, this is in a private room or office, free from distracting shop noise and activity. Sometimes a quiet corner in the sales area is used for consultations. Whatever area is chosen, it should be furnished

Notes

Notes

with a comfortable table and chairs that will accommodate a minimum of three persons. (When planning large functions, it is common for two or three party clients/coordinators to attend a consultation together.) Commonly used party props may be located within the consultation area if space allows. Samples of specialty items offered by the shop, including linens, invitations, and favors, should be readily available. All of the necessary items for conducting the consultation should be neatly assembled on the table or stored in a desk or cabinet. These items should include the site file (see Chapter 3), a photo album of party decorations designed by the shop, order forms, sketch pads, pens and colored pencils or markers, a telephone (with the ringer turned off to prevent interruptions), telephone book, and calculator. Refreshments, such as coffee, tea, or soda, might also be available. Festive, theme-oriented decorations may be used to accent the consultation area and display the florist's diverse design abilities. The key is to incorporate all of these elements into the available space without creating a cluttered look.

Consultation Sequence

The sequence of the party consultation should be logical and orderly. It should allow the florist to collect the information needed to formulate suitable design/decoration ideas. An order form or party planner, such as the sample provided in Appendix A, is helpful for keeping the florist on track and the consultation flowing smoothly. The consultation should be an open exchange of information and ideas; however, the florist should maintain control of the discussion in order to keep from getting sidetracked or bogged down in unnecessary details.

When beginning the consultation, general party information should be collected first. Some of this information may have been gathered when the consultation appointment was made. If so, this information should already be recorded on the order form. While gathering this general information, the client might be encouraged to look at the shop's party photo album or other idea books. A series of fact-finding questions, such as the following, will help the florist collect the basic information needed.

Fact-Finding Questions:

- *"What is the date of the party?"*

- *"Where will the party be held?"*

- *"What time will the party be held?"*

- *"How many guests will be attending?"*

- *"Is there a theme?"*

- *"Is there a color scheme?"*

- *"Is this a formal, semiformal, or casual affair?"*

- *"How many tables will be used for meals, cocktails, other?"*

- *"What size and shape will the tables be?"*

- *"What type of food, beverages, and entertainment are planned?"*

Once the basic information has been collected, a discussion of the client's decoration needs and preferences should follow. The florist might use the following question starters to gauge the client's feelings about the overall party style, as well as the decorations.

Question Starters:

- *"What style of party do you wish to hold?"*

- *"What impression do you want guests to have when they enter the party site?"*

- *"How do you feel about . . .?"*

- *"What do you like best about . . .?"*

- *"How important is that to you?"*

- *"What is your biggest concern regarding . . .?"*

- *"What would you like your party to achieve?"*

Once the fact-finding and information-gathering questions have been asked, the florist should begin sharing conceptual ideas regarding the look of the party. Discussion should revolve around the total party setting before keying in on specific areas. Once the florist and client have agreed on a general theme or concept, details can be determined.

There are two ways to begin discussing specific details. The florist can start with the party entrance, considering ideas for decoration of the parking area, doorways, coat check station, place card table, and so on, then moving to areas around the perimeter of the room, including walls, ceilings, stages, bandstands, dance floors, bars, windows, chandeliers, and even rest rooms. Finally, the florist should discuss individual table decorations, including guest tables, cocktail tables, buffet tables, and head tables. It is believed that this sequence of discussion results in a larger total flower order because clients are often focused on table flowers and are reluctant to add significantly to their order once these flowers are totalled. By saving the table flowers for the end, the client can be encouraged to order other extraneous decorations before the budget is depleted.

This sequence of discussion is not always comfortable for the client or the florist, however, since the style of the table design frequently sets the tone for the rest of the decorations. The alternative sequence, then, is the reverse. Guest tables would be discussed first, followed by head tables, buffet tables, and cocktail tables. Room decorations would be considered next, and, as the budget allows, exterior decorations, such as entrances, rest rooms, and parking areas, would be considered last.

Since much of the emphasis of the consultation revolves around the table centerpieces, the florist will likely find it helpful to show sample table setups using colorful linens and decorative accessories. An effective sales technique is to present at least two or three ideas in two or three price ranges each. This gives the client a choice and helps stay within his budget. An ordinary table setting can be progressively enhanced to help the client understand the difference between less and more expensive design concepts. The client can then see what adding extra dollars to the budget will add to the visual appeal of the designs.

Throughout the selling process, it is important to keep the budget in mind. One of the most difficult tasks in planning a special event is to stay within the budget. It is easy to enhance the decorations with more flowers than the price allows, thus diluting profits. The most difficult cost to determine is labor, because it is difficult to calculate how much time each job is going to take. Many shops have a set cost for installation and removal of party decorations. This charge is based on what day the function is held (usually higher for Sundays and holidays), difficulty of installation and removal, and the time involved in creating decorations on site.

For small parties, a single consultation may be sufficient to gather the needed details and reach an agreement regarding design ideas and price. For larger parties, the first consultation will likely result in a detailed list of decoration needs, flower and color preferences, room dimensions, and budget estimates. From this information, the florist will develop a party proposal and present specific ideas in a second consultation. The appointment for this consultation may be set up at the completion of the first or when the florist has completed preparation of the written proposal.

Proposals

Once a florist has completed the initial consultation and obtained the necessary information, he is ready to prepare a detailed proposal of the goods and services the shop can provide for the client's party. If a site analysis has not been conducted by this point, and the florist is not familiar with the party facility, he should visit the location before proceeding. Even if the florist has designed decorations at a given site in the past, it is a good idea to discuss plans and potential problems with the caterer or facility manager before presenting the client with an impossible proposal.

Proposals may be written in a variety of formats. Typically, they include a detailed description of the designs, props, and other decorations to be used in the different areas of the party site, along with prices. Sketches or photographs of proposed designs might also be included. Services to be provided and accompanying charges are also outlined and the total cost of the party listed.

Whenever possible, the party proposal should be presented in person so that the florist can explain his ideas and answer questions. A second consultation appointment is usually set up for this purpose. The second consultation should include presentations of table linens, napkins, floral decorations, props, accessories, and favors, as appropriate. Story boards are one of the most impressive methods of presenting a proposal at the second consultation. The story board is a board that is designed for an attractive presentation of the party. The board is usually made of foam board (approximately 18 inches by 24 inches) and is embellished in an attractive manner that will visually show the overall look of the party. This is achieved by making a collage of the invitations, napkins, ribbons, color scheme, and favors. This

Notes

story board helps sell the idea, look, and theme to the client. The professional presentation of story boards is often the difference between closing the sale or losing it to another shop.

Contracts

When the client accepts a party proposal, the florist should be prepared to have him sign a contract outlining not only the goods and services to be provided, but also the schedule for installation and removal, rental agreements, deposit requirements, and payment policies. The contract should be thorough and state all responsibilities of the florist and client. Additional charges that the client may incur for last-minute add-ons should be listed, along with cut-off dates for changes or cancellation.

Deposits and payment policies vary from shop to shop; however, a substantial deposit is usually required. This can range from 50 percent to 100 percent of the total order. Many shops require that a deposit of 50 percent of the total cost be paid 30 days prior to the party. This deposit is often 100 percent refundable until flowers, props, or accessories have been ordered. (This can be anywhere from 2 to 6 weeks before the party.) The balance of the order must usually be paid at least 2 weeks prior to the event and is nonrefundable. A sample party contract with common inclusions is provided in Appendix B.

Add-On Sales and Services

When a retail florist is providing flowers and decorations for parties, it provides an opportunity to expand sales and services that are not normally part of the florist's product line. For example, the florist may have the opportunity to provide printed materials, such as invitations and place cards. While the florist is working with the client, suggestions for some of the extras can be made. If the florist is going to provide such products and services, he needs to be familiar with the possibilities and have a network of sources and information established. Subcontracting can be a useful method of providing many of these services. (A sample subcontracting agreement is provided in Appendix B.) Rather than telling a client that a particular product or service is not available, the florist should have a list of people to call to provide the services the client desires. Following is a variety of add-on party sales and services that can be sold by the florist or subcontracted to other firms.

Printed Materials and Paper Goods

For many parties, there are needs for some type of printed materials, if nothing more than the invitations. This is an area in which the retail florists can become involved with relatively little effort. There are commercially available catalogs from which the florist can have clients choose from an array of available materials. These books have preestablished prices and minimums. All the florist need do is take the order and send it in to the printer. However, the florist can also choose to help design the invitations. The invitations can then be taken to a commercial artist for conceptualizing and printing.

Invitations

Invitations can be printed for any party, including graduation, 25th and 50th anniversary, and retirement. Invitations can include lined envelopes, printed outer envelopes, and envelope seals. Some may also include response cards and maps. (See Appendix C.)

- *Lined envelopes* - These are available with many different lining colors that will enhance the color and design of the invitations. (See Appendix C.)

- *Printed outer envelopes* - The printer can print the return address on all of the envelopes, assuring that all invitations that are not deliverable will be returned. This will also save the client the time required to hand write the return address on all the envelopes.

- *Envelope seals* - These add an elegant touch to the invitations and are available in a variety of colors and styles. (See Appendix C.)

- *Response cards* - These are the cards that the guests fill out and return so the client knows how many people to plan for. (See Appendix C.)

- *Map cards* - Map cards are included with the invitations when the client needs to communicate with the guests how to reach the party. (See Appendix C.)

Whenever invitations are being ordered, it should be ensured that the client proofreads and signs a sample of all products

Notes

ordered. This eliminates the florist's liability if there are misspelled words.

Thank You Notes

Thank you notes can be ordered to match invitations. These can be used to thank guests for attending the party and/or for gifts. (See Appendix C.)

Place Cards

Place cards can be ordered with the same theme as the invitations. These cards are used to assign guests to certain tables. This may be done by positioning a place card with a guest's name at each place setting or by lining up place cards with table numbers in alphabetical order on a table near the entrance. The second method also requires that table number markers be used on each table. The florist can accent the place cards by placing a ribbon or silk flower in the corner. (See Appendix C.)

Menus and Programs

Menus and programs may be laid on each plate, rolled into a scroll, tied with ribbon and placed above each plate or passed out at the entrance. These can also be decorated in the same theme as the invitations. The florist can accent these with a ribbon to match or a fresh or silk flower. (See Appendix C.)

Matches, Coasters, and Napkins

These utilitarian items are appropriate for certain types of parties and can be ordered in the same theme as the invitations. These are usually placed on the tables before the guests arrive or stationed on or near bars and food tables. (See Appendix C.)

Linens

The florist can also provide all the linens for a party without a great outlay of capital. Linen companies will rent tablecloths and napkins. They can provide the florist with a color card that has the sizes and swatches of the fabrics and colors available, along with the prices for each item. Some florists that do a considerable amount of party work prefer to buy their own stock of table linens for multiple rental uses. Chapter 7 provides additional information regarding the creative use of many types of table linens.

Napkins folded in a variety of ways can be provided by the florist. (See Chapter 7 for folding techniques.) These can be done ahead of time by shop staff or subcontracted to other businesses when large quantities are required. The florist should also consider selling double napkins, consisting of two napkins often of different sizes, and/or colors, which are folded, rolled, or tied decoratively. One napkin is used for dinner; the other is used for dessert.

Napkin rings can also be provided by the florist. They can be easily and inexpensively made with plastic floral tape rings covered with ribbons and fresh or silk flowers. The florist might also suggest a coordinating garnish of fresh or silk blossoms on the dinner or dessert plates.

Favors

Party favors are a popular add-on sale item. Many clients like the idea of giving guests a small memento to take home. Favors are usually somewhat simple and inexpensive. The florist might suggest a miniature vase with a single blossom for each place setting, a small blooming plant wrapped in foil, or a gift bag with nuts and candies, to name just a few. The favor does not have to be a floral item in order to be sold by the florist. Instead, the florist can use his creative abilities to package nearly any item to complement specific themes.

Escort Board

A decorative escort board can be designed by the florist and sold as a party add-on for clients who want a more formal system of communicating seat assignments to guests. Foam board can be used as a base with ribbons and floral accents decorating the border. A diagram of the floor plan with table numbers and seat assignments is included. Escorts dressed in appropriate formal attire (perhaps tuxedos) greet guests as they arrive, find their seat assignments, and escort them to their tables. The florist might provide only the board itself (propped on an easel) or, for an additional fee, provide the escort personnel as well.

Costumes

The florist might also suggest dressing the valet parking attendants and the waiters in costumes appropriate for the theme of the party. For instance, if the theme is a "Hoe Down," all the waiters and parking attendants would wear appropriate attire and the florist would provide everyone with a straw hat and a red kerchief. If the theme is an "Evening in Paris," everyone involved in serving the guests might wear a beret.

Depending on the theme of the party, the florist might also suggest having all the guests park at a certain location other than the party site and then transport them together in a special way to the location of the party. Again, if the party theme is country, all the guests could be transported in a haywagon.

Luminarias

Luminarias, often thought of as special outdoor Christmas decorations, add atmosphere to the entrance of a party location. Luminarias are typically paper lunch sacks with an inch of sand in the base for stability and a votive candle in the center, which provide a soft glow of light for hours when lit. Sometimes more decorative bags in festive colors and with theme-oriented cutouts are used for this purpose. In either case, the bags are usually lined up along sidewalks and driveways to create a luminous pathway. Depending on when the party starts, they can be lit at the beginning or the end of the party. If the florist has completed the setup hours before the party is to start, a parking attendant or someone else working at the party may be assigned the task of lighting the luminarias just before the guests arrive. Clients must be made to understand that this is a nonrefundable service. The florist will provide luminarias, but there is no refund if they cannot be used due to bad weather.

Custom Balloon Imprinting

The opportunity may arise for the retail florist to provide custom imprinted balloons for a client. This can be a relatively easy service to provide. The florist should contact a balloon distributor and become familiar with that company's policies regarding custom imprinting. In general, almost anything can be printed on latex or mylar balloons. Congratulatory messages, company names, and party themes are commonly used. The client needs to provide the florist with camera-ready artwork or a drawing of what is desired. If there is no camera-ready artwork available, the drawing will have to be sent to a typesetter to have it made camera-ready. The artwork is then sent to the balloon distributor. They will then send the order to a balloon manufacturer where a plate will be made from the artwork. (There is a charge up-front for the plate, but this can be reused, if desired.) The balloons are then imprinted with this plate.

One drawback to custom imprinting is that there are usually minimum orders that may make it prohibitive for small parties. However, each distributor has different minimums and policies. The florist should be familiar with the different services and policies of the balloon distributors in his area.

Guest Room Favors

Some parties attract many out-of-town guests that will be staying in hotels. Another add-on sale for the florist could be providing guest room favors. This can be as simple as a bud vase, a small fruit basket, or a mixed basket with candies and flowers. The favor does not always have to be floral related. It could include information on local attractions packed nicely in a gift bag with candy or bubble bath. When this service is being provided, it is important to coordinate it with the hotel so that the favors are placed in the rooms before the guests arrive.

Calligraphy

Calligraphy is a service that the retail florist can provide relatively easily. Calligraphy can be offered for addressing invitations, place cards, table numbers, and signage. This service can best be covered by subcontracting with a free-lance artist. A listing can usually be found in the Yellow Pages or by contacting the art department of a local college. Rates among artists vary. They may charge by the envelope, by the line, or by the word. The florist should become familiar with the quality and availability of these services before offering them to clients.

Limousine Services

Limousine services can be an easy additional sale for the party florist. Limousine services are usually contracted on an hourly rate with a usual 2 to 3 hour minimum. The florist can provide the service with the advantage of offering a floral decoration either inside or outside the limousine or both. Since few, if any, florists own limousines, this service is typically subcontracted to local companies.

Special Effects

There are many special effects that can be offered to enhance the overall effect of a party. These can be offered by the florist;

however, the florist needs to be aware of the availability of the effects from local sources. When renting special effects, it should be kept in mind that there is usually a deposit and that the customer needs to be aware that he is responsible for any damage or theft. Following is a list of possible special effects for use at parties.

- Fog machines

- Bubble machines

- Rainbow machines

- Black lighting

- Laser lighting

- Strobe lighting

Next Day Deliveries

Occasionally, a client may wonder what to do with the floral decorations after the party. The florist can suggest that these designs be delivered to area nursing homes or hospitals. As an add-on service, for a nominal fee, the florist can make arrangements for the pickup and delivery of the flowers.

Selling parties and special events requires specialized selling techniques, the ability to pay attention to details, preparation, and follow-through. To become a successful party florist, one must be an excellent communicator, a thorough fact finder, and a skilled problem solver. Planning a party from beginning to end and delivering the promised goods will ensure a happy client. Preparing complete proposals, realistic price estimates, and fair contracts will ensure the florist of smooth and profitable events. Interjecting specialized add-ons throughout the consultation will help boost the total order and increase revenue. The key is to create a look that pleases the customer and excites the party guests. Satisfied clients are repeat customers and the best advertisement for future functions with future clients.

Notes, Photographs, Sketches, etc.

Selling

Notes, Photographs, Sketches, etc.

Planning and Organization

*P*rofessional party servicing is more complex than simply knowing the correct location and time of an event. Construction and delivery of floral party products can entail a considerable amount of detailed steps, requiring months of work by numerous employees. Time and labor are two of the most crucial determinants of profit; therefore, special event work must be carefully orchestrated. Waiting until the "last minute" to order merchandise, hire needed employees, or rent additional delivery vehicles is an invitation to disaster.

Florists who wish to develop party business should familiarize themselves with local sites. They should not only be familiar with the areas within a site that will allow for marketable decorations, they should also know the best method of entry and delivery. Knowing how to plan for the purchase of materials, maintain prop inventories, and efficiently produce and deliver party pieces is essential to operating a successful party business.

This chapter explains methods of maintaining control in a manner that will minimize confusion and maximize shop profit when servicing parties. Appendix A contains many sample charts and checklists for use with party work, which are an extension of this chapter.

Planning for Purchase and Construction

During the selling process, a proposal or contract will have been accepted by the client. This may be written in very specific or in vague language. It will catalogue the varied floral pieces and custom work that the florist is expected to provide. For example, perhaps the client has simply asked that all the flowers be pink. Although having this in the proposal is enough to satisfy the request, it would not be sufficient information to allow for proper professional planning. Exact details must be formulated by the florist during or immediately following the consultation.

Immediately after the party sale has been made, detailed planning should be done. Sample floral arrangements may have been made for the consultation or they may now be made for the florist's own reference. Photos taken at this time will be invaluable later. A sketch of each type of finished product should be made, along with a description of the construction elements. *(Figure 3.1)* From the sketches, a list of specific ingredients will be formulated. Since each type of arrangement will be reproduced a number of times for the party, a materials list will tell the designers exactly what types of products and how much should be used in each design. This information will be taken from the sketch and filled into a production chart similar to the one in Appendix A. The production chart specifies exactly what will be used, how long it will take to make the design, and how far in advance it may be completed. Completing a production chart makes it easy for the florist to delegate the work. It tells, in writing, exactly how to reproduce the arrangements for the party. It also eliminates the designer's temptation to add additional merchandise at will.

In the production chart in Appendix A, the manner in which the design segments are broken down to make design time and purchasing information clear should be noted. As each type of party piece is sketched and charted, the party purchasing form and the party production calendar, both in Appendix A, can be updated.

Design segments that have an infinite shelf life should be completed as early as possible. They should be identified with the party name and stored carefully. The more segments completed in advance, the easier the job is for the florist.

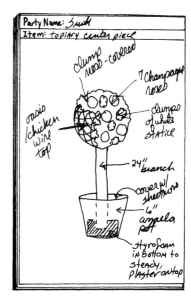

Figure 3.1 Example Sketch in Party Planning

Ordering

The information about products needed to complete the designs will be taken from the production chart, multiplied by the number of pieces of this type to be made for the party, and transferred to the party purchasing form. (See Appendix A.) The type of flower, color or variety, quantity needed, and the particular wholesaler will also be filled in. All of this information will then be available in one place, so that one employee may be assigned the job of ordering all necessary products. This employee may also be made responsible for ensuring that all products arrive in good condition and that they are separated from other shop stock.

The following ordering rules should be adhered to.

1. Order perishable materials well in advance, even though they may not be needed until shortly before the event.

2. Order perishables that need maturing, such as roses or lilies that need to be open for the event, so that they arrive with ample time for processing.

3. Nonperishable items should be ordered and obtained immediately upon customer request to ensure availability and lessen the chance of price changes.

4. Check all products as soon as they arrive to ensure that they are in good condition. If there is a problem with any product, make arrangements for replacement or substitution immediately.

Keeping Special Product Separate

To keep party product separate when it arrives in the shop:

• Put party flowers in a different color bucket from regular stock flowers.

• Color code parties and tie ribbons of the appropriate colors on the buckets of flowers for particular parties.

Scheduling

Production scheduling will ensure that each segment of each party design is completed on time. A party production calendar, such as the one provided in Appendix A, with specific information gathered from the various production charts should be completed.

Organizing Production

Once all of the products are assembled and the design staff is ready to produce the party pieces, an organized method should be agreed upon.

There are two methods of multiple production: move the people and move the designs. When designing by moving people, all of the designs should be set up in a row or in a circle. Each person is responsible for the insertion of one kind of flower or group of flowers. As the designers move down the line, or around the circle, they put in their particular flowers. The designs will all be completed at the same time and then all designers will perform quality control, checking for the correct number of materials and ensuring that mechanics are covered.

Using this method, the designers must move around more with their flowers, but the arrangements are not handled as much. This is often the preferred method when assembling heavy or large designs or ones with tricky mechanics. Following are tips for designers when using this method of multiple production.

- Wear an apron with pockets that will hold tools.

- Wear clippers and/or a knife on a ribbon around the neck so that they cannot get lost.

- Small carts or "microwave tables" on wheels can be used to move flower buckets around with designers.

When creating arrangements by moving designs, each designer should have at his work station the types of flowers or group of flowers he is responsible for inserting. As designers complete their insertions, they pass the arrangement on to the next designer who is responsible for inserting another type of flower. The last person is responsible for quality control. He ensures that the correct number of materials have been used and that the mechanics are perfectly covered. This method is less tiring for designers. They do not have to move around as much, and all of their products can stay in one place.

Following are tips for designers when using this method of multiple production.

- Have a central "waiting" table where designers may place the designs after they have finished their particular step.

- Set up products in the order in which they will be used so that they are easily reached by designers.

- Attach a ribbon to clippers and/or knives so that they can be easily found among the debris.

- Assign faster designers to the first and the most difficult jobs so that they will not be waiting for slower designers to finish.

Props

Props can be a large part of a florist's party business; they can also represent a large investment. The more times a prop is used, the more cost effective it becomes. Florists should use a prop

Notes

inventory form, such as the one provided in Appendix A, for props that are continually reused. The prop inventory form should be filled out to identify the props that are in inventory and where they are stored. It will also list when, where, and to whom they are rented and when they need to be retrieved. The form should be updated as soon as a party is sold to show where certain props will be needed in the future; this will ensure that a prop is not sold for two parties at the same time. An employee should be assigned to update the form; this will give everyone in the shop an idea of where the props will be and will act as an important reminder and confirmation of prop retrieval.

An employee should be assigned to prepping props. Prior to parties, he should be responsible for ensuring that props are still in good condition and are cleaned or prepped, if necessary.

When props are to be constructed in the shop, they should be sketched and laid out on the production chart as previously described.

If props are to be rented from an outside source, they should be contracted far enough in advance to guarantee there availability and to ensure that they will be available for the entire length of time needed, including prep work time before the party, time on the site, and time for pickup. Chapter 5 reviews extensive details regarding the use of props in party work.

Logistics of Party Work

Handling the logistics of storage and design for parties often requires special planning. The magnitude of some special events can create logistical nightmares. However, in most cases, advance planning can prevent major difficulties. Site analysis is the key to determining what problems might arise on location. Working with the party organizer or site manager in advance allows the florist to resolve problems before they arise. Within the floral shop, the logistics of space for both storage and design of large party pieces can also cause difficulties. Following are ideas for preventing common logistical problems.

Site Analysis

The florist must become familiar with the party site. Floor plans and seating charts of most catering establishments are available from their management. Copies of these may be embellished by the florist to show exact measurements and party piece locations to staff members.

Some locations are temporary: office buildings, malls, tents, patios, houses of worship. The florist should draw a detailed map with specific measurements. Likewise, annotated photographs will make the staff's job easier and more efficient.

If not completed before the consultation, a site investigation should be conducted immediately after the consultation. Most information may be obtained simply by observation; however, some will require meeting with others who are involved in the project. Refer to the event site checklist in Appendix A as a tool for recording specific details for each event.

The banquet manager or catering staff of a hotel, restaurant, or meeting hall can be very helpful. Florists should attempt to develop a good rapport with these people. Knowing the name of the customer's contact at the site can make it easier for florists to obtain important information about delivery. From observation and the site's personnel, florists may ascertain the best method of delivery; what loading dock or doors will be available for the delivery at the correct time; if items may be brought through a central loading facility; and at what time the event rooms will be available to the florist for setup. Obtaining answers to these questions will help smooth delivery and setup.

When there is much assembly work to be done on site, finding space in which to do it may be a problem. In many hotels and halls, not all of the public rooms are occupied at the same time for functions. Vacant meeting rooms, vacant ballrooms, or sections of divided ballrooms, loading and shipping areas, or unused kitchen areas can be effectively used by florists as setup areas. If a florist has developed a good relationship with site personnel, such space may be made available for preliminary setup free of charge.

The Site File

Florists who want to be prepared for selling party work will create an alphabetical (by site name) file of detailed information on common local party sites, along with their floor plans and seating charts. Room measurements, areas needing decoration, size of available tables, and other specific information will then be available at a glance. An example of a party site file is provided in Appendix A. Once it is filled out during the site analysis, it will save the florist considerable time in the future and will make things clear to other staff members who have not visited the sites. The addition of sketches, floor plans, seating plans, and pictures will make a complete file for the staff's future reference.

Work and Storage Space

Party pieces may require a work area that is separate from the one where daily shop operations take place. Likewise, props built for repeated rental will necessitate additional storage space. Renting extra retail space for design and storage can be very costly; shops without abundant square footage need to invent creative techniques for utilizing space. Following are examples of simple, inexpensive space utilization ideas.

- Build inexpensive outdoor sheds for prop storage.

- Rent or purchase immobile truck trailers to park in the shop's parking lot; the truck should be refrigerated, if needed.

- Use employees' personal basements, barns, or attics for temporary work or storage space.

- Rent inexpensive warehouse space.

- Use the party site for design prior to the event.

- Rent storage in warehouses on a weekly or monthly basis.

Delivery

Deliveries for parties often include a large number of oversized items and need to be accomplished within a relatively short period of time. To achieve maximum efficiency, organization is a must.

Vehicles

A florist will need to determine whether or not extra delivery vehicles are needed. If so, a common solution is to subcontract employees' vehicles; this is usually convenient and inexpensive. (See the sample subcontracting agreement in Appendix B.) If vehicle renting is necessary, all available options should be considered; prices and services vary. Some rental companies will offer free pickup and delivery services; this can reduce paid employee time. Many vehicle types, from sedans and station wagons to large trucks, are available. Florists should not pay for extra space that is not needed. Reserving well in advance will assure that an appropriate vehicle will be available when needed.

Tips for Loading Vehicles

- Place loose flowers in sturdy boxes. The boxes will form a base on which other items can rest, creating two levels in the vehicle.

- Items that will be needed first should be loaded last so that they will be closest to the door, making access easier.

- When making more than one trip between the site and the shop, determine which items will be needed first. This will allow a section of the setup to be completed before making the second trip.

- Do not load designs far in advance if the outside temperature is extremely hot or cold.

- If water is available on site, dump water out of designs before loading, then refill containers at the party location.

Delivery Instructions

Delivery people should have a master list of all items going to a site. This should include time information, directions to the site, the best method of entry and all pertinent details gathered and recorded on the event site checklist, such as the one in Appendix A. A party delivery chart, such as the one in Appendix A, will enumerate this information. This chart should be used by employees so that it is clearly understood what items are to be loaded and what items have been loaded. It also serves as a reminder of the items that need to be retrieved after the party. Utilizing the spaces for vehicle number, driver, and loading time, a separate chart may be used for each vehicle or each trip to the site.

Notes

Party Delivery Kit

Delivery people should ensure that the following items are on board before departure.

- Florist knives, wire snips, and foliage clippers in a tool chest

- Glue gun and glue pan with glues

- Drop cloths to work on and plastic garbage bags for cleanup

- Grounded extension cord

- Hammer and assorted nails

- Matches or candlelighter

- Collapsible saw

- Floral tape, duct tape, double-faced tape

- Hyacinth stakes and assorted wired wooden picks

- Extra floral foam

- Paper towels, tissues, first-aid kit

- Watering can to replenish the water in arrangements

- Portable hand vacuum

- Small whisk broom with dustpan

- Special tools appropriate for the present party's props and floral pieces

- Extra flowers of each type used, in case of transit damage

- Several wooden wedges to prop doors open

- Step stools or ladders, if appropriate

- Refreshments for the crew, if setup will be lengthy

- Floral shop business cards for people who inquire about the floral designs

Tips for Delivery and Setup

Following are suggestions for helping with the organization of delivery and setup for parties.

- Drivers should be sure to check fuel and other vehicle fluids 24 hours before delivery time.

- All delivery personnel should be given a brief tour of the site so they will know where to place each piece; this avoids lost time and confusion.

- Dollies, hand carts, mechanic's creepers, and other moving devices should be used when possible to decrease the amount of lifting that must be done by employees. These may be borrowed or rented. At hotels, often luggage movers may be used with permission. An inexpensive mover may be made by cutting a piece of 3/4-inch plywood to measure 2 feet by 4 feet. Screw-on casters should be placed at each corner. Holes should be drilled on one edge and rope added and knotted. *(Figure 3.2)* This mover can easily be stored against the wall of a vehicle and is not difficult to maneuver.

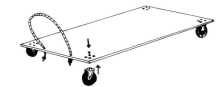

Figure 3.2 **Moving Device**

- Water, although necessary for flowers, can be heavy and messy. Arrangements can be made lighter by shipping them with little water. Take a watering can and find out in advance where to get water on site. Having a hair dryer with an extension cord can be useful for drying linens that have been made wet by spilled water.

- Wooden or plastic door wedges are useful for keeping heavy metal doors open while staff members are going in and out; they are usually available at hardware stores.

Notes

- Shop tools should be labeled and have a bright ribbon attached so that they can be located. One member of the staff should be assigned to tools. This person will be responsible for knowing the location of tools and for retrieving them after setup.

- Occasionally, a ladder may be needed; it may be brought along or a staff member should find out in advance how to obtain one from the site staff.

- When electrical cords need to be run along the floor, be sure to securely fasten them to the floor with appropriately colored tape to avoid creating a tripping hazard.

- Candles are easier to light if they have been lit before and blown out; light and extinguish them at the shop. Light other candles from a single candle, instead of a match, or use a hand-held, gas-powered charcoal fire lighter.

- If any type of fastening to walls, floors, or ceilings needs to be done, it should be cleared with site management. Failing to do so may result in an expensive repair bill for the florist.

- Bring proper cleanup tools. A small whisk broom with dustpan and a hand-held vacuum can help clear debris. Plastic bags are useful for waste foliage, mosses, etc.

- Put each employee in charge of a group of items: one person for the props, one for the rented trees, one for the foam board cutouts, etc. With assistance, this person will make sure they get to their location properly and will also be responsible for their removal as necessary (e.g., props that need retrieval).

- When setup is complete, one person should inspect the party area to make sure all ordered items have been set up properly. Also, check to ensure that tools and debris are removed.

After party setup is complete, personnel should be discharged as appropriate. If they have brought their own vehicles, a trip to take everyone back to the shop may not be necessary; likewise, they do not have to be paid for the time while they are returning to the shop. When props need to be picked up and the site needs to be cleaned after a party, some staff members will be needed again, usually 4 hours later. Besides cleaning and reorganizing the delivery vehicles and returning some products to the shop, there is rarely much productive work to do during the interim time period. The manager may wish to release them and have them return when cleanup begins, rather than paying them while they wait.

Efficient Movement

Wasted motion can take its toll on staff members during party delivery and setup. Repeatedly lifting and then putting items down can be very tiring. If several doors must be passed, propping the doors open with wooden wedges or having another person hold the doors can save time and effort.

Delivery Etiquette

Loading docks are available at many catering establishments. At times, these are blocked by large trucks or are not close to the party setup. In such cases, other entries may be more convenient, but entry through guests' doorways may be prohibited or inappropriate. This information, obtained when first investigating the site, must be passed on to delivery personnel.

Delivery Communication

At large hotels and other locations, it may be difficult for staff members to communicate. Distances between the loading area and the ballroom, for instance, may be large or on separate floors. In this case, a beeper or walkie-talkie system may be very helpful. These can usually be rented (sometimes through hotels) or may be purchased by the florist.

Delivery/Installation Staffing

Additional workers will make party setup easier. However, if not carefully controlled, this can greatly reduce profit. From sketches, plans, and a head designer's sample, less experienced personnel will be able to complete the party pieces. Temporary, per diem employees (in some cases, people who will work just for

Notes

the experience of being involved with party work), and students are valuable to florists as extra help for moving products and performing finishing jobs on party designs. Additional workers must be contacted far in advance of the event to ensure that they will reserve the date. The following individuals could be considered for temporary employment.

- Shop customers who get along well with staff members

- Relatives and friends of employees

- Temporary employment agencies

- Students

The shop should carry proper insurance for these additional staff members. Temporary employees should be scheduled well in advance of the party date, and should be scheduled for party removal time, as well as delivery time.

Work that must be done by designers is more costly than work done by temporary part-time helpers. Planning designs so that they may be easily assembled or completed without design staff on site will conserve profit for the shop.

It is essential that the florist who organizes the party be good at delegating duties. He should be able to let other people attend to their assigned details, while overseeing the general "look," organization, and timeliness of the installation and removal.

Delivery people must realize that they represent the shop to potential customers at all times. Their manner should be businesslike and polite. A professional identity may be achieved when all delivery personnel wear the same style and color apron or shirt, which has been monogrammed with the shop logo. As an alternative, clearly printed name tags may be supplied for staff members.

Frequently, clients who are planning parties may inspect sites while other events are taking place. Therefore, appearance and manners can make a difference in obtaining other business for the shop. Staff members should always carry business cards to distribute to potential clients.

If a party requires a great deal of time for setup, the shop may want to bring along snacks for the staff or arrange for the client to provide food.

Personnel may be encouraged to drive to the site in their own vehicles, following the main delivery vehicle. This will leave more room in the main vehicle for equipment and supplies and will make it easier to move people after the event is set up.

At times it is necessary for a party delivery team to wait while another event is cleared out before entering a site. The florist should plan to keep out of the way of departing guests and other removal staff. It may be possible to schedule small parts of the party assembly while waiting, such as napkin folding, balloon inflating, etc.

Time Schedule

For each event, a separate time schedule should be prepared. A daily event schedule, such as the one shown in Appendix A, should be filled out to show all the appropriate actions that should be taken during the event day and to identify the person responsible for each action.

The following information should be included on the daily event schedule.

- Rental vehicle pickup time and who will pick it up

- Vehicle loading time and identification of the driver (There may be more than one.)

- Site availability time

- Site arrival time

- "Finish by" times for items to be completed

- Setup ending time

- Pickup time and who will pick it up

- Times subcontractors are due to arrive and/or complete jobs and who they are

All personnel should be provided with a copy of the schedule, so that everyone is aware of what his responsibilities are and when specific events need to occur.

Notes

Party Removal and Cleanup

The party finishing time should be known in advance. Usually the catering staff can provide this information because they are hired for a certain period of time. The removal staff should know what items they will be retrieving. Storage boxes, moving tools, and ladders should all be kept in the delivery vehicle to be used for removal. Staff members should be assigned responsibility for specific aspects of the removal and cleanup. Party sites should be left in the state originally encountered. In other words, no extra debris or damage should result from the florist's activities during removal. Water, foliage, or debris dropped by the floral staff should be cleaned up by staff members.

Props and linens should be counted and carefully examined for damage. Damaged or lost items will usually be charged back to the client. Cleaning and re-storage may be done at the shop immediately following tear down or may be left for the regular daytime staff.

Employees in charge of each aspect of the removal should be sure that all items are picked up. Often there is no second chance to retrieve valuable props and tools.

Subcontracting

Some parts of special event work (balloons, linens, delivery, etc.) may be done by a subcontractor, a company which uses its own merchandise and employees. Subcontractors can relieve a florist from performing unfamiliar or laborious tasks. An agreement will list the duties and liabilities of both the florist and subcontractor. A sample subcontracting agreement is provided in Appendix B.

Coordinating production and setup of props, floral pieces, tenting, and the other parts of event decor is a time-consuming operation. Florists must be willing to spend a considerable amount of time in planning if a profitable, repeat party business is to be established. Being familiar with local party sites and keeping a file on them are important steps to becoming a local party expert. Planning for ordering and production are also vital aspects of a profitable party business. The use of checklists and written charts will free the florist from remembering all types of details and will make the delegation of various aspects of the party work easier. The professional, organized delivery, setup, and removal of party work will assist florists in pleasing clients and assuring the shop of a profitable party work venture.

Notes

Planning and Organizing

Notes, Photographs, Sketches, etc.

Notes, Photographs, Sketches, etc.

Planning and Organizing

Notes, Photographs, Sketches, etc.

PARTY THEMES

*P*lanning a theme party can be a wonderful challenge to the creativity of a florist. Sometimes, however, it is difficult to think of creative party themes or theme interpretation. This chapter is designed to provide a multitude of theme ideas that can be used by florists and/or clients when planning a special party. There are several popular, as well as unusual, themes. When considering themes for a client, florists should be open to suggestions. Imaginations can soar when freed of preconceived limitations.

To start planning, a list of the various components of the party should be organized. The suggestions within this chapter can then be modified in accordance with the needs of the client. Not every component is recommended for each party. The following categories are addressed within each suggested party theme.

- The themes within this chapter may be interpretations of a specific subject or they may be actual titles for a party.

- Colors are combined to immediately convey the mood and spirit of the event. Colors that are not available in floral materials can be included in containers, candles, accessories, tablecloths, etc.

- The floral materials listed are suggestions for inclusion in the theme party. From the list, the florist should create his own combinations.

- Props are considered to be decorations within the room that establish the theme. They may be made of any material.

Notes

- Accessories are intended to be used on table tops. They are important in establishing the theme in each table floral arrangement. They may serve as containers, or the ideas may be developed by using pictures, miniatures, or other representations of the theme.

- Table setting ideas are intended to spark ideas about the total look of the table. This might include the flowers and container or tablecloths and napkins.

- Special effects are the unexpected and delightful touches that truly make an event memorable. This might include costumed food servers, dancers, lighting, indoor fireworks (pyrotechnics), etc.

- Sounds allow those attending a party to sense the atmosphere even before they see it. For themes where special sound effects are required, it may be difficult to find exactly the desired sound track. Look for special effect sound recordings in large record stores. Frequently, even the local library will stock a limited number of such recordings.

After compiling a list of possible themes, the florist should look realistically at the limitations of time, space, labor, and money. This will allow a few strong themes to emerge for consideration by the client. The selection of a theme can be simplified when the florist presents a limited number of options that meet the needs of the client and his budget.

The remainder of this chapter has been designed as a quick-reference source for theme ideas.

Alice in Wonderland Tea Party

Colors

Pink, yellow, blue, and white.

Floral Materials

Daisies, gerberas, sunflowers, roses, delphinium, larkspur, and peonies.

Props

Oversized playing cards, formal English garden, and a Mad Hatter's Tea Party setting.

Accessories

Red paper money pockets, pagodas, artificial firecrackers and sparklers, fiber optics, folding fans, fortune cookies, noisemakers, looking glass (mirror), hats, teapots, mushrooms, Cheshire cats, caterpillars, White Rabbit, and Queen of Hearts.

Table Setting Ideas

Tables set to look like an English tea party with china and silver.

Special Effects

Instruct the waiters to wear whimsical hats and gloves while serving.

BACK TO SUMMER CAMP

Colors

Tan, khaki, red, and yellow.

Floral Materials

Solidaster, monte casino, lilies, alstroemeria, pompon mums, asters, and weedy grasses.

Props

Camp fire, tents, canoes, rowboats, archery target, suitcases, backpacks, and canteens. Score 4-foot by 8-foot sheets of foam board crosswise and fold to make pup tents. Tape them to the floor from the inside.

Accessories

Popsicle™ stick crafts, feathers, mosquito repellent, bats, letters from home, flashlights, marshmallows, frogs, turtles, raccoons, popcorn, s'mores, and jars of lightning bugs.

Table Setting Ideas

Put each table under a canvas tent-like canopy. Use a lantern that holds a candle in the center of the table with rocks and flowers surrounding it.

BEACH PARTY

Colors

Blue, yellow, and orange.

Floral Materials

Tritoma, bachelor buttons, seafoam statice, dune grasses, larkspur, daisies, and coreopsis.

Props

Surfboards, beach umbrellas, lifeguard stands, bathing beauty pavilion, beach chairs, and beer kegs. Signs indicating various areas within the party, such as "Shark Cove," "Body Builders Beach," and "Bikini Contest - Judges Wanted."

Accessories

Sand, pails and shovels, sea glass, glass floats, portable radios, blankets, towels, beach balls, sunglasses, tanning lotion, and flip-flops.

Table Setting Ideas

Blue tablecloths, beach umbrella over each table with sea gulls suspended from the umbrella struts.

Special Effects

Hire models to pose with guests for photos taken in front of a wave and surfboard backdrop.

Chinese New Year

Colors

Red, black, and metallic gold.

Floral Materials

Ginger, carnations, gerberas, protea, dendrobium orchids, fuji mums, and gold-painted foliage.

Props

Pagoda through which the guests enter the party. (To construct, use foam board. Pieces can be taped together and suspended from hooks in the ceiling.) Emperor and Empress life-size props. (Make them out of foam board. Add fabric and glitter accents. Cut out holes for the faces. Guests can pose behind them and be photographed as a personalized favor or to be used as a fundraiser.) Chinese garden, moon gates, red flags with gold calligraphic symbols for good luck, laser lights, and dragon to be carried by a train of people beneath it. Symbols of the animal whose year is being celebrated.

©DG 1990

Accessories

Red paper money pockets, pagodas, artificial firecrackers and sparklers, fiber optics, folding fans, fortune cookies, noisemakers, and anything metallic gold and festive.

Table Setting Ideas

Red and/or gold mylar cloths. (Use mylar from a roll. Measure the diameter of the finished cloth, using 3-inch wide tape on the back. Fasten the sheets together to achieve the proper dimensions, then cut to shape.) Try to adjust lighting to take advantage of the sparkly surfaces. A Chinese junk (boat) can be made of a gold painted dry palm spathe. Fill it with plaster and insert a gold-painted cardboard tube to serve as a mast. The sail can be made of red foam board, with struts made of river cane glued to it. The inside can then be filled with low red and purple flowers and gold-painted foliage.

©DG 1990

Christmas Around the World

Colors

Red, green, and gold.

Floral Materials

All evergreens and metallic accent materials.

Props

Christmas decorations from various countries. Graphics of Santa as he is known in various countries.

Accessories

Sweden - straw and red yarn; Mexico - piñata; Scotland - tartan fabric; America - Santa Claus; and Germany - Saint Nicholas.

Table Setting Ideas

Each table represents a country. Small Christmas trees decorated according to the customs of each country. Guests might enjoy decorating a bare tree at their table with ornaments that are displayed in charming beribboned baskets.

Sound Effects

During the evening, appropriate ethnic Christmas music is played and dedicated to the corresponding table.

COME AS YOUR FAVORITE STAR

©DG 1991

Colors

White and silver.

Floral Materials

Roses, lilies, dendrobium orchids, freesia, callas, and carnations.

Props

Stretch limousines, spotlights, mirror-like plastic or mylar on stair risers, Gruman's Chinese Theater, and movie cameras.

Accessories

Stars, glitter, rhinestones, mirrors, sunglasses, cigarette holders, graphics of stars, movie posters, and a 6-foot Oscar made of gold mylar to serve as a photo site.

Table Setting Ideas

Have each table represent a different movie star. Use large rhinestone accents on the floral containers or use mirrored containers. Set the head table with personalized directors' chairs.

Special Effects

Allow the guests to make their own "Gruman Theater Style" handprints in plaster. They can sign the finished casts and take home a special remembrance. Make sure cleanup is easy for the guests. Make an experimental set of prints first so that the amount of help needed to do this efficiently can be determined. This could be a fundraiser. Invitations should tell guests to "come as your favorite star." Use rhinestone sunglasses and movie contracts for prizes.

Dreamscapes

Colors

All white.

Floral Materials

Queen Anne's lace, bouvardia, astilbe, baby's breath, caspia, and campanula.

Props

Clouds made of cotton batting wrapped over chicken wire and dusted with diamond dust glitter and gauze draped from the ceiling.

Accessories

Combine elements that would depict specific dreams; for example, a dream of wealth could have a pot of gold, a chest of jewels, gold-paved streets, hundred dollar bills, $ signs, a letter informing the reader that they just inherited a billion dollars, etc.

Table Setting Ideas

White gauze over white linen. Gather, and puddle the gauze so that it drapes over the top and cascades almost to the floor. (Fabric that touches the floor may be tripped on an therefore would be hazardous.) Crushed glass can be mounded and bonded with heavy coats of casting resin to create an irregular base for flowers. A clear plastic dish may be mounted, asymmetrically on top of the mound to support a candle and a floral cage with flowers.

Special Effects

Place fog machines at the entrance so that guests walk into the misty realm of dream time. Use white candles from 18 inches to 36 inches in height on all tables and have them tiered on risers draped in gauze so that they flank the entrance and exit areas. A less expensive version is to use tea lights (candles in low metal cups). The tea lights can be placed in votive cups for additional safety. Votives also work well. Make sure that the lit candles are a safe distance from the guests.

Eighteenth Century Christmas

Colors

Red, dark green, orange, yellow, and lime green.

Floral Materials

Minimal flowers, focus instead on fruit and greens. Magnolia, boxwood, pine, apples, pineapples, lemons, oranges, limes, nuts and kumquats.

Props

Overhead entrance door piece, garlands, swags, oval wall hangings, wreaths, candle lampposts with bows and greens, and fireplace mantles.

Accessories

Blue and white Chinese bowls, Revere pewter bowls, and brass containers.

Table Setting Ideas

Create the effect of a garland running along the length of the table by laying on greens and fruit. Use a punch bowl in the center and add an abundance of fruits to the base. Use lots of candles throughout. Luminaries (sand-filled paper bags with votive candles inside) may be used in the driveway and lit just before the party is over.

FANTASIA

Colors

Rainbow: violet, blue, green, yellow, orange, and red.

Floral Materials

Snapdragons, tulips, liatris, bear grass, and weeping willow.

Props

Sorcerers' hats, Bald Mountain backdrop, dancing hippos, castle, and oversized flowers in pots.

Accessories

Wands, mops, buckets, water well, vulture, mirrors, and a book of magic.

Table Setting Ideas

Bucket with flowers spilling out over the table and down to the floor. This may require that one place setting be eliminated.

Special Effects

Dancing waters show (can be subcontracted from a prop or special event company).

Sound

Musical score from *Fantasia*.

Fifties Sock-Hop Be-Bop Do-Wop Shu-Bop!!!

Colors

Pink, gray, and white.

Floral Materials

Carnations and daisies.

Props

Juke boxes, root beer stands with car hops, Elvis silhouette, soda fountain, and a beauty shop.

Accessories

Poodle skirts, ponytails, bobby socks, curlers, pink telephones, sugar cube corsages, dog bone corsages, and records.

Table Setting Ideas

Make tablecloths from pink and gray felt. Glue white felt poodles to the tablecloths. Use full-size 33 rpm records under the plates. Use 45 rpm records for saucers under black cups. Slide 45 rpm records over bud vases. They may also be used in the centerpieces.

Special Effects

Have costumed beauty shop operators fluffing the guests hair by adding bows or small scarves, making spitcurls and ponytails, or inserting foam and metal curlers and pin curls. For the men, provide combs and have the beauty operators offer to spray their hair with water and then slick it back.

Flying High

Colors

Red, dark blue, and airplane silver.

Floral Materials

Cockscomb, alstroemeria, anemone, carnations, monkshood, bachelor buttons, tulips, poppies, echinops, and irises.

Props

Full-size (foam board) bi-plane, suspended from the ceiling. A banner with an appropriate message should be tied to the tail of it.

Accessories

Goggles, toy planes, pilot wings, propellers, and beanie hats with propellers.

Table Setting Ideas

Use the dull gray side of colored mylar to cover the tables. Arrangements should have small, lightweight airplanes attached to long, stiff wires that are inserted into the design after being secured to a wooden pick. Each arrangement may be placed on a slow-moving electrical turntable (available from hardware stores), which will allow the planes to fly high above the guests.

Football Tailgate Party

Colors

Blue, gray/silver, and white.

Floral Materials

Football mums, pompon mums, eryngium, and echinops.

©DG 1991

Props

Locker room with blackboard and plays indicated, cheerleader posters, and goal post. Banners with slogans, such as, "Go, fight, win!!!" are also effective. Drive actual station wagons into the ballroom. Serve submarine sandwiches and beverages in thermal jugs from the open tailgates.

Accessories

Shoulder pads, footballs, trophies, megaphones, and cheerleader pompons.

Table Setting Ideas

Cover rectangular tables with artificial turf and mark the football field with adhesive tape. Place 10-foot tall goal posts made of PVC pipe at each end of the table. Centerpieces should have trophies in their centers with the name of the guest of honor inscribed on each.

©DG 1991

Futurescape

Colors

Silver, pink, and aqua.

Floral Materials

Protea, anthuriums, ginger, carnations, fuji mums, and silver leaf foliage.

Props

Asteroids made of carved Styrofoam™, flying saucers, murals of the solar system, and a dryer hose painted silver for an astronaut look.

Accessories

Lucite rods with Styrofoam™ meteorites, spaceships, rockets, and mirrors.

Table Setting Ideas

Silver cloth with neon-like glow sticks under opalescent mylar.

Special Effects

Decorate the ceiling by suspending mylar stars from balloon ceiling walkers. (See Chapter 6.) Also, light-colored flowers may be dipped into a solution of liquid taken from florescent magic markers. Open the top of the markers and mix the ink with approximately 3 cups of water. The flowers will glow when placed in a room with black lights.

Ghosts, Goblins, Witches, and Warlocks Coven

Colors

Orange, black, and bronze.

Floral Materials

Pumpkins, miniature pumpkins, gourds, oak leaves, straw, gerberas, safflower, red rover mums, calendula, marigolds, pompon mums, lilies, gladioli, spider mums, and football mums.

Props

Entrance door with a spider web around the edges, which is made of string or rope. Hang spiders from the ceiling. Spray chandeliers with artificial spider webs. (Read instructions on the can carefully to make sure it will not affect any surface adversely.) Place a huge cauldron on logs that appear to be glowing from an artificial fire. The "fire" is created with fire retardant red cellophane over white string lights. Make an artificial flat bottom inside the cauldron, if necessary, to support fifteen or twenty votive candles deep inside. Have bats swirling above the cauldron. Place dead branches all around. Hang gauzey white ghosts from the ceiling.

Accessories

Candles, brooms, cauldrons, bats, witch hats, crystal balls, astrological symbols, crescent moon, scary jack-o-lanterns, black cats, the number 13, skeletons, and rubber chickens. Paint dry materials and branches bronze to glisten in the dark.

Table Setting Ideas

Black paper tablecloths with white fluorescent paint can be covered with spider webs. Hang a 2-foot diameter spider over each table. The centerpiece is a bronze cauldron with a twisted, curved branch in it. From the top of the branch to the base of it, make a half of a spider web. In some arrangements, use grave stones instead of spider webs. Finish with bold flowers. Use black and orange pillar and Gothic candles on each table.

Special Effects

Have coats checked by white-faced ghouls. Waiters could be costumed as witches, warlocks, ghosts, or gremlins. A visiting vampire with a candelabra may seat guests as they arrive. Black lights also add an eerie cast to props that are highlighted with florescent paint. At midnight, select an honorary grand witch to preside over an improvisational coven.

Sounds

Have guests approach the outside entrance listening to the eerie sounds of screams and howls. (Record stores and some libraries have sound effects records.)

© DG 1992

Hole in One Party

Colors

Green, yellow, and white.

Floral Materials

Tulips, euphorbia, carnations, daisies, and lilies.

Props

Sand traps, ponds, putting green, and miniature golf obstacles (clubs may possibly be rented during off season from a miniature golf course or driving range). Make a putting green out of artificial turf.

Accessories

Golf clubs, tees, balls, bags, pennant hole markers, and score cards.

Table Setting Ideas

Use artificial turf for table tops over green cloths. On some tables, create sand traps, woods, ponds, and other obstacles. Use pennant hole markers to indicate the table numbers.

Special Effects

Use golf carts to transport guests from the parking lot to the entrance.

Hот! Hот! Hот!

© DG 1992

Colors

Red, orange, and yellow.

Floral Materials

Tritoma, birds of paradise, anthuriums, agave flowers, eremurus, ginger, and banksia.

Props

Sun, cellophane flames (red, orange, and yellow), and overhead fans.

Accessories

Hot peppers, paper fans, and lots of candles (red, yellow, and orange).

Table Setting Ideas

Open grills may be used if well ventilated. Food service is ethnic food varying in intensity of spiciness. Some should be mild. Large arrangements should be amply weighted but narrow enough to avoid interfering with the food display. Very tall showy arrangements work well. In the "Not So Hot" area (see "Special Effects" below), cooling refreshments should be served. Lush use of green plants will add a soothing contrast.

Special Effects

Meet guests in the parking lot with fire trucks that will transport them to the party entrance. (This can sometimes be arranged with a volunteer company as a fundraiser for the company.) When guests first walk in, have heaters cranked up to give a brief blast of hot tropical air to a limited area. Various areas will have different expressions of the hot themes: Hot and Tropical (Brazilian), Hot Tamale (Mexican), Sweltering Hot (India), and Hotter than _ _ _ _ (Hell), and finally, Not So Hot (a relaxing, low key area).

Sounds

Loud, hot, and tropical music should establish the mood.

Hot Jazz on the Mississippi

Colors

Red and glitter gold.

Floral Materials

Gerberas, amaryllis, cockscomb, amaranthus, and Spanish moss.

Props

Silhouettes of jazz musicians, musical notes, "Help Wanted" signs for Dixieland jazz musicians, and stylized curved piano keyboards. Make the entrance to the party look like guests are boarding the deck of a paddlewheel boat. The paddlewheel may be made of cardboard and painted inexpensively or covered with self-sticking wood grain plastic. Remember to add an arrangement to the piano.

Accessories

Riverboats, paddle wheels, saxophones, pianos, trombones, banjos, and drums.

Table Setting Ideas

Red tablecloths with a plastic keyboard swirling through the center of the table. To make this, cut a pattern for the keyboard so that it looks like it is flexible. Use liquid plastic (from a craft store) to outline the black keys; fill in the remaining keys with the white liquid plastic. When dry, they keyboard can be placed on the table and flower arrangements in inexpensive reproductions of brass instruments added. Musical notes could be incorporated into the flower arrangements. Pages of jazz sheet music can be photocopied for use as placemats. Finish with clusters of ball candles on low copper or brass candle holders.

Huck Finn Party

Colors

Blue, red, and yellow.

Floral Materials

Sunflowers, weeds, and grasses.

Props

White picket fence, white wash buckets, steamboat paddle wheel, tree stumps and logs, and Injun Joe's Cave.

Accessories

Straw hats, used paint brushes, sling shots, fishing poles, fishing hole signs, and swinging rope.

Table Setting Ideas

Denim cloths with red-checked napkins.

Special Effects

Build an "ol' fishin' hole" and allow guests to fish for floating toys that have numbers on the bottom symbolizing specific prizes. This could be a fundraiser if games of chance or skill are legal in the state where the party is held. To simply build the fishing hole, fill rectangular design dishes with full blocks of presoaked floral foam. Use them to outline the shape desired. If the water is to be shallow, dry foam blocks may be alternated (without a container) between the wet blocks. (This is lighter and allows recovery of the dry bricks at breakdown.) Use a black, heavy gauge plastic (visqueen) to line the hole and drape over and tuck it under the foam-filled dishes. Slit the top of the plastic where wet foam is used and insert ferns to totally cover the edges of the fishing hole. Place a tree stump or fallen log over the fishing hole. Add a stick fishing pole and a "no fishing" sign. Surround it with tall plants and branches.

Italian Bistro

Colors

Red, white, and green.

Floral Materials

Pots of geraniums, oregano, basil, thyme, parsley, dusty miller, etc.

Props

Wooden vat filled with grapes, grapevine trellis, black and white tile floor, large terra-cotta pots with tomato plants. Strawberry pots with strawberry plants and artificial strawberries, if none are in season.

Accessories

Italian flag, chianti wine bottles with candles, loaves of bread in varied shapes, bread baskets, raffia, salami, pepperoni, cheese, 5-gallon jars of cherry peppers, and clear jars filled with varied pasta shapes.

Table Setting Ideas

Red and white checked tablecloths; centerpieces may be baskets filled with plants, breads, and vegetables.

Special Effects

Fill a vat with fresh grapes and allow guests to have fun stomping them into "wine." Plan to have an assistant close at hand during the process. Provide a vat of water and ample towels to expedite cleanup of festive feet.

JUNqLE NiqHTs SAFARi PARTy

Colors

Intense hues of green, orange, red, yellow, purple, and black.

Floral Materials

Dense use of tropical foliage, reeds, and vines. Anthuriums, orchids, gladioli, ginger, allium, and birds of paradise.

Props

Eight-foot tripod of crossed spears, tied with raffia. (Spears are constructed of yucca poles with foam board blades at the top. Trim with animal skins and feathers.) Jungle huts made with thatched roofs.

Accessories

Spears, cauldrons, and jungle animals (check with client before using snake motifs). Containers can be primitive clay pots, baskets, vines, etc.

Table Setting Ideas

In cocktail areas, use thatched grasses around the table edges. (They are too stiff to use on a table where people are seated.) Cover dining tables with animal prints.

Special Effects

Food servers dressed in safari shorts and hats with binoculars around their necks.

Kingdom of Neptune

Colors

All white with shadowy blue green lighting on mother of pearl glitter.

Floral Materials

Allium, agapanthus, white branches, succulents, and mosses.

Props

"Coral" made of aerosol insulation, and a curtain made of long white paper strips. (The strips taper at the base and have gently curving edges. Dust with glitter and light for sparkling movement.) Giant fantasy fish, suspended from balloons as ceiling walkers. (See Chapter 6.) Mermaids and Neptune, oversized pearls made of strings of large, chilled onions, and Davie Jones's locker.

Accessories

Sponges, Neptune's golden pitchfork, fishnet, plastic pearls, shells, and ice carvings of mermaids with lighting underneath.

Table Setting Ideas

White tablecloth with the top two-thirds covered with opalescent mylar. Cut blue vinyl to conform with the edge of one-third of the table top. The vinyl edges should be wavy to symbolize the ocean. On the vinyl, place clusters of vertical, aqua mist, and taper candles that are 30 inches tall. The candles may be secured into heavy, and low glass holders, which are covered with loose shells. Add fish (made of foam board) on wire to look as if they are swimming through kelp (represented by the tall candles). Make sure that the fish are not placed within 3 inches of the burning candles. Design arrangements in or around shells that are on the opalescent part of the table top. Pour sand around the arrangements and add votive candles in clam shells.

M*A*S*H B*A*S*H

Colors

Army green and tan with accents of bright colors.

Floral Materials

Sunflowers, cattails, rice grass, weeds, reeds, solidaster, daisies, and poppies.

Props

Klinger's closet, the Swamp, the mess tent, the operating room, the colonel's office, the main road through camp, tents, Rosie's Bar, signposts, and shower stalls.

Accessories

Army and medical uniforms, trunks, a makeshift still, picnic tables and benches, Sophie's saddle, jeeps, Radar's teddy bear, victrola, grape NeHi, tin trays, dry rice, loud speakers on poles (used for announcements during the party), swinging light fixture, and kerosene lanterns.

Table Setting Ideas

Use camouflage canvas with brightly colored arrangements. Parts from old cars (jeeps) can be used to hold the flowers. Rocks from the edge of camp may be included. Use rice at the base of the arrangements and spill it onto the tables.

Special Effects

Make a shower stall setting to be used as a photo site. Paint a 3-foot by 8-foot sheet of foam board to look like the doors of a row of shower stalls. Suspend it from overhead so that it hangs about 2 feet from the floor. Suspend a shower head over each door. Have guests pose for pictures by standing behind the doors, barefooted, with shower caps on (optional), and with their pant legs or dresses pulled up behind the doors.

MEDIEVAL COURT

Colors

Deep jewel tones: emerald, ruby, sapphire, amethyst and topaz.

Floral Materials

Open roses, gloriosa lilies, scabiosa, ranunculus, pendulous amaranthus, peonies, eremurus, herbs, fruits, and nuts.

Props

Massive furniture and chests, throne, and knights in shining armor.

Accessories

Trumpets, flags and banners, and court jesters.

Table Setting Ideas

Massive banquet tables, bare or with tapestry-like fabric. Forks and spoons should be optional with places set with knives only. Lots of extra napkins are required and may be tied with jewel tone ribbons and a sprig of fresh herbs.

Midnight at the Oasis

Colors

Blue, lavender, pink, yellow, and peach.

Floral Materials

Carnations, centaurea, celosia, banksia, protea, kangaroo paw, and yarrow.

Props

White gauze tents, camels, palm trees, moon, stars, rough blankets with merchants wares of brass, leather, and fruits.

Accessories

Leather or chamois-wrapped containers and sand (grits may substitute).

Table Setting Ideas

For each table, individual palm trees made of yucca poles with tepee foliage inserted into the top. The base should have a pool of water to create the appearance of an oasis.

Special Effects

Drape midnight blue gauze from the ceiling and use nets of white lights behind it, so that it gives the effect of a starry night. Have costumed belly dancers and roving Middle Eastern musicians mix with the guests during the evening.

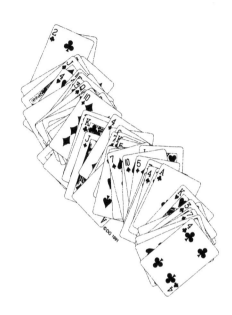

Monte Carlo Magic

Colors

Red, green, white, and yellow.

Floral Materials

Roses, gerbera, lisianthus, and lilies.

Props

Roulette wheel, gaming tables, and slot machines.

Accessories

Dice, cards, champagne and glasses, and poker chips.

Table Setting Ideas

Green felt cloths (make sure that they are colorfast when wet). Make arrangements in oversized champagne glasses with accents of playing cards. Cluster play money on the table with poker chips and dice.

Special Effects

Have the waiters wear visors and rolled up sleeves. Intersperse a few card trick specialists, who look like waiters, to entertain the guests at the tables with their antics.

Musical Christmas

Colors

Green and gold.

Floral Materials

All evergreens, including pine, boxwood, oregonia, cedar, juniper, and mistletoe.

Props

Garlands and pedestals with greens and various musical instruments, accented with dark green and gold ribbon woven through the designs.

Accessories

Musical instruments, sheet music, and millimeter balls.

Table Setting Ideas

Dip pages from Christmas sheet music in tea to age the paper. Make them into fan shapes and add to the arrangements. Top with gold bullion thread. Use five individual brass candle holders on each table with tall hunter green candles in various widths.

Mystery on the Orient Express

The Orient Express is a luxury train, still in operation, which at the turn of the century ran between Paris and Istanbul. A party with this theme should be divided into two rooms. One is a Paris dance hall and the other is a desert marketplace. Guests are invited to wear period costumes. During the evening, a "murder" is committed and the guests, who are also suspects, must solve the mystery.

Colors

Red and purple.

Floral Materials

Poppies, fritillaria, euphorbia, dendrobium orchids, vibirnum, plume celosia, and pincushion protea.

Props

Paris - columns with fabric festoons around the dance floor. (See Chapter 8.) Plant and tree clusters, with miniature white lights. Clusters can be used to form intimate settings for small groups of chairs. Morocco - striped tents, striped canopies over the buffet tables.

Accessories

Paris - Eiffel Tower, feathers, urns of flowers, highbutton shoes and petticoats, dance hall posters, candelabras. Morocco - leather, brass, camel blankets, sand/cornmeal, Fez hat with tassel, billowing gauze, palm trees, oil lamps, and goatskin bags for wine.

Table Setting Ideas

Paris - red checked café cloths. Arrangements can include bread, wine, and cheese. Morocco - Place "pipe and drape" supports on each side of the table and drape with white gauze. Use white cloths, top-dressed with gauze. Tie the edges with leather cords. Five-foot palm trees, made from yucca poles and palm foliage, may be placed in the center of the tables. (Scale down those found in Chapter 5.)

Special Effects

The cocktail area can be decorated like a train station waiting area. Use bench seats and "ticket windows" for the bar. When guests leave Paris and Morocco, they should be given a ticket. This can be a raffle ticket as a charity fundraiser or for a complimentary door prize. The setting between the two rooms can be made to look like the coach or dining car of the train. Conductors (waiters) announce "all aboard," collect tickets, and allow passengers to "travel" through the train. Use soft lighting, candles, abundant flowers, and red carpet to convey the ambience of the luxury travel. Paris - waiters with handlebar moustaches. Morocco - waiters in turbans.

NUTCRACKER CHRISTMAS

Colors

Red, white, blue, and gold.

Floral Materials

Carnations, holly, pine, miniature carnations, Star of Bethlehem, and roses.

Props

Toy nutcracker soldiers, ballerinas, giant Christmas tree, snowy forest, sled, and Giant Rat soldiers.

Accessories

Wrapped presents, toy wooden soldiers, ruffled bed, snowflakes, nuts and nutcrackers.

Table Setting Ideas

Gold lamé fabric billows around the base of a miniature boxwood tree accented with sprigs of pine, clusters of whole nuts, and nutcrackers. Gather a length of lamé around the edges of the table and accent with sprigs of greens, gold painted nuts, and ballerina and soldier Christmas tree ornaments. Alternate hunter green and red 24-inch candles in low, clear glass candle holders on each table.

©DG 1990

Oktoberfest

Colors

Orange, yellow, and brown.

Floral Materials

Football mums, pompon mums, wheat, hops, barley, and oats.

Props

German beer signs, backdrop of a village on the Alps, and wooden tables and benches.

Accessories

Pretzels and bratwurst, steins, and cuckoo clocks.

Table Setting Ideas

Arrangements can be placed in clusters of beer steins or mugs that will break apart so that each couple may take one home. Cluster beer pretzels on the table. Tablecloths can be as simple as brown craft paper with irregularly torn edges.

PIRATES ANd WENCHES

Colors

Black, red, purple, and metallic gold.

Floral Materials

Anthuriums, ginger, liatris, and gold-painted foliage.

Props

Wooden gangplank (make any walkway very stable) upon which guests walk through a darkened area. Use candles for lighting and to create dim spots on the path to reveal skeletons, treasure chests, and rum bottles.

Accessories

Pirate flags, gold coins, treasures, skulls, plumed hats, swords and scabbards, and parrots.

Table Setting Ideas

Black cloths with treasure chests or skulls as containers for flowers. Gold chocolate coins and treasures spread around the table. Ship masts and figureheads can be included in the setting.

Special Effects

Waiters wear eye patches and bandannas tied on their heads.

Sounds

Music is the bawdy chanting of pirates.

Polynesian Delights

Colors

Pink, purple, red, yellow, and orange.

Floral Materials

Orchids, ginger, birds of paradise, heliconia, calathea, and ti leaves.

Props

Tiki statues, drums, huts, and palm trees.

Accessories

Flower leis, grass skirts, coconuts, pillar candles, and torches.

Table Setting Ideas

Cover tables with woven palm bark or grass cloth wallpaper. Cluster large ti leaves in the center and carefully arrange tropical fruit and flowers to look like an offering to the gods.

Special Effects

To create a thatched hut, make the supports first. Sink a cluster of 8-foot bamboo poles into plaster in a papier-mâché container. Make a frame of 1-inch by 2-inch boards to match the desired size of the finished roof. Stretch ready-made thatch mats (available from floral wholesalers or visual display houses) over the frame and staple. Lash and glue the roof to the tops of the poles. Tie the joints with raffia to cover the mechanics. Cover the plaster pots with burlap and accent with raffia.

PROSPECTOR'S PARTY

Colors

Gold, yellow, and red.

Floral Materials

Succulents, goldenrod, calendula, gerberas, marigolds, solidaster, and wild grasses.

Props

Wagon wheels, pick axes, shovels, mules, mine entrance, stream bed with gold-painted rocks, foam board mountains and hills.

Accessories

Pans with screen bottoms or holes, rocks and pebbles painted gold, and old hats and bandannas.

Table Setting Ideas

Piles of gold rocks with mining tools and wildflowers. Use burlap for tablecloths. Serve food and drink in tin or enamel pans and cups. After the party, the tinware may be donated to a local chapter of Boy Scouts or Girl Scouts.

©DG 1990

Reach for the Sky (American Skyscrapers)

Colors

Black and white.

Floral Materials

Callas, orchids, gladioli, allium, agapanthus, and liatris.

Props

Suspended clouds (made of fiberfill or balloons), intermittently spaced and suspended from the ceiling, and skyscrapers.

Table Setting Ideas

Each table should have an 8-foot foam board skyscraper from various American cities. (Build a base of 2-foot by 4-foot boards that rise 30 inches above the table. Reinforce the top and base with strips of wood. Cover the base with white, fire-retardant tulle or other fluffy fabric. Cut four skyscraper profiles out of foam board and attach them to the upper part of the painted wood frame.) Overhead lights can be directed into the buildings to illuminate any windows that are cut out of the foam board. Consider New York's Chrysler and Empire State Buildings, Seattle's Needle, Chicago's Sears Tower, the Washington Monument, and San Francisco's Coit Tower. Use several votive candles to add shadow drama to the skyscrapers.

RETURN OF THE DINOSAURS

Colors

Green, orange, and yellow.

Floral Materials

Centaurea, succulents, cycas palm, palmetto, tritoma, eremurus, echinops, and cockscomb.

Props

Dinosaurs, such as triceratops, stegosaurus, brontosaurus, pterodactyl, and tyrannosaurus rex, made of foam board. Rocks can be made of opened, crumpled paper bags with the seam side down. If the budget allows, top dress the "rocks" with a textured spray finish. Caves can be made of crumpled brown craft paper. Stalagmites can be made of aerosol spray insulation over twisted newspaper forms.

Accessories

Newspapers announcing the discovery of live dinosaurs at the site of the party, toy dinosaurs, and caves made of papier-mâché.

Table Setting Ideas

Create a prehistoric landscape for each table; swamps, caves, volcanos, and ice masses might be used.

Rio Carnivale!!!

Colors

Hot, intense colors, including red, orange, and pink.

Floral Materials

Anthuriums, heliconia, euphorbia, eremurus, cymbidium orchids, lilies, giant allium, and carnations.

Props

Costumed mannequins, columns topped with masses of feathers, and oversized masks.

Accessories

Feathers, glittered accents, sequins, masks, balloons, and streamers.

Table Setting Ideas

Use mylar to top the tablecloths and scatter large palettes (sequins) on the fabric. Have 4-foot long dry sticks or river cane bursting from the arrangements with long, fluttering streamers in hot colors cascading from the ends.

ROARING 20's SPEAKEASY

Colors

Hot pink and black with white accents.

Floral Materials

Nerines, Uchida lilies, callas, gerbera, and black-painted foliage dusted with black glitter.

Props

Bar from the 1920's, secret doors, limousines, foam board shadows of gangsters and their molls, bathtub with ice to hold drinks or with bubbles and models.

Accessories

Machine guns, spats, derby hats, garters, rhinestones, pearls, and gangster "Ten most wanted posters." (Pictures of guests may be used with client's permission.)

Table Setting Ideas

Top hats filled with flowers and feathers. Accent the arrangements with pink or lace gloves. Large corsages of cattleya orchids, plumosa, roses, or carnations as favors for the ladies.

Special Effects

Show old silent movies in different areas of the room.

Sadie Hawkins Barn Dance

Sadie Hawkins Day is in October and, traditionally, is a day for things being opposite the usual. It became famous through the comic strip Li'l Abner. The most memorable part of this day is that women become the aggressors and are able to ask men to marry them. If this is being planned for a fund raiser, the guests may find themselves in jail for breaking the inane rules of the day. **(See the sample list of rules to the left.)** Of course, bail must be posted to get out of jail. An impromptu wedding can be arranged for a nominal fee. Prizes may be given to the people who get married the most times by Marrying Sam and can prove it with the fake gold wedding rings from each ceremony. People impersonating the major characters should act accordingly and interact with the guests throughout the evening. A library can provide additional information about the comic strip and its zany cast.

SADIE HAWKINS DAY RULES
(ENFORCED BY HAND OF JUSTICE!)

1. Everyone must have at least 7 freckles on each side of their face.

2. Freckles may be purchased at the entrance.

3. You may sit with the right leg crossed over the left, but NOT the left leg crossed over the right.

4. In designated areas smoking is allowed, but the Sheriff can arrest anyone caught while lighting up.

5. A man must say yes to anything a woman asks for, but the answer becomes invalid after 10 minutes.

6. All rules must be obeyed.

7. The Sheriff has the right to put anyone in jail who breaks the rules or gives the Sheriff a dirty look.

8. The Judge may release any prisoner for any reason.

9. Everyone else must pay bail to get out.

Colors

Orange, red, and yellow.

Floral Materials

Sunflowers, daisies, poppies, anemones, montbretia, nigella, pompon mums, bachelor buttons, miniature carnations, dahlias, and bouvardia.

Props

Bales of hay (sprayed with fire retardant), barn doors, hay wagon, straw hats, graphics of characters from "Li'l Abner" comic strip including, Li'l Abner, Mammy Yokum, Marrying Sam, the Sheriff, the Judge, and, of course, sexy Daisy Mae.

Accessories

Wedding rings, miniature hay bales, and Abner's suspenders and work boots.

Table Setting Ideas

Red tablecloths with casual flower arrangements accented with straw or raffia.

Sights and Sounds of New York

Colors

Black and yellow; white and red.

Floral Materials

Yellow and white callas, oncidium orchids, gerberas, dendrobium orchids, roses, and tulips.

Props

Food stands - hot dogs, shish kebabs, pretzels, fruit, egg creams, and bagels. The entire room can be divided into identifiable neighborhoods. (See listing under "Accessories.") Plastic ceiling tile grids can be cut and glued into the shape of the skyline and then lit with strings of white lights.

Accessories

Subways, yellow cabs, theater tickets and programs, *New York Magazine*, parking tickets, reproductions and/or graphics of Little Italy, SoHo, Central Park, Harlem, South Street Seaport, Central Park, Chelsea, the Staten Island Ferry, Empire State Building, Statue of Liberty, Brooklyn Bridge, big apples, and sports memorabilia from the New York teams.

Table Setting Ideas

Alternate tablecloths in black and white. Use flowers and accessories to add the red and yellow. Use apple-shaped containers with flowers and include fresh apple branches or wire apples to natural branches.

Special Effects

Rap dancers, mimes, and street musicians.

Sounds

Combinations of sound effects - horns, music, jackhammers, crowds, fire engines, trains, boats, and street vendors.

"A Star is Born" Christening

Colors

Grass green, raspberry, sky blue, and silver.

Floral Materials

Tulips, Bells of Ireland, baby's breath, monte casino, snapdragons, sweet Williams, hyacinths, delphinium, bachelor buttons, miniature carnations.

Props

Star-shaped balloons clustered with rattles tied to the streamers and storks carrying silver stars with the baby's name.

Accessories

Star-shaped rattles, teething rings, and bottles with star decals.

Table Setting Ideas

Blue or pink tablecloth topped with a stork or star flat crib sheet. Each place card should have one side with the saying, "When you wish upon a star, dreams come true . . . ." The baby's name can be printed repeatedly in the background and napkins folded into a diaper shape and pinned with diaper pins that have silver stars glued to them. The same pins can be used to attach ribbon streamers to the edges of the tables.

The Sun God (Louis XIV)

Colors

Gold, white, and green.

Floral Materials

Roses, white irises, peonies, delphinium, and ornamental kale.

Props

Large urns, candelabras, topiaries, columns, and fountains.

Accessories

Volumes of fabric to be draped and cascaded as room decorations. Hunter green candles to be used in varying heights and diameters. Use tapers in candelabras and groups of pillar candles in individual gold candle stands.

Table Setting Ideas

Seat all guests at one massive, long banquet table. Space a variety of urns and candelabras down the center of the entire table. Puddle gold lamé at the base of the pieces and nestle additional masses of fruit on the table. The look is opulent and excessive. (In advance, discuss with the client whether or not the leftover fruit is to be delivered to a local charity.)

A Taste of the 20's

Colors

Pink, black, and silver.

Floral Materials

Nerine lilies, callas, ornithogalum, French tulips, bear grass, and palms.

Props

Architectural motifs from buildings of the 1920's, stylized art deco motifs, such as flamingos and palm trees, or standing cutouts of women. Egyptian-inspired motifs, such as the pyramids, the sphinx, and scarabs. Eagles, wolfhounds, sleek cars, steamships, and geometric designs could also be used.

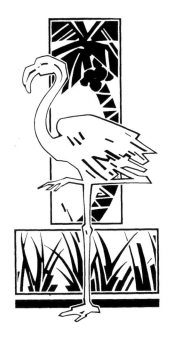

Accessories

Statues of women and dancers, prints of work by Erté, long cigarette holders, cigarette cases, pink neon-like plastic tubing, and pink glow in the dark luminous sticks.

Table Setting Ideas

Use hot pink lamé tablecloth squares over long black tablecloths. Make 2-foot tall pedestals, with a base of at least 9 inches in diameter for stability. They may taper to approximately 6 inches and then increase in diameter at the top. Use foam board and draw or trace a symmetrical, flat-topped pattern. Make a slot, one-half the way down from the top on one piece and one-half the way up from the base on the other. Slide them together. Cut out a top of foam board or use an inverted plastic saucer and glue securely. Attach the arrangement securely to the top. (Any time a new pattern for a design is created, make a sample well in advance and test for visual and mechanical balance.) Accent the arrangement with pink neon glow sticks just before the guests enter. Tie black napkins with pink glow sticks and a dendrobium orchid blossom.

TROPICAL RAINFOREST

Colors

Predominantly green with occasional brilliant color accents in purple and orange.

Floral Materials

Tropical flowers and lush foliage, including monstera, ti leaves, palmetto, tepee, hala, pandanus, fishtail palm, coconut fronds, vines, etc.

Props

Rope bridge and swinging ropes hanging from the ceiling; black banana and coconut trees.

Accessories

Exotic birds, alligators, monkeys, tigers, bananas, black coconuts.

Table Setting Ideas

Use dark green tablecloths with a minimal overhang. Pin or tape the cloth edge underneath the table. Cover legs of the tables with fresh bundles of grasses and reeds.

Special Effects

Lighting to form shadows of trees.

Sounds

Sounds of a rainstorm that fade to jungle noises, such as birds and monkey sounds.

Vienna Ball

Colors

Peach, ivory/white, and copper.

Floral Materials

Open roses and fresh peaches.

Props

Formal garden plantings, balustrades.

Accessories

Copper containers. Use clusters of 24-inch, 30-inch, and 36-inch "shell pink" candles in arrangements with elegant masks on the handles.

Table Setting Ideas

Use rectangular tables with peach colored tablecloths. Add a soft, draped length of copper tissue lamé so that it goes under the centerpiece and cascades down the side of the table. Tie the copper lamé with French wired ribbon. Use a pair of candelabras to flank the arrangement. Request that no chair or place setting be placed where the lamé cascades toward (but stopping short of) the floor.

Wild Wild West

Colors

Yellow, orange, brown, and red.

Floral Materials

Sunflowers, wheat, tall weeds, red rover chrysanthemums, safflower, calendula, tansy, montbretia, protea, succulents, black cacti.

Props

Covered wagon with arrows piercing it, wagon wheels, cowboys, rodeo riders, saloon doors, dance hall, card tables, railroad tracks, pony express, horses, and howling coyotes.

Accessories

Cowboy boots, spurs, pistols, sheriff's badge, horseshoes, saddles, lassoes, and bandannas.

Table Setting Ideas

Burlap potato bags and flour sacks on top of the tables. Flowers in whisky bottles, tin skillets, or pots wrapped in copper screens with other accessories.

Winter Wonderland

Colors

White and silver.

Floral Materials

Fuji mums, Queen Anne's lace, hyacinth, ornithogalum, and snow drift pompon mums.

Props

Stands of tall white painted birch branches for backdrops. Lace with white miniature lights.

Accessories

Snowflakes, artificial snow, cotton batting with opalescent mylar flakes, and balloons with white streamers and lightweight snowflakes attached. Subcontract for lighted ice sculptures and create an environment for the sculptures with additional birch branches and snowflakes.

Table Setting Ideas

Rent a tablecloth with a snowflake pattern. Place it over a manufactured net of miniature white lights (available through the special events industry), which have been taped to the edges of the table and draped to just above the floor. When the expense of lighting is a factor, use it in a highly visible area, such as the front of a buffet table. For simple arrangements, use clear glass bubble balls with white pillar candles inside. Add 1/2 inch of water and float a small amount of opalescent snowflakes within. Surround the outside with white pine that has been dusted with artificial snow and glitter. Accent by tucking in short, loose stems of wilt-resistant flowers just before the party starts.

Wizard of Oz

Colors

Red, blue, yellow, green, and white.

Floral Materials

Daisies, poppies, red roses, monte casino, asters, bachelor buttons, miniature carnations, yarrow, dock, and wheat.

Props

Tin Man, Lion, Scarecrow, Wizard, Emerald City, yellow brick road, munchkins, Dorothy, Toto the dog, and the wicked and good witches. One backdrop can depict a simple farmhouse in a wheat field with a descending tornado. Another can depict the Emerald City. (Watch the movie for more inspiration.)

Accessories

Picnic basket, ruby slippers, magic wand, straw, scrap metal, tin funnel, and lion's mane.

Table Setting Ideas

Green tablecloth with yellow vinyl brick road laid on top. Use a permanent marker to draw the bricks. Arrange flowers in red-painted and glittered shoes.

Notes

Fabulous parties are a magical blend of creativity and a desire to dazzle and delight each and every guest. The glamour of a party is not dictated entirely by the budget. An ample budget may result in an incredibly boring fete. The florist has the opportunity to start with flowers and his imagination to take his clients on fanciful flights on the wings of his dreams. The limitations of time and money can stimulate a totally new approach to any theme. Use this chapter to acquire new sources of inspiration that can be part of the florist's reputation for creating not just memorable parties, but *magic!*

Notes, Photographs, Sketches, etc.

Party Themes

Notes, Photographs, Sketches, etc.

Props

*W*hen designing party decorations, props are an important ingredient. Props can be the stuffed animals tucked into trees in a safari or rainforest party, the elegant candelabras placed throughout a ballroom, or the elaborate construction of Egyptian tombs, Russian villages, or tropical beaches. The word prop is a shortened form of the word property. Property is defined by Webster's Dictionary as "any of the moveable articles used in a stage setting." Props, when referred to in party design work, are those materials that are used to help transform an ordinary space into a theatrical setting that fits the mood of the party. The props can be anything from the mechanics used to raise a centerpiece off of a table to great fiberglass sculptures used to decorate a grand hall.

Elaborate props are most often rented or subcontracted from commercial production companies. Others are bought and used repeatedly so that their cost is amortized over a given period of time. On the other hand, others can be easily and inexpensively created so that they can be used for one particular event.

This chapter offers tips for locating props that are available to buy or rent. Suggestions for care and handling of props, including storage ideas, are also provided. Construction techniques are provided for props that even a beginner can create.

Prop Resources

Florists who design elaborate parties on a regular basis have a need for a wide variety of props. Some props, such as candelabras and table-top mirrors, may be used many times. Other props that relate to specific themes (bunnies for Easter, umbrellas for showers, etc.) may be used only once or very infrequently. Therefore, most florists purchase or build those props that are frequently needed and rent more unique or one-of-a-kind props as needed for special theme events. Each option has advantages and disadvantages.

Maintaining an in-house prop inventory allows the florist to have particular props that he might often use available at all times. Props can be built or modified to the florist's particular specifications, altered without penalties, and, in the long run, may be more profitable. The disadvantages include the costs of storage, maintenance, and capital outlay. Also, one may think that a certain prop will be reused, only to find that future party clients find the prop unacceptable.

Renting props from other companies is another alternative for providing florists with access to a variety of props. The advantages of using a rental company include savings on capital outlay, labor for maintenance, and costs of storing the various items. Disadvantages include the limited availability of props, quality, costs to the florist, and, ultimately, the customer.

In-House Prop Inventory

Buying one's own props is a good investment when those props are used frequently. Many companies that service the floral industry have a variety of products available for purchase. These companies exhibit at floral industry trade shows and their sales representatives visit shop locations during the year. Candelabras, arches, canopies, table risers, and columns are just a few of the available items. When buying props, it is important to see them (not just a picture) and to be able to examine the items for durability and stability. If one can only buy from a picture and a description, he should be sure that the item can be returned. Items that appear to be satisfactory in a picture may actually be too bulky or unprofessional in appearance.

Display companies that specialize in visual display merchandise are another viable source for props. These companies are frequently represented at trade shows for the visual display industry, as well as being advertised in trade journals. A list of prop resources is provided in Appendix A. Also, second-hand props can sometimes be purchased from the visual display department of local department stores.

Architectural restoration firms are still another resource for party props. These companies salvage items, such as fireplaces, columns, banisters, moldings, windows, doors, etc., from buildings that are being razed or renovated. These parts are then re-sold. With a little creativity and some refinishing, they can often be used to create props.

Building props can be rewarding or frustrating, depending on one's abilities. Sometimes props can be built at a lower cost than renting. This also allows greater customizing options for individual

Notes

parties. The second half of this chapter includes several suggestions for props that can be easily constructed within a floral shop.

Renting from Sub-Contractors

For florists who do not have adequate storage space for props or who might only infrequently need party props, renting from specialty companies is a valuable alternative.

Local Rental Companies

Local party rental companies, which can be found in the telephone Yellow Pages under "Rental" and/or "Party," often supply dividing screens, candelabras, linens, umbrellas, wishing wells, arches, and many other items. Inventory lists and prices from such companies should be kept on file in the floral shop.

Florists might also consider contacting local rental companies and proposing a reciprocal agreement. Although commissions are often considered appropriate, it is also possible to arrange for each to recommend the other's services without financial considerations.

Reservations with rental companies must be made in advance. If possible, the rental company should be contacted as soon as the party is booked and a deposit has been received. The rental company should be provided with a written list of prop needs, the dates needed, and delivery instructions. Times, addresses, and any other pertinent information that the rental company may need to know should be included in this written request. The company can be asked to send a written confirmation of the reservation. This attention to detail is important and can reduce the possibility of errors on the day of the party.

Fellow Florists

Another good source for "renting" props is from other florists. Many of the unique wedding props, such as a clam shell canopy, a chuppah, or candelabras, can be either rented or borrowed from one's colleagues. If there is a local industry organization, a list of props that each florist might be willing to loan or rent could be established. This is best for those types of props that a florist may use only once or twice a year. It is usually best to purchase materials, such as mirrors for tables or centerpiece risers, that will be used often.

Professional Display Companies

Another source for rental props is professional display companies. These commercial production companies specialize in large, customized props. For example, they may have carousel horses, life-size wooden clowns, fiberglass cactus plants, or rodeo scenes that can be rented. Some of these companies can be found in the Yellow Pages; however, a magazine devoted to party planning would be an even better source. Special Events is published monthly by Miramar Publishing Company (6133 Bristol Parkway, Culver City, California 90230) and includes not only articles on various types of parties and party planning, it also features many advertisers who could be terrific resources. As with local rental companies, these companies should be sought out before they are needed. What they offer, what they charge, and how far in advance reservations are needed should be determined. Likewise, some companies simply rent their props, while others are actually party planners and will develop the party in its entirety and offer the florist a commission. For a list of prop resources, see Appendix A.

Pricing

Props that are owned by the florist are priced to reflect the capital outlay, the cost of storage, and the cost to transport the items to the party and back to storage. While the first cost is usually a known figure, the costs of the two latter items may be difficult to accurately estimate. Therefore, it is easier to use a percent markup than a set dollar figure. To do this, the florist should attempt to determine the approximate number of times he thinks he can rent an item during a year. Then he can set the rental charge at 30 to 100 percent of the wholesale cost of the item. Props that can be rented multiple times, such as mirrors and votives, should be priced at a lower percentage (30 to 40 percent). Items that can be rented only a limited number of times before wearing out (tablecloths, plants, foam board props, etc.) should be rented at a higher percentage. Some florists, for example, rent linen tablecloths at 100 percent of the wholesale cost. This way, even if the cloth is damaged during its first use, the initial capital outlay is recouped.

Rental companies are convenient adjuncts to the floral industry. When using such a company's products, one is no longer concerned with capital outlay, storage, maintenance, and pickup and delivery costs. The florist can afford to charge a percentage (10 to 15 percent minimum) plus the florist's cost of the rental when billing the customer. Some rental companies have wholesale prices that might allow the florist to use a greater markup and still be competitive.

Frequently, rental companies will deliver and pick up the required items to and from the party location. This will assist in saving the florist labor costs. If this service is not available or not convenient for the florist, the added percentages should be increased to cover such expenses.

It is a good practice to require a refundable deposit on all rental items. The deposit should be at least 90 percent of the total replacement cost of the equipment. Taking a deposit on a major credit card makes it easier to collect the full value of a rental item if it disappears.

Renting props, plants, or other items to a client can be a profitable venture or costly disaster. To avoid the latter, the florist should draft a rental contract before renting anything. This contract should clearly state the client's responsibility for rented items and for their return to the florist. Consequences of damage to, or loss of, items should be stated as well. A sample rental contract is provided in Appendix B.

Care and Handling of Props

Care and handling of the props that a florist owns are very important to the life of the prop. If a florist spends hundreds of dollars on fiberglass columns, for example, he must use them many times for the columns to be profitable. Therefore, they must be cared for so that they are not damaged when being used, delivered, picked up, or stored.

Storage

Adequate storage is mandatory if a florist plans to purchase or build props for long-term use. Storage space can quickly become a problem in many floral shops because props are often large and bulky. Some florists rent additional space specifically for prop storage. Warehouse storage is often the most affordable option. One florist in New York City rents space in Pennsylvania because the difference in rental cost more than outweighs the transportation cost. This florist has a very large inventory of props, which makes this arrangement more cost effective.

Besides warehouse space, other storage alternatives include leasing local mini storage space, building outdoor storage sheds, renting a garage, or perhaps even utilizing an employee's garage or basement. Depending on the geographic location and the economic situation at any specific time, a florist may find warehouses with excess rental space. These facilities may offer short-term leases at lower rates; however, it may be necessary to relocate if economic conditions change and the landlord is able to fill space and raise rates.

Storage space should be easily accessible, especially on weekends and holidays. The space should also be dry and free from moisture to avoid mold and other damage. If a basement is the chosen space, it should be determined whether or not the props can be taken down the stairs and if the width of the staircase is too narrow for large, bulky items.

Related props should be kept together. Shelving and/or floor space should be sufficient so that all candelabras can be stored in one place, all the mirrors in another, and so on. An inventory list with the quantity and location of each prop noted should be maintained. When an item is used, the driver should account for the number of pieces taken, and then make certain that that number is returned when the party is over. (See the prop inventory form in Appendix A.)

Assigning one person responsibility for the storage area may be desirable. That person is assigned the task of seeing that all props are stored neatly, with like products together, and inventoried for future accessibility. This person could also be responsible for the maintenance of the props.

Maintenance

As each prop is returned from a party, it should be examined for damage. For example, if the paint is chipped on a candelabra, if the hinges on the dividing screens have loosened, or if mirrors have melted wax on them, they should be repainted, repaired, and/or cleaned before being stored. However, if it is not possible to repair an item when it is returned to storage, it can be tagged with a note describing the care needed and stored in a separate area.

Props that are assembled with screws and bolts or other hardware, such as an arch, should be stored with the hardware in an airtight plastic bag. A label should be inserted in the bag that names the prop the hardware is for, as well as the number and types of pieces necessary to construct the prop. This bag should be secured to one of the largest pieces of the prop. Making sure that all the pieces are there when needed should be the responsibility of the prop manager. When each item is stored, these pieces should be checked. If any part is missing it should be replaced immediately rather than waiting until the next party.

It is recommended that items such as candelabra globes be contained in a moveable and storable box or crate. Keeping all the glass together means that when it is time to load the delivery

Notes

P_{ROPS}

Notes

vehicle, no one has to locate all the pieces and find something in which to transport them. This saves time and reduces the chance that something will be missing or forgotten.

Periodically, those items that are painted should be repainted so that they always look clean and fresh. If there are adhesive tape marks, they can be removed with a small amount of spray hand cleaner or nail polish remover (check for finish damage in an inconspicuous place first). Traces of melted wax can be removed with hot water and/or a cleaning product. On brass items, care should be taken not to remove the lacquer finish that prevents tarnishing.

Foam board and foam board figures should be stored flat, if possible. The shipping cartons in which foam board is frequently delivered will make good storage containers. Foam board has a tendency to warp; therefore, it is necessary to store the board in an area that is dry and where the edges will not get bent or damaged.

Creating Props

Each new party brings a need for unique and creative use of floral materials and props. New ideas must constantly be developed, new materials used, and yet each party must be commercially profitable. On the following pages are specific examples of props that can be used to create a mood, camouflage a room's decor, add to the dramatic presentation of the floral decorations, and assist in developing the uniqueness of each party.

The materials recommended are lightweight, easy to move, and inexpensive so that costs can be kept to a minimum. If props are stored with care, many can be reused and/or altered for other parties. No special skills with complicated power tools are required to create these props. Tools readily available in a floral shop are all that are required.

Suggestions and how to's are offered, but the key to creating successful party props is being able to take these ideas, modify them, and create props that are tailored for each specific event.

Free-Standing Space Enhancers

Parties are held in many different types of spaces. To personalize that space, it should be enhanced or its boundaries redefined. Party decorators often use free-standing space enhancers. Dividing screens, lattice screens, shoji screens standing cutouts, plants, and moveable walls can all be used to alter the space or environment of a chosen location.

Dividing Screens

Dividing screens are used to conceal areas of a room that might not be as attractive as desired, to separate space so that available square footage is reduced, and to direct traffic patterns. Many different types of dividing screens are available, such as lattice folding screens, shoji (Oriental-style) screens, and folding screens that can be made from foam board. Instructions for making foam board screens follow.

Foam Board Screen

The following instructions are for constructing a foam board dividing screen that is scored and folded into accordion-type folds. The screens can be easily covered with fabric, paint, and/or wallpaper for a decorative finish.

Materials Needed

- Two sheets of foam board, 6 feet by 4 feet

- X-ACTO® knife or very sharp razor blade tool

- Yardstick

- Pencil

- Masking tape

Construction Steps

1. Lay each sheet of foam board on a flat surface and measure each so that it is divided in half lengthwise. **(Figure 5.1a)**

2. Score each board down the length of the board with the knife; be careful to only cut one side of the paper. **Do not cut through the back of the board.**

3. Bend each board down the cut. Position the boards side by side with one board so that the cut side is facing up and the other board so that the cut side is

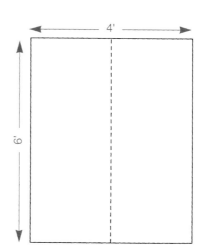

Figure 5.1a Constructing a Foam Board Screen Step 1

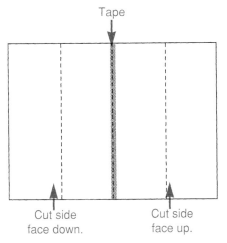

Figure 5.1b **Constructing a Foam Board Screen Step 3**

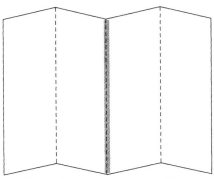

Figure 5.1c **Constructing a Foam Board Screen Step 4**

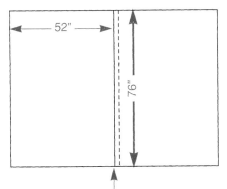

Sew together 2 panels - right sides together along this edge. Results = 4 panels 102" x 76"

Figure 5.1d **Constructing a Foam Board Screen Step 5**

facing down. With masking tape, secure the two boards together lengthwise. *(Figure 5.1b)*

4. The boards can now be bent accordion-style and stood up. *(Figure 5.1c)*

5. The board can be covered with one of the following.

   • *Paint* - Use latex or tempera paints and be sure to paint both sides so that the boards do not warp.

   • *Fabric* - The fabric can be shirred and adhered with hot glue and/or staples. A changeable fabric cover can be easily made according to the following steps.

      a. Cut eight panels of fabric each 52 inches by 76 inches.

      b. Sew every two panels together lengthwise with 1-inch seams. *(Figure 5.1d)* When completed, there should be four large panels, each 102 inches by 76 inches.

      c. Place the right sides of two panels together and sew a 1-inch seam along three of the edges. The fourth unsewn edge should be a 76-inch side. *(Figure 5.1e on page 118)*

      d. Turn the panel right side out, press the seams, and slip the pillowcase over the edges of the board, gathering the fabric as it is slipped over. The unfinished edge should be on the inside of the dividing screen. *(Figure 5.1f on page 118)*

      e. Repeat Steps 1 through 4 for the second side of the screen. Be sure to keep the fabric pattern going in the same direction on all of the pieces.

   • *Wallpaper* - Wallpaper can be attached with wallpaper paste, a glue gun, or with spray adhesive, if the paper is not too heavy.

- *Photocopied pictures* - Photocopy and enlarge the desired picture, such as a Greek column, in sections. Glue the sections to the board to form a large column. *(Figure 5.1g)* Other photos to consider copying are those of skylines or natural scenes.

- *Murals* - Purchase a commercial mural backdrop paper from a party decorating store. Secure onto the board with glue.

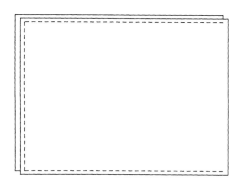

Figure 5.1e Constructing a Foam Board Screen Step 5

Tips for Using Foam Board

- An opaque or overhead projector can be used to project an image onto foam board. The image can be traced with a pencil. **Do not use a ballpoint pen** - it will leave a permanent mark. Alternatively, a slide can be made of the desired image and then a slide projector can be used to project the image.

- Use a utility knife, X-ACTO® knife, jigsaw (with a knife blade) or a Cutawl™ power tool (available through the Cutawl Company, Bethel, Connecticut) to cut foam board.

- Scoring can be used to create a variety of curves, corners, and creases. To score a piece of foam board, cut the top layer of the foam board with parallel lines 3/4 inch apart. Remove the paper strip, exposing the foam center; score the foam and remove the foam, but **do not cut or damage the bottom paper liner.** The board can then be folded with the cut-out section to the inside of the fold.

- A variety of paints can be used to finish the boards. Both sides of the board must be painted so that the board will not warp. Poster paints, acrylic paints, tempera, and latex-based pigments may be used successfully. Enamel sign paint, which is available at art supply houses, is very true and bright and does not fade easily.

- White glue, hot melt glue, and floral adhesive can all be used to connect pieces of board. Corsage pins can be used to hold the boards together until the adhesive dries.

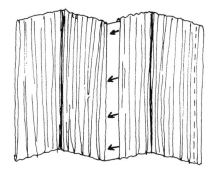

Figure 5.1f Constructing a Foam Board Screen Step 5

Figure 5.1g Constructing a Foam Board Screen Step 5

Shoji Screen

This Oriental-inspired area divider features a wooden frame and a covering of cotton muslin. When a floodlight is placed behind the screen and a grouping of green plants to the front and sides of the screen, a particularly warm and elegant space enhancer is created.

Materials Needed

- Four 72-inch pieces of 1-inch by 3-inch white pine boards

- Six 43-inch pieces of 1-inch by 3-inch white pine boards

- Four 44-inch pieces of 1-inch by 3-inch white pine boards

- Fifty-four inch or 60-inch unbleached cotton muslin cut into two pieces 72 inches long

- Three sets of 2 1/2-inch hinges

- Nails (corrugated nails are recommended)

- Wood glue

- Paint (traditionally either white or black)

- Saw

- Hammer

- Screwdriver

- Staple gun

- Two paint brushes

Construction Steps

1. Lay out the two wooden frames in the pattern shown in *Figure 5.2a*. Glue and nail all pieces of wood together.

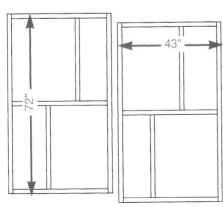

Figure 5.2a Creating a Shoji Screen
Step 1

2. Paint the frames and let them dry completely.

3. Dilute the wood glue with a small amount of water and brush it along the back of each frame. Lay the muslin straight along the outer edges of the frame and staple it in place every 3 to 4 inches. Be sure to pull the fabric taut as it is stretched over the frame.

4. Trim the excess material.

5. Attach the hinges to the back of the two sections of frame making sure they are properly aligned. *(Figure 5.2b)*

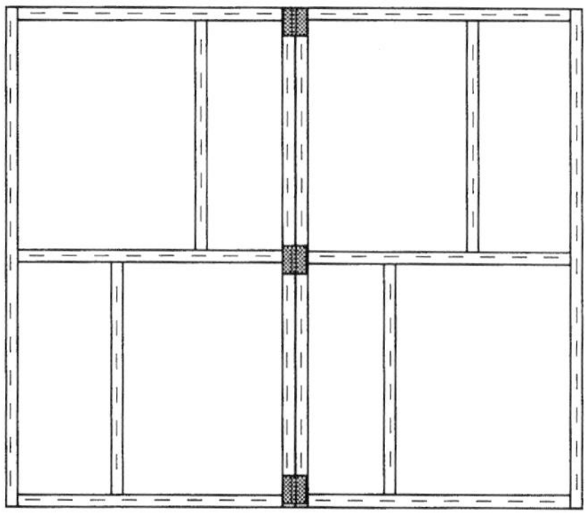

Figure 5.2b **Creating a Shoji Screen** Step 5

6. Additional panels can be made and hinged to the original set if a larger screen is desired. However, if more than three panels are hinged together, the screen could be too heavy to move easily.

Foam Board Cutouts

Theme parties and children's parties are only two examples of occasions when a florist might need to create standing cutouts. Sports figures, cartoon characters, model cars, rocket ships, fairy tale figures, and holiday emblems can all be created with foam board and paint. By enlarging a pattern and tracing it onto the foam board with an overhead projector, cutting out the shape, and then painting in the details, almost any character can be created. Coloring books, greeting cards, story books, art illustrations, magazine pictures, and posters are filled with pictures that can be enlarged with an overhead projector onto foam board. (A selection of patterns is also provided in Appendix D.) Overhead projectors are available for a variety of prices from art supply houses, can be rented from audio-visual stores, or can be borrowed from schools and libraries. Following are instructions for creating foam board cutouts.

Materials Needed

• One sheet of foam board 4 feet by 8 feet

• Line drawing of desired figure

• X-ACTO® knife

Figure 5.3a **Constructing a Foam Board Cutout Step 2**

Figure 5.3b **Constructing a Foam Board Cutout Step 5**

Figure 5.3c **Constructing a Foam Board Cutout Step 5**

- Overhead projector

- Latex or tempera paints

Construction Steps

1. Have the desired line drawing made into a transparency. (This service is available for a nominal cost at print shops, libraries, and schools.)

2. Using an overhead projector, superimpose the transparency on the foam board. Adjust the distance of the machine until the size of the figure is as large as desired. Focus the image and trace the outline of the figure with a soft pencil. Do not press hard onto the board. Add any details that might be appropriate to copy or outline later in the finished figure. **(Figure 5.3a)**

3. With an X-ACTO® knife, cut the outer outline of the figure, pressing hard enough to go through both sides of the board. The knife blade must be very sharp and may need to be changed frequently. (This cutting may also be done with a jigsaw, using a knife blade.)

4. Using the paints, add details to the figure. Be sure to paint both sides of the figure to avoid warping.

5. Create a stand for the figure by cutting two pieces of foam board into half circles. Cut a notch in the center of the curved side of each half circle and cut two notches, well spaced from each other, into the base of the figure. **(Figure 5.3b)** Align the base pieces perpendicular to the foam board figure and slip them into the cutout notches. **(Figure 5.3c)** The larger the figure, the larger the base pieces will need to be.

Note: The completed figure may be enhanced with decorations, as desired. Various materials can be glued onto the board to add texture. For example, a Sesame Street Big Bird might be covered with yellow Easter grass, with pampas grass glued to the board for the tail. Fabric can also be glued to the figure with batting underneath to add a puffy quality to the desired areas.

Stained Glass Windows

A stained glass window, or perhaps a pair of windows, could be used to flank a dais. The stained glass adds a play of color and light that might be appropriate at either a religious celebration or for a party atmosphere depicting an atrium setting. Using PVC pipe (found in the plumbing section of hardware stores) and colored cellophane paper, one can create inexpensive and lightweight windows. The PVC pipe can be bent with the aid of a heat gun, secured with a PVC angle joint, and glued into a base. The cellophane is leaded with black electrical tape. (Porterfield, 80) Following are instructions for constructing stained glass windows.

Materials Needed

- Two 6-foot long pieces of 3/4-inch PVC pipe

- One 45-degree 3/4-inch elbow joint

- One 3-foot long piece of 2-inch by 4-inch wood

- One 3-foot long piece of 2-inch by 6-inch wood

- Three or more colors of cellophane paper

- Black electrical tape

- Heat gun

- Drill

- Hammer

- Three-inch nails

- Plumber's glue (specifically for the PVC pipe)

- White paint

Construction Steps

1. Bend the two sections of PVC pipe until a curved arch is created. By heating the pipe with a heat gun (the

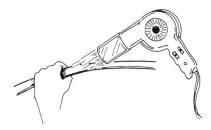

Figure 5.4a Creating a Stained Glass
Window Step 1

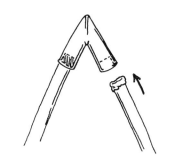

Figure 5.4b Creating a Stained Glass
Window Step 2

Figure 5.4c Creating a Stained Glass
Window Step 3

Figure 5.4d Creating a Stained Glass
Window Step 5

same type of gun used to shrink wrap fruit baskets) and gently bending the heated area, one can create a gentle curve. *(Figure 5.4a)*

2. Insert one end of each piece of PVC into the 45-degree angle joint. Apply plumber's glue before inserting to assure that the pipe will not slip out. *(Figure 5.4b)*

3. To create the base, take the 2-inch by 4-inch wooden board and drill two 3/4-inch holes about 30 inches apart. Put the 2-inch by 4-inch board on top of the 2-inch by 6-inch board and nail the two together. *(Figure 5.4c)*

4. Spray paint the base with white paint.

5. Cut sections of the various colors of cellophane paper and lay one next to the other until a sheet approximately 6 feet by 36 inches is achieved. Use black electrical tape to tape the sections together. Most stained glass windows do not have perfectly even panes, so make one pane larger than the other. *(Figure 5.4d)*

6. Using hot glue, secure the cellophane panel to the PVC frame. *(Figure 5.4e on page 124)*

7. Trim the excess cellophane that extends beyond the PVC frame.

Table Risers

When placing table arrangements in a ballroom with a very high ceiling, it is often desirable to raise the centerpieces high in the air above the tables. This allows the visual space of the room to be filled, along with providing a focal area on each table. However, care must be taken to ensure that the prop is stable and that the arrangement is not precariously positioned. Following are suggestions for creating several different types of table risers.

Glass Vase Riser

A tall glass vase that is approximately 17 inches or higher can be placed in the center of the table and an arrangement placed on top of the vase. The arrangement should be designed in a low, shallow tray or dish. The container can then be fixed to the top of the vase with floral adhesive clay. *(Figure 5.5a)*

Flower Pot Riser

Turn a flower pot, of any height desired, upside down and cover it with a fabric square, making sure the fabric drapes in a pleasing fashion. *(Figure 5.5b)* The edges of the fabric should be finished either with a rolled hem or with pinking shears. Centerpieces designed in standard utility containers can then be positioned atop the risers. The height of the flower pot should not be so high that it obstructs the view of the guests seated at the table. For an additional party sale, matching fabric can be used to create napkin ties for a coordinated table setting.

Clear Plastic Riser

Clear plastic risers can be built in a variety of configurations. The one described here is the simplest and can be modified by using longer or shorter rods. Clear plastic can be purchased from plastics manufacturers. Often, the materials needed by the florist can be found in a manufacturer's scrap bin, reducing the cost considerably. If old, clear plastic risers need an update, either because they are dirty or scratched, they can be spray painted with a coat of pearlized paint. A quality clear plastic can also be taken to a plastics manufacturer to be re-polished. Following are instructions for building clear plastic risers.

Materials Needed

- Two 8-inch round clear plastic disks

- Four 21-inch clear plastic rods with end caps

- Sandpaper

- PVC pipe cement

- OASIS® Glue or Pan Melt Glue

Construction Steps

1. Measure the disk and divide it into four parts. *(Figure 5.5c on page 125)* This can be done on a piece of

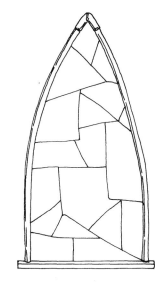

Figure 5.4e **Creating a Stained Glass Window Step 6**

Figure 5.5a **Table Risers - Glass Vase Riser**

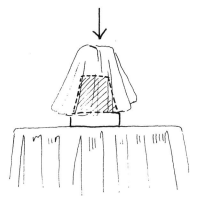

Figure 5.5b **Table Risers - Flower Pot Riser**

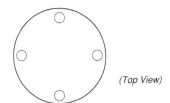

(Top View)

Figure 5.5c Table Risers - Constructing
a Clear Plastic Riser Step 1

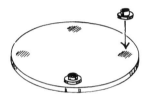

Figure 5.5d Table Risers - Constructing
a Clear Plastic Riser Step 3

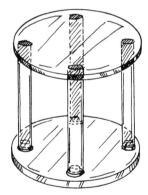

Figure 5.5e Table Risers - Constructing
a Clear Plastic Riser Step 4

white paper with the markings on the paper. The pattern is then placed underneath the disk and the rods are cemented to the lucite disk at the marks on the pattern.

2. Roughen the spots on the disk were the pattern marks indicate, using a piece of fine sandpaper. The glue will hold better if the plastic is slightly roughened. Be careful not to make marks that will be visible and detract from the finished product. The caps on top of the rods should also be roughened with the sandpaper.

3. Glue the end caps to the disk. *(Figure 5.5d)* PVC pipe cement works very well; however, it is blue in color and may show through if not applied sparingly. OASIS® Glue is an excellent adhesive; be sure to let it dry thoroughly before using. Pan melt glue will also work; however, since the glue is not clear, care must be taken to avoid getting any excess on the plastic because it will not come off.

4. When the caps are glued to the disks and the glue has hardened, insert the rods into the cap ends. *(Figure 5.5e)*

Wood and PVC Riser

A riser made of wood and PVC pipe is convenient because the riser can be stored, disassembled, and can be assembled quickly and easily when needed, either in the shop or at the party location. The riser consists of two flat squares held apart by a piece of PVC pipe. The unit can be spray painted, covered in fabric, covered in decorative contact paper, or covered in mosses and natural materials for a woodsy look. Following are instructions for creating a riser made of wood and PVC pipe.

Materials Needed

- One 10-inch square of 1/4-inch plywood

- One 6-inch square of 1/4-inch plywood

- Two 6-inch pieces of 1-inch by 1-inch parting strip (lumber)

- One piece of 2-inch PVC pipe as long as desired. (If taller than 2 feet, the parting strip may need to be longer than 6 inches for balance.)

- Four 2-inch wood screws with flat heads

- Thin black rubber sheeting

- Saw (if lumber is not cut to size)

- Screwdriver

- Black spray paint

Construction Steps

1. Secure the parting strips to the center of each square (so that they are perpendicular to the base) with two screws in each. Be certain that the head of the screw is very flat and will not interfere with the stability of the prop. The smaller square will have the parting strip attached to the bottom of the wood, while the larger square will have the parting strip attached to the top part of the wood. *(Figure 5.6a)*

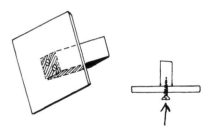

Figure 5.6a Constructing a Wood and PVC Riser Step 1

2. Spray paint all the pieces with an even coat of black spray paint. The PVC pipe should be sanded first with a fine grade of sandpaper. This will help the paint adhere to the surface.

3. Cover the top of the 6-inch square with a thin piece of black rubber so that the centerpiece placed on top will not slide off.

4. Insert the PVC pipe over the rod segment of the parting strip and insert the smaller square and its rod into the top of the PVC pipe. *(Figure 5.6b)*

5. Position a centerpiece on the top level of the riser.

Note: A fabric tube can be created to cover the PVC pipe, if desired. Fabric can also be draped over the base and flowers and/or foliage used to enhance the base and pole.

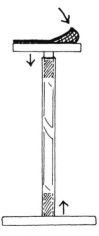

Figure 5.6b Constructing a Wood and PVC Riser Step 4

Props

Columns

Columns are an effective way of displaying plants and arrangements throughout a room. They can be used to frame a head table by placing one on either end and slightly to the back of the table. Columns can also be used to create a focal area with a grouping of columns, floral arrangements, and green plants.

The columns constructed in the following directions begin as cardboard packing tubes (or construction tubes known as sonotube) and are capped with Styrofoam™ wreaths and squares. The entire column is then covered with papier-mâché and spray painted. A variety of finishes can be developed, ranging from "faux marble" to stucco. (<u>Florist's Review</u>, June 1988, 45) Following are instructions for constructing a column.

Materials Needed

- Cardboard packing tube (These can be obtained from companies that specialize in commercial packaging. sonotube, available from construction company suppliers, can also be used.)

- Two Styrofoam™ wreath ring forms (The inside diameter of the wreaths should equal the diameter of the packing tube.)

- Two pieces of square 2-inch Styrofoam™ board slightly larger than the wreath ring forms

- White tissue paper

- Spray paints

- Spray adhesive

- Sabre saw with cardboard blade or hand band-saw

- Hot glue pan

Construction Steps

1. Cut the tube to the height desired. Secure a wreath ring to both ends of the tube with hot glue. Glue the Styrofoam™ square on top of the ring form. *(Figure 5.7a)*

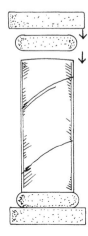

Figure 5.7a Creating a Column Step 1

2. Tear the tissue paper into strips approximately 2 to 4 inches in width. Spray the tube with adhesive glue and cover it with a layer of tissue paper. Try to place the paper so that there are no wrinkles in the finish. Paper the entire column form with the tissue, spraying adhesive on either the form or just the back of the tissue paper. The paper should cover the joints of the tube and the Styrofoam™ and the end result should appear to be created out of one piece of material. Allow the column to dry. **(Figure 5.7b)**

3. Using spray paints, create the desired finish. One suggestion is to spray the entire unit with white paint. Next, spray lightly with cottage green, then with teal green, and finally with a layer of black deco lace. The webbing of the deco lace gives the column the appearance of a marble finish. An alternative finish is to use Fleckstone™ paints that produce a textured finish.

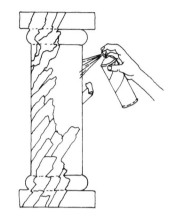

Figure 5.7b Creating a Column Step 2

Arches

Arches can create exciting and dramatic entryways. Three different types of arches are presented in this section. The first is created with PVC pipe and a choice of coverings. The second is constructed with tall birch tree branches. The third uses curly willow and illustrates an asymmetrical design rather than the traditional symmetrical arch.

PVC Arch

This arch has the advantage of being able to be disassembled and stored for repeated use. The pipes are connected with the PVC connectors sold with the pipe. The fabric covering can be coordinated with the table linens or it could be yards of ribbon fabric. (Many ribbon manufacturers sell ribbon fabric by the yard before it is cut into the ribbon widths.) Following are instructions for creating a PVC arch.

Materials Needed

- Four poles - 7-foot by 3/4-inch PVC pipe

- Two poles - 6-foot by 3/4-inch PVC pipe

- Six poles - 24 to 36-inch by 3/4-inch PVC pipe

- Four female-female ended 90-degree elbow joints for the 3/4-inch PVC pipe **(Figure 5.8a)**

Figure 5.8a Constructing a PVC Arch - Female-Female Elbow Joint

Props

Figure 5.8b Constructing a PVC Arch - Male-Female Elbow Joint

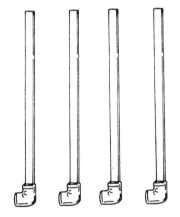

Figure 5.8c Constructing a PVC Arch Step 1

Figure 5.8d Constructing a PVC Arch Step 2

- Four male-female ended 90-degree elbow joints for the 3/4-inch PVC pipe *(Figure 5.8b)*

- Eight T-connectors for the 3/4-inch PVC pipe

- Six yards of fabric at least 45 inches wide

- Corsage pins

- Plumber's PVC cement

- Electric saw or a hand band-saw (if the pipe needs to be cut)

Construction Steps

1. Glue (with the plumber's PVC cement) the female-female elbow joints to the ends of the 7-foot poles. *(Figure 5.8c)*

2. Glue the bases of four of the T-connectors to the tops of the same 7-foot poles. Make certain that the connectors are lined up perpendicular to the opening of the elbow joint on the other end as shown. *(Figure 5.8d)*

3. Insert the male end of the male-female elbow joint into one end of each T-connector so the joints are lined up as shown. *(Figure 5.8e on page 130)* Glue the joints in place.

4. Slide two T-connectors onto each of the two 6-foot poles. The inner ends of the connectors should be 24 inches from the ends of the poles. Place a small amount of glue onto the 6-foot pole just before sliding the connector into place. Make sure that the connectors all line up as shown. *(Figure 5.8f on page 130)*

5. Insert the ends of the 6-foot poles into the open ends of the T-connectors atop the 7-foot poles. *(Figure 5.8g on page 130)*

6. Insert the 24 to 36-inch poles into the elbow joints and T-connectors as shown. **Do not glue. *(Figure 5.8h on page 130)***

7. Cover with fabric in one of the following ways.

Method I:

a. Drape the fabric over the frame. The fabric can then be pinned into place so that it is pulled taut or gathered as it passes over the pipes.

b. Swag the fabric and tie with bows and ribbons.

c. Sew a long tube from the fabric and slip the tube over the pipes, gathering the material as if hanging a curtain.

Method II:

a. Wrap Spanish moss around all the poles; use paddle wire to secure the moss strands to the pipes. Make sure that the connectors are well hidden.

b. Unroll grapevine wreaths and use the grapevine to wind around the pipes and over the moss.

c. IGLU® Holders can be wired into the corners and floral sprays created in the holders.

Note: Several of these arches lined up one after the other will create a grand entryway.

Birch Branch Arch

Birch branches are used to create a tall arch of natural branch material through which tiny white lights are strung. The arch is then decorated with floral materials, such as autumn leaves and berries, as well as fresh flowers woven throughout the branches. This same technique could be used with wisteria branches or with birch logs gathered from the woods. The taller and heavier the branch material, the heavier and wider the cement base must be for the arch to be stable. Following are instructions for creating a birch branch arch.

Materials Needed

- Two to four bunches of 8-foot tall birch branches, either natural or painted white, depending on the designer's needs

- Two papier-mâché pots

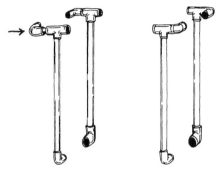

Figure 5.8e Constructing a PVC Arch
Step 3

Figure 5.8f Constructing a PVC Arch
Step 4

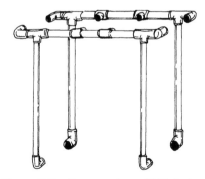

Figure 5.8g Constructing a PVC Arch
Step 5

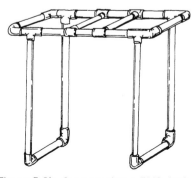

Figure 5.8h Constructing a PVC Arch
Step 6

Figure 5.9a Constructing a Birch Branch Arch Step 2

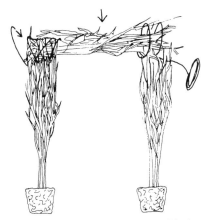

Figure 5.9b Constructing a Birch Branch Arch Step 5

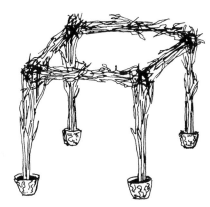

Figure 5.9c Constructing a Birch Branch Arch Step 7

- Plaster of Paris

- Wire

Construction Steps

1. Divide the branches into four bundles.

2. Fill each papier-mâché pot with plaster of Paris. As soon as the plaster begins to harden, insert one bundle of branches into the plaster. **(Figure 5.9a)** Allow the plaster to dry.

3. Wire the remaining two bundles in two or three locations to hold the stems together.

4. Lay the two bundles so that they overlap and wire them together horizontally in opposite directions.

5. Position the two papier-mâché pots 8 feet apart. Lay the double bundles of birch branches on top of the vertical birch columns and weave the stems among the birch tips. Wire the horizontal bundle in place. **(Figure 5.9b)**

6. Before displaying, cover the papier-mâché pots with an appropriate material. If using the woodsy, natural look, drape sheet moss over the pots, and add dried lichens, pods, etc., to complete the base. If a winter wonderland look is desired, cover with batting material and sprinkle with artificial snow.

7. For added impact, a second arch can be constructed. Place one in front of the other to obtain greater depth within an entry. If desired, additional branches can be wired to connect the two arches and create a canopy. **(Figure 5.9c)**

8. If the birch branches are white, use miniature lights with white cords. If the branches are natural, remove the light bulbs from the string and spray paint the cords brown. (Try painting the light cords before removing them from the cardboard packaging, cover the lights with masking tape, and then spray paint the cord.)

9. String the lights throughout the trees. Make sure that the plugs end up at the bottom of the trees.

Curly Willow Arch

This arch made of curly willow is actually only three quarters of an arch. A floral arrangement placed on the opposite side of the arch completes the arch shape. The curly willow adds grace and movement as guests walk under this arch. Instructions for constructing a curly willow arch follow.

Materials Needed

- Curly willow branches - at least 8 feet tall

- Papier-mâché pot

- Plaster of Paris

- Mosses

Construction Steps

1. Gently bend the curly willow branches by twisting the trunk and pushing against the thumbs. If necessary, prune the branches until there is a dramatic and graceful *C* curve. *(Figure 5.10)*

2. Fill the papier-mâché pot with plaster of Paris; when the plaster begins to harden, place the branches in the pot. Position the branches so that the bottom trunk leans toward the left side. This is important for the balance of the material.

3. Cover the pot with mosses.

Figure 5.10 Curly Willow Arch

4. Design a tall, upright floral arrangement to reach up to the end of the willow arch. *(Figure 5.10)*

Note: Fresh stock heads can be suspended from the branches to imitate a wisteria vine.

Canopy

A canopy can be used over the head table at a party or as an entryway to the ballroom. It can also be used to bring attention to important locations within the party setting, such as food tables or a bandstand. Following is a simple PVC canopy that can be dismantled and reused for many occasions.

Materials Needed

- Four 12-inch squares of 1/2-inch plywood

- Eight 8-foot 3/4-inch PVC pipes

- Four PVC flanges

- Four 90-degree 3/4-inch elbow joints

- Screws 3/4 inch long

- Drill

- Wire

- Chenille stems

- White paint

- Fabric - 20 yards 60 inches in width

Figure 5.11a Building a Canopy Step 1

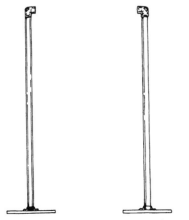

Figure 5.11b Building a Canopy Step 4

Construction Steps

1. Screw the four PVC flanges to the centers of the four 12-inch squares of plywood to create the bases. *(Figure 5.11a)*

2. Spray paint the bases white.

3. Attach the elbow joints to the tops of four pieces of PVC pipe.

4. Insert the opposite end of each PVC pipe into the flanges. *(Figure 5.11b)*

5. Insert the remaining four pieces of PVC pipe into the elbow joints, forming a square top on the canopy.

6. Drill holes through each end of the elbow joints and wire the PVC frame together for security. *(Figure 5.11c)*

7. Cut the fabric into two pieces, each 10 feet by 60 inches, and then sew the fabric together so that the finished piece is 10 feet by 120 inches. Cut four additional pieces that are each 10 feet in length.

8. Cover the top of the frame with the large piece of fabric. Banking pins can be used to secure the fabric to the canopy.

9. The remaining lengths of fabric can be swagged along the lengths of the poles to cover them. Chenille stems can be used to secure the fabric to the poles.

Note: Wrap rubber bands around the poles before assembling the canopy. The rubber bands should be placed at the same height on each of the poles. *(Figure 5.11d)*

When the fabric is gathered around the pole, the rubber bands not only keep the fabric from sliding, they are also a measure so that the draping is at equal heights.

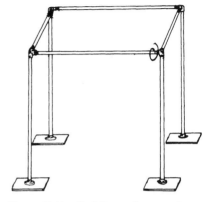

Figure 5.11c Building a Canopy Step 6

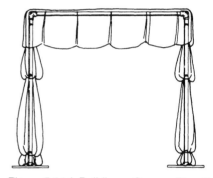

Figure 5.11d Building a Canopy Step 9

Topiary Forms

Topiary forms are used for table arrangements, as well as floor or entry arrangements. The arrangements are based on the topiary trees that are commonly found in formal English gardens. The bases can be terra-cotta, wooden garden planters, ceramic cache pots, or even plastic flower pots that are wrapped in fabric or other materials. The main stem of the topiary can be a wooden dowel, a birch branch, a heavy curly willow branch, or even a piece of pipe. Small topiaries can be secured in floral foam or Styrofoam™, but most need to be embedded in plaster of Paris for stability.

Materials Needed

- Two to 3-foot piece of 1-inch diameter curly willow trunk (see other options above)

- One IGLU® Grande Holder (or substitute a wedge of floral foam that has been wrapped in chicken wire)

Props

Figure 5.12a Constructing a Topiary
Form Step 3

Figure 5.12b Constructing a Topiary
Form Step 4

Figure 5.12c Constructing a Topiary
Form Step 4

- Plastic wrap

- Waxed string

- Base container, i.e., plastic flower pot or papier-mâché container (Terra-cotta and ceramic pots are not recommended for use with plaster of Paris, as expansion may cause the pot to break.)

Construction Steps

1. Cut the bottom of the branch with a straight cut, and whittle the top into a point.

2. Mix the plaster of Paris according to directions. Fill the plastic flower pot or papier-mâché container with the plaster of Paris.

3. As soon as the plaster begins to thicken, insert the branch into the center of the pot. Make sure the branch is straight and centered. **(Figure 5.12a)**

4. Remove the cutout center of the bottom of the IGLU® Grande Holder and position the holder on the top of the branch. **(Figure 5.12b)** Using waterproof tape, secure the holder to the branch. **(Figure 5.12c)** If using floral foam wrapped in chicken wire, it may be necessary to cut one or two wires in the base of the chicken wire in order to wedge the mechanic onto the branch.

5. Wrap the holder or the floral foam once with plastic wrap. This prevents the foam from drying out too quickly and allows the floral material to last longer. Secure the wrap by tying with waxed string.

6. The plastic pot or the papier-mâché pot can be placed inside a decorative pot, such as a terra-cotta pot or a ceramic cache pot. The size of the base should be proportionate to the height of the tree. The plaster of Paris and any space between the two pots can be covered with sheet moss.

7. For design directions, see Chapter 7.

Artificial Palm Trees

Palm trees are great props to fill corners, disguise tent poles, and develop focal areas throughout a ballroom. Constructed of tall yucca poles and tepee palm leaves, the trees are inexpensive and lightweight. Following are instructions for making an artificial palm tree.

Materials Needed

- Yucca poles - height as desired

- Fresh or preserved palm leaves, such as tepee

- One-half block of floral foam

- Chicken wire

- Papier-mâché vase

- Plaster of Paris

- Plastic corsage bag

- Greening pins

- Sheet moss

Construction Steps

1. Mix the plaster of Paris according to the directions on the package. Fill the papier-mâché container with the plaster of Paris. Make sure the container is large enough to support the height of the yucca pole. The width of the container is as important as the height.

2. Insert the yucca pole into the plaster of Paris. The tree should have a natural bend, but should be stable enough not to fall over when the weight of the floral foam and foliage is placed on top. *(Figure 5.13a)*

3. Soak the floral foam block and place it inside the corsage bag. Use greening pins to seal the bag closed.

Figure 5.13a **Constructing an Artificial Palm Tree Step 2**

Figure 5.13b Constructing an Artificial Palm Tree Step 4

Figure 5.13c Constructing an Artificial Palm Tree Step 6

4. Wedge the floral foam brick onto the top of the pole. Cover the foam with chicken wire and use waterproof tape to secure it to the pole. *(Figure 5.13b)*

5. Insert the foliage into the floral foam, making sure that the leaves are placed in the natural growth positions of a palm tree. Any areas that are not covered with the foliage can be covered with sheet moss.

   Alternative: Instead of tepee leaves, the tree can be created with long dendrobium orchid sprays.

6. At the bottom of the tree, cover the plaster with sheet moss. If weight is needed to stabilize the tree, place shallow dishes filled with wet floral foam on top of the plaster base. Insert fern foliage into the floral foam to imitate smaller ferns growing at the base of the tree. *(Figure 5.13c)*

Jumbo Bows

Tent poles and entrances are often enhanced with oversized bows. Butcher paper, which comes on rolls and is available in several widths, is an inexpensive material to use for this purpose. The paper has enough flexibility to make the bows, yet enough weight so that the loops will not flop. The paper can be spray painted to coordinate with any color scheme. Tulle fabric can be added for a romantic effect, if appropriate for the party theme. Following are instructions for constructing jumbo bows.

Materials Needed

- Twenty-four inch roll of butcher paper (Butcher paper can be purchased from wholesale meat supply companies.)

- Chenille stems

Construction Steps

1. Unroll the paper, and as if making a bow with standard ribbon, make a bow with at least two loops on either side and very long streamers. The size of the paper

makes the bow oversized; however, it is necessary to make the outer loops at least 18 inches in length. It is not necessary to twist the paper as when making a ribbon bow; simply gather the material in the center after making each loop.

2. Secure the bow with chenille stems. Connect two together if necessary to go around the center of the bow. Pull as tight as possible before twisting the chenille stem.

Alternative: Lay tulle fabric over the butcher paper and make the bow, using both layers of material (tulle and paper). When using two materials at once, it is necessary to twist the layers between loops to keep the tulle on top of the paper.

Using props when decorating a party area helps change the atmosphere of the space. Props can be purchased from companies that specialize in equipment and display, or they can be borrowed from friends, colleagues, and/or rental companies. They can also be built by the florist allowing for personal customization. Appendix A provides a list of useful resources for props and prop ideas.

Knowing where to find props and how to build one's own props can prove profitable. They become profitable when they are rented repeatedly to a florist's clients. Since each party needs to be unique, props can be altered to meet these needs.

Props

Notes, Photographs, Sketches, etc.

Notes, Photographs, Sketches, etc.

Props

Notes, Photographs, Sketches, etc.

Balloon Decorations

*I*n recent years, the popularity of balloons has grown immensely. Although balloons have long been associated with parties, until recently, they were used only in rather traditional ways. Contemporary creative florists and balloon artists, however, have devised numerous ways to use balloons to create looks for parties that are fun and festive or elegant and sophisticated. Balloons have become a great addition to the party florist's product line and design selection. They can be used to turn an otherwise plain room into a party atmosphere. Balloons also offer a rainbow of colors that before were difficult to provide. In large ballrooms or convention centers, balloons can fill vast areas more quickly and at a significantly lower cost than flowers. When used in combination with fresh flowers, however, the appeal of balloon decorations is significantly enhanced.

As with floral design, there are certain specialty techniques involved when working with balloons. It is very important that the florist be familiar with different types of balloon products and the techniques for using them. In this chapter, different design ideas and special effects are given for use as room enhancements and other party decorations. For additional information on designing with balloons, including basic inflation and design techniques, refer to Redbook Florist Services' *Designing with Balloons and Flowers.*

Note: The specific designs and instructions for the balloon spiral, square garland, candy cane, puffed balls (small, medium, and large), heart arch, puffed heart, stuffed wall, and Christmas ornament are reprinted from the Decorator Series published by Pioneer® Balloon Company, Wichita, Kansas.

Supplies

When a florist is planning on creating balloon decorations for a party, consideration must be given to the tools, materials, and props that may be needed for inflation, construction, and installation. A checklist should be made to ensure that everything is at the job site when it is needed. If the florist is including balloon decorations in the shop's party work on a regular basis, a toolbox

labeled "Balloon Decor" should be put together. The following materials should be included in the toolbox.

- Spare helium nozzle

- Monofilament line (fishing line)

- Corsage pins

- Duct tape

- Drapery hooks

- Balloon clips

- Scissors

- Curling ribbon

- Rigid paper clips

- Wire cutters

- Screwdriver

- Helium tank carrier

Atmospheric Considerations

When decorating with balloons, a few things should be kept in mind to prevent surprises at the job site. For example, balloons can be greatly affected by atmospheric changes. Following are specific occurrences that the florist can expect.

Outdoors

When latex balloons are used outdoors in sunlight, the sunlight will cause the balloons to oxidize. This is a natural process balloons go through as the latex ages and dries out. It is evident when the balloons take on a cloudy or powdery look. Oxidation does not necessarily cut down the float time but it does change the balloon's appearance. When planning decorations for outdoor use, balloons with an opaque matte finish should be used. When using helium outdoors in the sunlight, it is also important to remember that the helium will expand in the heat. Balloons should be slightly underinflated to allow for this expansion.

Indoors

When decorating with balloons indoors, air conditioning can cause some colors of balloons to oxidize. Also, some textured ceilings, such as fiberglass ceilings, are especially prone to have sharp edges that will frequently cause balloons to burst.

Inflation

When designing extensive balloon decorations, it is often preferable to inflate the balloons on site. It is much easier to deliver and carry in a few boxes and a helium tank as opposed to bags and bags of inflated balloons. This also ensures that the balloons are inflated in the environment in which they will be displayed, which reduces the likelihood of shrinkage or expansion due to temperature changes.

When inflating on site, the question often arises as to where to put the inflated balloons until they are needed. An easy solution is a lightweight plastic drop cloth tied and/or taped to the corners of four different chairs. The chairs should be placed far enough apart so that the plastic is spread to about half of its capacity or until the plastic hangs in the air. The helium-inflated balloons can then be placed under the plastic until needed. *(Figure 6.1)*

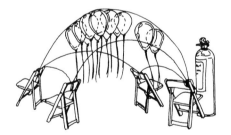

Figure 6.1 Helium Balloon Tent for On-Site Inflation

Table Uses

Balloons are a tremendous complement to fresh flowers. They can add a subtle or dominating spark to a party table. Whether using balloons strictly with helium or as a design element in the table centerpieces, they can offer the color needed to complete the look and theme. Following are several balloon looks that can be used to enhance party tables.

Balloon Bouquets

The term balloon bouquet implies a collection of multiple balloons clustered in a group. However, balloons do not always have to be grouped together and tied. There are several ways to create unique balloon bouquets floating in centerpieces. Following are some examples.

One Large Helium Balloon

One large helium balloon, such as a 40-inch latex, can be very effective by itself. Balloons of this size hold 16 cubic feet of helium, which provides for a substantial float time. This technique can be exemplified by a ballroom full of tables and flowers with one 40-inch balloon floating 5 to 6 feet above the center of each table. This method of balloon decoration can lower a tall ceiling and give the room a glow of color with the lights reflecting through the balloons. *(Figure 6.2)*

Figure 6.2 Single Balloon on a Party Table

One Large Balloon and Trim

The same 40-inch balloon can be accented with a variety of different treatments. As stated previously, a 40-inch balloon will hold 16 cubic feet of helium. This is a substantial amount of helium, which will allow the balloon to hold up a pound or more of trim. The following are suggestions for lightweight balloon trims.

Fabric or Illusion

First, the balloon should be tied and weighted to the table in the traditional manner. Then, the center of a piece of sheer fabric or illusion can be tied around the knot of the balloon. The fabric or illusion can then be draped decoratively onto the tabletop. *(Figure 6.3)*

Figure 6.3 Large Balloon with Fabric Trim

Ribbon

A single 40-inch balloon can be secured to the table and a shower of ribbon attached, allowing it to drape to the table. *(Figure 6.4b)* Wired ribbon can also be used. The ribbon can be formed into interesting spirals and curves. Fishing line securing the balloon to a weight with the ribbon cut above the tabletop could create the effect of the balloon floating in midair. *(Figure 6.4b)*

Figure 6.4a Balloon with Trim - Ribbon Shower

Hanging Balloons

Using a 40-inch balloon, 5-inch balloons can be filled with air and hung from ribbons tied onto the knot. This will create the effect of bubbles. *(Figure 6.5 on page 147)*

Figure 6.4b Balloon with Trim - Wired Ribbon

Figure 6.5 Hanging Balloons

Figure 6.6 Multiple Balloon Cluster

Figure 6.7 Fanned Balloon Cluster

Multiple Balloon Clusters

Multiple balloons can be used to float above tables to create different effects. They can be evenly spaced and anchored into small floral arrangements on the tables. *(Figure 6.6.)* Following are two ideas for unique variations on the traditional cluster style.

Fanned Balloon Cluster

Three to five balloons can be inflated with helium and tied with ribbon. They should be positioned so that they are directly next to each other. Using a small piece of double-faced tape, the balloons should be secured to each other wherever they touch. The ribbons should be pulled together and inserted into a design on a wood pick. More balloons can be added as desired. *(Figure 6.7)*

Inverted Balloons

Balloons can add many different effects while floating over a design. One special look can be created by floating the balloons upside down. This gives the balloons a teardrop appearance. This is done by inflating the balloons with helium and tying them as usual. A piece of fishing line should then be taped to the top of each balloon and the balloons allowed to float with the knot on top. The balloons can then be tied into the design individually at different points and heights. *(Figure 6.8 on page 148)*

Chair Ballcons

An alternative to using helium balloons in the center of the table is to use them on the backs of the chairs. A single latex balloon could be tied to the back of each chair around the table. This can give an interesting all-over effect with circles of balloons around each table. *(Figure 6.9 on page 148)*

Balloon Structures

Balloons can be used to create a wide variety of structures for use as party room decorations. Simple arches and columns are described in Redbook Florist Services' *Designing with Balloons and Flowers.* This section focuses on more complex garlands, sculptures, and other structures that require specialized construction techniques and intense labor.

Spiral Garland

There are several ways to create a balloon spiral. The paper clip and wrap methods are explained here. When deciding which method to use on a given job, the florist should consider the following:

1. The paper clip method may be advantageous when working outdoors under windy conditions because this method allows the clusters some movement along the line without stressing the main part of the balloon.

2. The wrap method may be quicker since it involves fewer steps to assemble each cluster.

The following instructions are for four-color, four-balloon cluster spirals; however, the instructions can be adapted to any color combination, from one to four. A balloon can be added to each cluster to incorporate up to five colors.

To create balloon spirals of a particular length, Table 1 can be used to determine the number of balloons and clusters needed.

Figure 6.8 Inverted Balloons

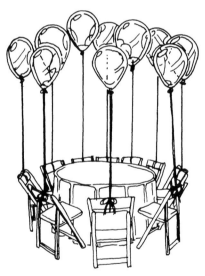

Figure 6.9 Chair Balloons

TABLE 1

CALCULATING NUMBER OF BALLOONS FOR CLUSTERS

Balloon Size	Balloons Per Foot (Four-Balloon Clusters)
5-inch	13
7-inch	9
9-inch	7
11-inch	6
14-inch	5
16-inch	4

The number of clusters needed may be calculated by multiplying the "finished" length of the spiral in feet by the number of balloons per foot (refer to chart on page 148). The total is then divided by the number of balloons in each cluster.

> Example: A 12-foot spiral of 9-inch balloon clusters would require: 12 x 7 = 84 ÷ 4 = 21 four-balloon clusters.

> Example: A 10-foot spiral of 5-inch balloon clusters would require: 10 x 13 = 130 ÷ 4 = 33 four-balloon clusters.

<u>Paper Clip Method</u>

Materials Needed

- Qualatex® (latex) balloons

- Fifty-pound test monofilament line (fishing line)

- Rigid paper clips

Construction Steps

1. Cut a piece of monofilament line the length of the desired spiral plus 3 feet. Attach one end of the line to a stationary object (doorknob) against a flat surface (door), leaving approximately 18 inches of extra line. Then stretch the line horizontally so it is taut and attach the other end to a sturdy structure, leaving approximately 18 inches of extra line. This is the "balloon line."

2. Properly inflate and tie-off four balloons (one of each color). When inflating balloons, a template (which can be made or purchased from a balloon distributor) is recommended. **It is important to maintain a consistent size. (Figure 6.10a)**

3. To assemble the cluster, hold a paper clip in one hand with the double-rounded end pointing down. With the other hand, gently pull away the outer stem of the paper clip approximately 1/8 inch so that the sharp end is exposed. **(Figure 6.10b)**

Figure 6.10a Constructing a Spiral Garland - Paper Clip Method Step 2

Figure 6.10b Constructing a Spiral Garland - Paper Clip Method Step 3

4. Hook the four (or five) balloons onto the paper clip by sticking the sharp end of the paper clip through the neck of each balloon between the knot and neck roll. Move all four balloons around the clip to the inside, opposite the double-rounded end. *(Figure 6.10c)*

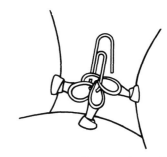

Figure 6.10c Constructing a Spiral Garland - Paper Clip Method Step 4

5. Attach the paper clip to the end of the line nearest to the flat surface, making sure the line is completely inside the clip. Then return the clip to its original shape. *(Figure 6.10d)*

6. Secure the cluster to the line by wrapping any balloon in the cluster around the line. Make sure to wrap the balloon between the knot and clip to avoid bursting. This will secure the cluster snugly to the line and prevent the cluster from slipping once in place. Once the cluster is on the line, position colors in the desired pattern. *(Figure 6.10e)*

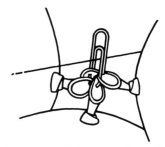

Figure 6.10d Constructing a Spiral Garland - Paper Clip Method Step 5

7. Push the cluster into place at the end of the line next to the flat surface. Make sure the cluster lies flat against it. **The cluster must lie flat in order to "nest" the following clusters.** *(Figure 6.10f)*

8. Push the second cluster firmly against the first cluster, rotating the second cluster so it is nested (at a 45-degree angle) into the first cluster, with balloons of the same color adjacent to each other to achieve the spiral effect. *(Figure 6.10g on page 151)*

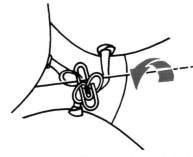

Figure 6.10e Constructing a Spiral Garland - Paper Clip Method Step 6

9. After the second cluster is properly positioned, be sure to push its paper clip farther toward the first cluster to hold the two clusters firmly together. **Take care to nest the spirals firmly, but not to pack too tightly as the spiral will begin to warp.**

10. Continue adding clusters to the line in this manner until all the clusters are in place. **If necessary, any balloon in the column can be replaced by attaching a single-balloon on a paper clip to the line.** *(Figure 6.10h on page 151)*

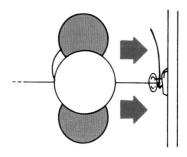

Figure 6.10f Constructing a Spiral Garland - Paper Clip Method Step 7

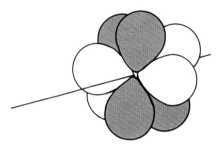

Figure 6.10g Constructing a Spiral Garland - Paper Clip Method Step 8

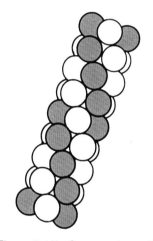

Figure 6.10h Constructing a Spiral Garland - Paper Clip Method Step 10

Figure 6.11a Constructing a Spiral Garland - Wrap Method Step 2

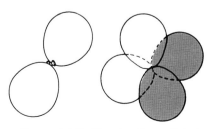

Figure 6.11b Constructing a Spiral Garland - Wrap Method Step 3

Wrap Method

Materials Needed

- Qualatex® (latex) balloons

- Fifty-pound test monofilament line (fishing line)

Construction Steps

1. Prepare a "balloon line" as described in Step 1 of the paper clip method.

2. Inflate one balloon and pinch the neck closed. Inflate the second balloon and pinch the neck closed. Hold the balloons with their necks crossed and twist one balloon over the neck of the other and back to its original position. *(Figure 6.11a)*

3. Tie the necks together. This is a two-balloon cluster. Make a cross with two 2-balloon clusters, pushing the centers together. Twist two balloons together, one balloon from each side. This is a four-balloon cluster. *(Figure 6.11b)*

4. If a five-balloon cluster is desired, tie the neck of the fifth balloon (which has been inflated and tied off) to the neck of one of the balloons in the four-balloon cluster. *(Figure 6.11c on page 152)*

5. To attach the cluster to the balloon line, separate two of the balloons and push the line inside the cluster. Push the cluster to the end of the line, against the flat surface. Once in place, secure the cluster to the line by twisting the two balloons that were separated together. This step secures the cluster snugly to the line and keeps the cluster from slipping. *(Figure 6.11d on page 152)*

6. Push the line inside of the second cluster and position it snugly against the first. With the wrap method the cluster should be close to its final position on the line before securing. Pushing the cluster along the line too

much once it has been secured may cause pin holes to develop. Once secured, the balloons may be arranged to produce the desired color patterns or spiral effect. **The cluster must lie flat so the following clusters will "nest" properly.** Once the balloons are arranged in the desired pattern, make sure the cluster fits snugly against the previous cluster. **Take care to nest the spirals firmly, but not to pack too tightly as the spiral will begin to warp.**

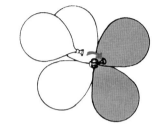

Figure 6.11c Constructing a Spiral Garland - Wrap Method Step 4

Square Garland

The square garland is a slightly more complicated balloon structure than the spiral garland. It is made with two different sizes of balloon clusters. For instance, one may choose to use 7-inch balloons for the large clusters and 5-inch balloons inflated to four inches for the same cluster. To create balloon garlands of a particular length, use the following chart and formula to determine the number of balloons and clusters needed.

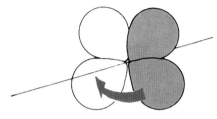

Figure 6.11d Constructing a Spiral Garland - Wrap Method Step 5

TABLE 2

CALCULATING NUMBER OF BALLOONS AND CLUSTERS NEEDED FOR GARLANDS

Balloon Sizes		Approximate
Small	Large	Balloons Per Foot
5-inch	3 1/4-inch (5-inch*)	12
7-inch	4-inch (5-inch*)	10
9-inch	5-inch (7-inch*)	9
11-inch	5 3/4-inch (7-inch*)	7
14-inch	7-inch (9-inch*)	4
16-inch	7 3/4-inch (9-inch*)	4

*Original balloon size.

To calculate the number of clusters needed, multiply the "finished" length of the spiral in feet by the number of balloons per foot. (Refer to Table 2.) Then divide the total by the number of balloons in each cluster.

Example: A 12-foot square garland of four 9-inch and four 5-inch (7-inch) balloon clusters would require 12 x 9 = 108 ÷ 4 = 27 four-balloon clusters; fourteen 9-inch clusters and thirteen 5-inch (7-inch) clusters.

Materials Needed

- Qualatex® (latex) balloons (half large and half small in the same color or different colors)

- Fifty pound test monofilament line (fishing line)

- One roll heavy duty duct tape

- Tempered aluminum rod, Code 6061T-6 (available from local steel distributors, look under "Steel" in the Yellow Pages) (optional zigzag)

- Bolt cutters (optional zigzag)

Construction Steps

1. Prepare a balloon line as described in Step 1 for the paper clip method of the spiral garland. (See pages 149 through 150.)

2. The square garland is constructed of fully inflated 5-inch balloons for the large balloon clusters and underinflated 5-inch balloons (3 1/4-inch) for the small balloon clusters. A template (can be made or purchased from balloon distributors) is recommended. It is important to maintain a consistent size. To create the large balloon clusters, inflate one balloon and pinch the neck closed. Inflate the second balloon and pinch the neck closed. Hold the balloons with their necks crossed and twist one balloon over the neck of the other as shown and back to its original position. *(Figure 6.12a)*

3. Tie the necks together. This is a two-balloon cluster. *(Figure 6.12b)*

4. Make a cross with two 2-balloon clusters, pushing the centers together. Twist two balloons together, one balloon from each cluster. This is a four-balloon cluster. *(Figure 6.12c)*

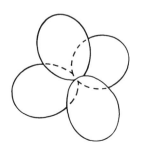

Figure 6.12a Creating a Square Garland Step 2

Figure 6.12b Creating a Square Garland Step 3

Figure 6.12c Creating a Square Garland Step 4

5. To attach the cluster to the line, separate two of the balloons and push the line inside the cluster. To secure the cluster to the line, twist the two balloons that were separated together as shown. This will secure the cluster snugly to the line and prevent the cluster from slipping once in place. *(Figure 6.12d)*

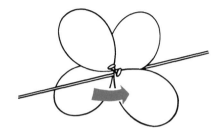

Figure 6.12d **Creating a Square Garland Step 5**

6. Prepare the second cluster as before (Steps 2 through 4). The 5-inch balloons should be inflated to 3 1/4 inches for the smaller four-balloon clusters. To attach the cluster to the line, separate two of the balloons and push the line inside the cluster. Rotate the second cluster so it is nested (at a 45 degree angle) into the first cluster. Before securing the small balloon cluster to the line, push its center firmly against the larger balloon cluster's center. Twist the two balloons that were separated together. This will secure the cluster snugly to the line and prevent the cluster from slipping once in place. *(Figure 6.12e)* Continue adding clusters to the line, alternating sizes, until all the clusters are in place, as shown.

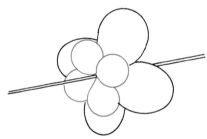

Figure 6.12e **Creating a Square Garland Step 6**

Optional Zigzag

7. To create a zigzag pattern, place the square garland on a flat surface, count five clusters from one end, pop two adjacent large balloons (5-inch) on the fifth cluster, and pop the two small balloons (3 1/4-inch) in clusters four and six, on each side of and between the large balloons just popped. *(Figure 6.12f)* This will allow the garland to bend.

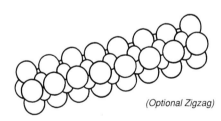

(Optional Zigzag)

Figure 6.12f **Creating a Square Garland Step 7**

8. Count down six more clusters, starting with cluster six, and pop the two adjacent large balloons (5-inch) of the eleventh cluster on the opposite side of the garland, and pop the two small balloons (3 1/4-inch) in clusters ten and twelve, on each side of and between the large balloons just popped. *(Figure 6.12g)* This will allow the garland to bend in the **opposite** direction. Continue this process, in intervals of six, along the garland, alternating sides, to create more bends.

Note: It is important to pop only the balloons shown, alternating sides. If a mistake is made, balloons can be added by using the wrap method.

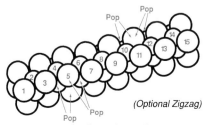

(Optional Zigzag)

Figure 6.12g **Creating a Square Garland Step 8**

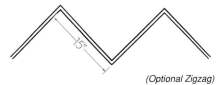

(Optional Zigzag)

Figure 6.12h **Creating a Square Garland Step 9**

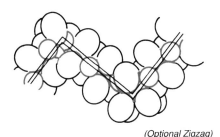

(Optional Zigzag)

Figure 6.12i **Creating a Square Garland Step 10**

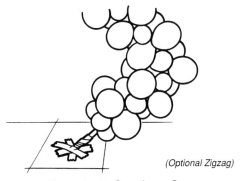

(Optional Zigzag)

Figure 6.12j **Creating a Square Garland Step 11**

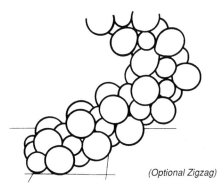

(Optional Zigzag)

Figure 6.12k **Creating a Square Garland Step 12**

9. Bend the aluminum rod into 15-inch sections at 90-degree angles on a flat surface. *(Figure 6.12h)*

10. Test the aluminum rod frame to see that it fits in the planned space. Leave 10 to 12 inches of rod and monofilament line at the ends for securing the garland to the floor, ceiling, and/or wall. Cut the excess rod with bolt cutters. Slightly open the weave of the balloons, from the side, and gently push the rod into the garland. *(Figure 6.12i)* Carefully push and pull the balloons into their original square pattern.

11. Secure one end of the rod, which extends from the garland, to the floor with duct tape or a drapery hook (for carpeted floors), or by attaching a heavy weight to the rod. Secure the other end to the ceiling or the wall with monofilament line or duct tape. *(Figure 6.12j)*

12. Finish out the spiral by using the wrap method to attach clusters to the remaining monofilament line or rod. *(Figure 6.12k)*

Candy Cane

This candy cane can be easily made and used in party decorations at Christmas time. It incorporates a spiral garland on an aluminum cane-shaped frame. Red and white balloons are recommended for a realistic candy cane look. With a team of two people, frame assembly takes from 45 minutes to 1 hour, inflation takes from 45 minutes to 1 hour, and assembly from 15 to 30 minutes each. Once made, the frames can be stored and used repeatedly.

Materials Needed

- One-half gross 9-inch Ruby Red Qualatex® (latex) balloons

- One gross 9-inch White Qualatex® (latex) balloons

- Fifty-pound test monofilament (fishing line)

- One 6-foot 3/16-inch tempered aluminum rod, Code 6061T-6 (available from local steel distributors; look under "Steel" in the Yellow Pages)

- One 6-foot length electrical metallic tubing (available from hardware stores)

- Heavy duty duct tape

- Twelve-inch x 12-inch x 1-inch plywood

- One-inch floor flange

- One-inch by 6-inch nipple

- Four wood screws

- Screwdriver

Construction Steps

1. Use a prefab base or make your own: Place the floor flange in the center of the plywood square. Using wood screws, secure the flange with a screwdriver. *(Figure 6.13a)*

2. Screw the nipple into the threads of the floor flange. Hand tighten. *(Figure 6.13b)*

3. To create the cane shape, bend the 6-foot aluminum rod into a half-circle. *(Figure 6.13c)*

4. Tape the rod to the 6-foot length of metallic tubing. Insert the support pole into the base; tape securely. *(Figure 6.13d)*

5. Create a 12-foot red and white spiral garland using the wrap method. (See pages 151 through 152.) Use two red balloons and three white balloons in each cluster. Approximately twenty-five to twenty-six balloon clusters will be needed.

6. Cover the support pole with the balloon garland. Slightly open the weave of the balloons, and gently push the garland onto the rod, starting at the base. Carefully push and pull the balloons into their original

BASE ASSEMBLY

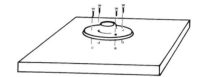

Figure 6.13a Constructing a Candy Cane Step 1

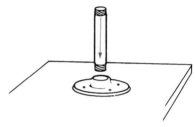

Figure 6.13b Constructing a Candy Cane Step 2

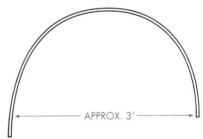

APPROX. 3'

Figure 6.13c Constructing a Candy Cane Step 3

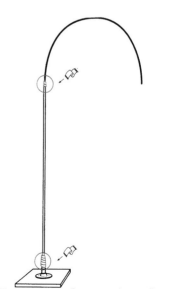

Figure 6.13d Constructing a Candy Cane Step 4

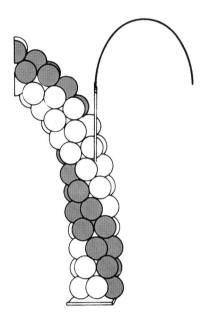

Figure 6.13e Constructing a Candy Cane Step 6

Figure 6.14 Puffed Balls

Figure 6.15a Creating a Small Puffed Ball Step 2

spiral pattern. The balloons may have to be popped to make the garland curve at the top of the cane. To keep the spiral effect, pop white balloons instead of red ones. **(Figure 6.13e)**

Puffed Balls

Balloon balls of different sizes can be created to hang from the ceiling or incorporate into floral decorations. Three construction methods are described here for creating small (14-inch diameter), medium (28-inch diameter), and large (35-inch diameter) balloon balls. The smallest ball is the simplest to create, the largest is the most complicated and labor intensive. With a team of two people, sculpture and assembly time for a large ball takes 3 to 5 hours. However, once the frame is made, it can be reused, reducing construction time to 2 hours. Balls of all three sizes in different colors and hung at different heights are especially effective decorations in a large party room. **(Figure 6.14)**

Small Puffed Ball

Materials Needed

- Twenty-two 5-inch Qualatex® (latex) balloons

- Fifty-pound test monofilament line

Construction Steps

1. Inflate the 5-inch balloons to 3 1/2 inches. Use a template, if necessary, to maintain a consistent size.

2. Create eleven 2-balloon clusters using the wrap method described for the spiral garland. (See pages 151 through 152.) **(Figure 6.15a)**

3. Make a cross with two 2-balloon clusters, pushing the centers together. Twist two balloons together, one balloon from each cluster. To introduce a third two-balloon cluster, push its center (stretching the linked necks) into the center of the four-balloon cluster. Twist

two balloons together, one balloon from each cluster. To introduce the fourth two-balloon cluster, push its center (stretching the linked necks) into the center of the six-balloon cluster. Twist two balloons together, one balloon from each cluster. Continue this process until all eleven 2-balloon clusters have been used.

Note: To create a uniform shape, it is important to maintain a constant center. *(Figure 6.15b)*

4. Push or pull the balloons to create a uniform surface. If balloons are not adjusted, the ball's surface will appear uneven where balloons have not been pulled into position. Tension between the balloons holds them in place. *(Figure 6.15c)*

Medium Puffed Ball

Materials Needed

- Two gross 5-inch Qualatex® (latex) balloons

- One 40-inch paddle balloon

- Eighteen to 20 square feet (1-inch square grids) nylon garden netting (available at garden centers)

- Two hundred fifty rigid paper clips

- Scissors

- Fifty-pound test monofilament line (fishing line)

Construction Steps

1. Inflate a 40-inch paddle balloon to 14 inches and tie.

   Note: The 40-inch paddle frame requires special care when attaching paper clips. *(Figure 6.16a)*

2. To create the base surface, double the nylon netting and stretch it tightly over the balloon's surface. Tie the ends of the netting together at the balloon's knot. Trim excess netting with scissors. If the puffed ball will be hung, tie monofilament line to the neck. *(Figure 6.16b)*

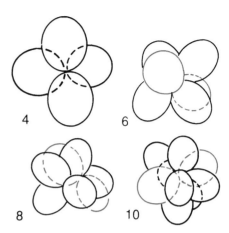

Figure 6.15b Creating a Small Puffed Ball Step 3

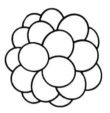

Figure 6.15c Creating a Small Puffed Ball Step 4

Figure 6.16a Creating a Medium Puffed Ball Step 1

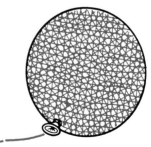

Figure 6.16b Creating a Medium Puffed Ball Step 2

Figure 6.16c Creating a Medium Puffed
Ball Step 3

Figure 6.16d Creating a Medium Puffed
Ball Step 4

Figure 6.16e Creating a Medium Puffed
Ball Step 5

Figure 6.16f Creating a Medium Puffed
Ball Step 6

Figure 6.16g Creating a Medium Puffed
Ball Step 7

3. The 5-inch balloons should be inflated to 4 3/4 inches. A template (can be made or purchased from balloon distributors) is recommended. **It is important to maintain a consistent size.** Inflate one balloon and pinch the neck closed. Inflate the second balloon and pinch the neck closed. Hold the balloons with their necks crossed and twist one balloon over the neck of the other and back to its original position. *(Figure 6.16c)*

4. Tie the necks together. *(Figure 6.16d)*

5. To attach the balloons to paper clips, hold a paper clip in one hand with the double-rounded end pointing down. With the other hand, gently pull away the outer stem of the paper clip approximately 1/4 inch so that the sharp end is exposed, and hook two balloons onto the paper clip by sticking the sharp end of the paper clip through the neck of each balloon between the knot and neck roll. This is a two-balloon cluster. *(Figure 6.16e)*

6. To attach a cluster to the base surface, hook the clip onto the netting so the strand of net rests in the same area as the balloon necks. (Position of net is the same as monofilament line when building a spiral.) Close the hook of the paper clip to hold the cluster in place and prevent it from bursting balloons. *(Figure 6.16f)*

7. Continue attaching clusters to the base surface. The balloon clusters should fit very tightly against each other. *(Figure 6.16g)*

8. Push or pull the attached balloons to create a uniform surface. Fill any holes with additional balloons. If balloons are not adjusted, the ball's surface will appear uneven where balloons have not been pulled into position. Tension between the balloons holds them in place. *(Figure 6.16h on page 160)*

Large Puffed Ball

Materials Needed

- Two gross of 5-inch Qualatex® (latex) balloons

- Fifteen to 20 feet of a 3/16-inch tempered aluminum

rod, Code 6061T-6 (available from local steel distributors; look under "Steel" in the Yellow Pages)

- Eighteen to 20 square feet (1-inch square grids) nylon garden netting (available at garden centers)

- Two hundred fifty rigid paper clips

- One roll heavy duty duct tape

- Bolt cutters

- Fifty-pound test monofilament line (fishing line)

Construction Steps

1. To create the basic ball shape, form a hoop approximately 2 feet 1 inch in diameter by bending the aluminum rod on a flat surface. Connect the rod lengths by overlapping approximately 6 inches and taping. *(Figure 6.17a)* Use bolt cutters to cut the excess rod.

2. Form a 2-foot 1-inch hoop with aluminum rod to create the first vertical hoop and tape it at the top and bottom of the ball's axis. *(Figure 6.17b)*

3. Form a 2-foot 1-inch hoop with aluminum rod to create the first horizontal hoop and tape it midway between the top and bottom. *(Figure 6.17c)*

4. Form a 2-foot 2-inch hoop with aluminum rod to create the second vertical hoop and tape it at the top and bottom of the ball's axis. *(Figure 6.17d on page 161)*

5. Form two 1-foot 6-inch hoops with aluminum rod to create the second and third horizontal hoops. Tape them midway between the first horizontal hoop and the top and bottom of the ball's axis. *(Figure 6.17e on page 161)*

6. To create the base surface, double the nylon netting and attach it, **stretching it tightly** to the frame with

Figure 6.16h Creating a Medium Puffed Ball Step 8

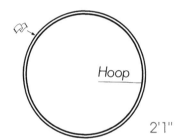

Hoop

2'1"

Figure 6.17a Creating a Large Puffed Ball Step 1

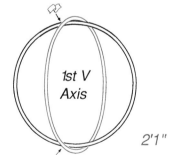

1st V Axis

2'1"

Figure 6.17b Creating a Large Puffed Ball Step 2

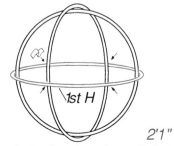

1st H

2'1"

Figure 6.17c Creating a Large Puffed Ball Step 3

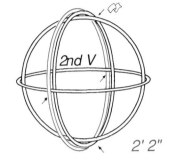

Figure 6.17d Creating a Large Puffed Ball Step 4

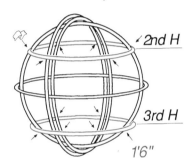

Figure 6.17e Creating a Large Puffed Ball Step 5

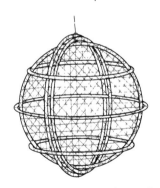

Figure 6.17f Creating a Large Puffed Ball Step 6

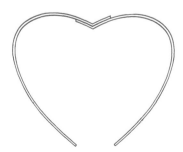

Figure 6.18a Constructing a Heart Arch Step 1

duct tape. *(Figure 6.17f)* Cable ties can be used to attach the net to the frame. If the puffed ball will be hung, tie monofilament line to the frame.

7. To cover the ball frame with balloons, follow Steps 3 through 8 for the medium puffed balloon ball. *(Figures 6.16a through 6.16h on pages 158 through 159)*

Heart Arch

The heart arch is a complicated balloon structure which can be used as an entrance decoration or other room enhancement. The frame may be prepared at the shop, but the balloon construction is best done on site. When completed, these instructions create a 9-foot by 9-foot heart-shaped arch. For smaller or larger heart arches, adjust the material and time requirements. With a team of two people, frame assembly takes from 2 to 3 hours and inflation and sculpture assembly 2 to 4 hours.

Materials Needed

- Two to three gross of 5-inch Qualatex® (latex) balloons

- Fifty feet of 50-pound test monofilament line (fishing line)

- Thirty feet of 3/16-inch tempered aluminum rod, Code 6061T-6 (available from local steel distributors, look under "Steel" in the Yellow Pages)

- One hundred rigid paper clips

- Hammer

- Two nails

- One roll heavy duty duct tape

Construction Steps

1. To create the heart frame, form two sections by bending the aluminum rod on a flat surface. *(Figure 6.18a)* Connect the rod lengths by overlapping 10 to 12 inches and taping in several places.

2. Follow the instructions for the spiral garland on **pages 151 to 152** to create an 18-foot spiral (2 feet shorter than the frame length).

3. Test the frame to see that it fits in the planned space, allowing for the addition of balloons. Lay the frame down on an area of clean floor. Slightly open the weave of the balloons, from the side, and gently push the rod into the spiral. **(Figure 6.18b)** Carefully push and pull the balloons into their original spiral pattern.

Figure 6.18b Constructing a Heart Arch Step 3

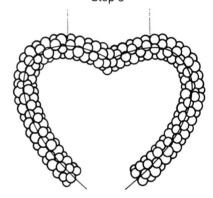

Figure 6.18c Constructing a Heart Arch Step 4

4. Leave 10 to 12 inches of rod and monofilament line at the ends for securing the arch to the floor. **(Figure 6.18c)** Cut two 12-foot lengths of monofilament line. Tie one to the center of each upper lobe. Loop the lines over an existing structure or tie them to nails placed above the lines. Hoist up the arch until it barely contacts the floor's surface. Make certain the lobes are level and tie the lines.

5. Secure the rods, which extend from the spiral, to the floor with duct tape, a drapery hook (for carpeted floors), or by attaching a heavy weight to the rod, such as a water balloon. **(Figure 6.18d)**

6. Finish out the spiral by attaching clusters of four, three, two, or one balloon(s) to the remaining monofilament line. **(Figure 6.18e)**

Puffed Heart

These instructions will create a 4 1/2-foot high by 5-foot wide by 2-foot thick puffed heart. For smaller or larger puffed hearts, adjust the material and time requirements. With a team of two people, frame assembly takes from 4 to 8 hours and inflation and sculpture assembly 6 to 8 hours. Once made, the frame can be stored and used repeatedly.

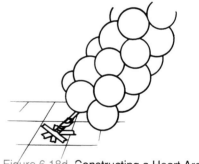

Figure 6.18d Constructing a Heart Arch Step 5

Materials Needed

- Six to seven gross of 5-inch Qualatex® (latex) balloons

- Two hundred ten feet of 3/16-inch tempered aluminum rod, Code 6061T-6 (available from local steel distributors, look under "Steel" in the Yellow Pages)

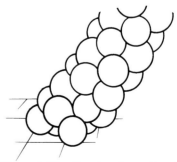

Figure 6.18e Constructing a Heart Arch Step 6

Figure 6.19a Creating a Puffed Heart
Step 1

8'8"

Figure 6.19b Creating a Puffed Heart
Step 2

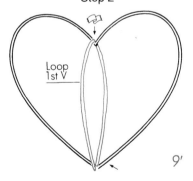

Loop
1st V

9'

Figure 6.19c Creating a Puffed Heart
Step 3

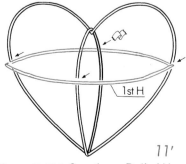

1st H

11'

Figure 6.19d Creating a Puffed Heart
Step 4

- Fifteen square feet (1-inch square grids) nylon garden netting (available at garden centers)

- Five hundred fifty rigid paper clips

- One roll heavy duty duct tape

- Bolt cutters

Construction Steps

1. To create the basic heart shape, form two 8-foot 8-inch sections by bending the aluminum rod on a flat surface. **(Figure 6.19a)**

   Note: The red figure is the approximate length of the shape(s) created and **does not include overlaps**.

2. Connect the rod lengths by overlapping approximately 6 inches and taping. **(Figure 6.19b)** Use bolt cutters to cut the excess rod.

3. Form a 9-foot loop, with a slightly tapered bottom, with the aluminum rod to create the first vertical loop and tape it. **(Figure 6.19c)**

4. Form an 11-foot loop with aluminum rod to create the first horizontal loop and tape it midway between the top and bottom. **(Figure 6.19d)**

5. Form two 9-foot 1-inch loops with aluminum rod to create the second and third vertical loops. Tape them a third of the distance from the first vertical loop to the heart's edge. **(Figure 6.19e on page 164)**

6. Form two 3-foot 8-inch arches with aluminum rod. Cross them at the heart's cleft, and join each end to the first horizontal loop and the second and third vertical loops and tape them. **(Figure 6.19f on page 164)**

7. Form two 7-foot 5-inch loops with aluminum rod, each placed half the distance from the second and third vertical loops and the heart's edge, and tape them. **(Figure 6.19g on page 164)**

8. Form two 6-foot 6-inch loops, which join at the heart's cleft and the heart's edge a few inches above the first horizontal loop, and tape them. *(Figure 6.19h)*

9. Form two 5-foot 6-inch loops which join at the heart's cleft and the heart's edge to create a horizontal line and tape them. *(Figure 6.19i on page 165)*

10. Form an 8-foot 6-inch loop, placed midway between the first horizontal loop and the heart's tip, and tape it. *(Figure 6.19j on page 165)*

11. To create the base surface, double the nylon netting and attach it, **stretching it tightly** to the frame with duct tape. Cable ties can be used to attach the net to the frame. *(Figure 6.19k on page 165)*

12. Inflate the 5-inch balloons to a uniform size. The balloons should be slightly underinflated and shaped as shown in *Figure 6.19l on page 165*. A template (can be made or purchased from balloon distributors) is recommended. **It is important to maintain a consistent size.**

13. Create two balloon clusters on paper clips following Steps 3 and 4 for the paper clip method of the spiral garland. (See pages 151 to 152.)

   Note: Use only **two** balloons per paper clip instead of the four as described. *(Figure 6.19m on page 166)*

14. To attach a cluster to the base surface, hook the clip onto the netting so the strand of net rests in the same area as the balloon necks. (Position of net is the same as monofilament line when building a spiral.) Close the hook of the paper clip to hold the cluster in place and prevent it from bursting balloons. *(Figure 6.19n on page 166)*

15. Continue attaching clusters to the base surface. The balloon clusters should fit very tightly against each other. *(Figure 6.19o on page 166)*

16. Push or pull the attached balloons to create a uniform surface. Fill any holes with additional balloons. If

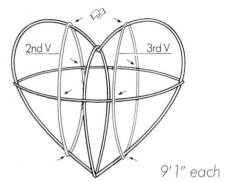

9'1" each

Figure 6.19e Creating a Puffed Heart
Step 5

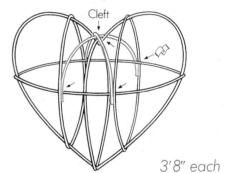

3'8" each

Figure 6.19f Creating a Puffed Heart
Step 6

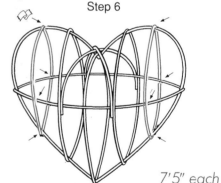

7'5" each

Figure 6.19g Creating a Puffed Heart
Step 7

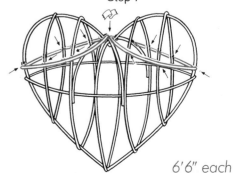

6'6" each

Figure 6.19h Creating a Puffed Heart
Step 8

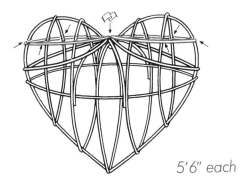

5'6" each

Figure 6.19i Creating a Puffed Heart
Step 9

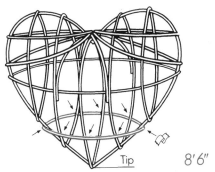

Tip   8'6"

Figure 6.19j Creating a Puffed Heart
Step 10

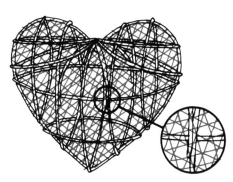

Figure 6.19k Creating a Puffed Heart
Step 11

Figure 6.19l Creating a Puffed Heart
Step 12

balloons are not adjusted, the heart's surface will appear uneven where balloons have not been pulled into position. Tension between the balloons holds them in place. *(Figure 6.19p on page 166)*

Stuffed Wall

Balloon walls are used as a creative way to back a stage or platform. Words or decorative patterns can be designed into a balloon wall by using different colors of balloons. Balloon walls can be made with the same technique as the spiral garland described earlier. The garlands are constructed on upright poles and then placed next to each other forming a wall. A second technique to construct a stuffed balloon wall is described below. These instructions are for a 4-foot by 8-foot wall. Walls of other sizes may be constructed by changing the number and lengths of the boards used.

With a team of two people, frame assembly takes from 1 to 2 hours and inflation and sculpture assembly 3 to 4 hours. Once made, the frame can be stored and used repeatedly.

Materials Needed

- Four gross of 5-inch Qualatex® (latex) balloons

- Sixty-four square feet (1-inch square grids) nylon garden netting (available at garden centers)

- Three hundred rigid paper clips

- Three 2-inch by 2-inch by 8-foot boards

- Two 1-inch by 2-inch by 8-foot boards

- Saw

- Staple gun

- Hammer

- Nails

- Spray paint (optional)

Construction Steps

1. To create an 8-foot panel, place two 2-inch by 2-inch by 8-foot boards on a flat surface parallel to one another and 4 feet apart. *(Figure 6.20a on page 167)*

2. Cut the remaining 2-inch by 2-inch by 8-foot board in half. *(Figure 6.20b on page 167)*

3. To create the 4-foot sides of the panel, nail the two 2-inch by 2-inch by 4-foot boards at the top and bottom. *(Figure 6.20c on page 167)*

4. Cut the two 1-inch by 2-inch by 8-foot boards in half. *(Figure 6.20d on page 167)*

5. Nail the four 1-inch by 2-inch by 4-foot sections 1 foot and 6 inches apart from each other. *(Figure 6.20e on page 168)*

6. To create the base surface, double the nylon netting and attach it, **stretching it tightly** to the frame and staple. *(Figure 6.20f on page 168)*

7. (Optional) To create patterns (stripes, waves, shapes, letters, etc.) spray paint the net. Use this pattern as a guide when attaching different colored balloons. *(Figure 6.20g on page 168)*

8. The 5-inch balloons should be inflated to 4 3/4 inches. A template (can be made or purchased from balloon distributors) is recommended. **It is important to maintain a consistent size.**

9. Create two-balloon clusters on paper clips following Steps 3 and 4 for the paper clip method of the spiral garland. (See pages 151 and 152.)

   Note: Use only **two** balloons per paper clip instead of the four as described. *(Figure 6.20h on page 169)*

10. To attach a cluster to the base surface, hook the clip onto the netting so the strand of net rests in the same area as the balloon necks. (Position of net is the same

Figure 6.19m Creating a Puffed Heart
Step 13

Figure 6.19n Creating a Puffed Heart
Step 14

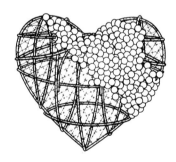

Figure 6.19o Creating a Puffed Heart
Step 15

Figure 6.19p Creating a Puffed Heart
Step 16

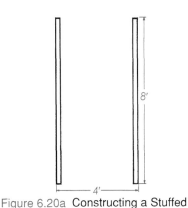

Figure 6.20a Constructing a Stuffed Wall Step 1

Figure 6.20b Constructing a Stuffed Wall Step 2

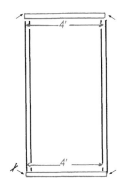

Figure 6.20c Constructing a Stuffed Wall Step 3

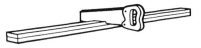

Figure 6.20d Constructing a Stuffed Wall Step 4

as monofilament line when building a spiral.) Close the hook of the paper clip to hold the cluster in place and prevent it from bursting balloons. *(Figure 6.20i on page 169)*

11. Continue attaching clusters to the base surface. The balloon clusters should fit very tightly against each other. *(Figure 6.20j on page 169)*

12. Push or pull the attached balloons to create a uniform surface. Fill any holes with additional balloons. If balloons are not adjusted, the wall's surface will appear uneven where balloons have not been pulled into position. Tension between the balloons holds them in place. *(Figure 6.20k on page 169)*

13. Since the materials used to create this structure are lightweight, the panels will stand against a wall on their sides or ends easily. To use the panels in a free-standing position, L-irons can be screwed into the back of the frame at the base. Monofilament can be attached to the top and secured to the ceiling for added stability. *(Figure 6.20l on page 170)*

Special Effects

Balloons not only offer many possibilities for use as structures, they also provide a variety of ways to enhance a party room with special effects. Special effects are decorations that create drama. Most of these effects can be achieved with very little effort and can greatly add to the floral decor of a party.

Balloon Releases

A balloon release is a special effect which involves the release of a mass of helium-filled latex balloons at a desired time during a party or other special event. Due to environmental concerns, be sure not to use metallic ribbon ties or plastic clips to seal balloons which will be released outdoors.

One form of balloon release is performed by party guests. For this release, the balloons are distributed to the guests and released at a specific time. This is most familiar as a wedding ritual outside the church or reception site. However, the same idea can be used to kick off or close special events of many kinds.

Another type of balloon release occurs when latex balloons are inflated with helium and knotted. String or ribbon is **not** added to the balloons. The balloons are placed in a large bag or tube that can be opened on cue, releasing all the balloons. The type of containing device can vary from large garbage bags to highly sophisticated containers available from balloon distributors.

When planning a balloon release, the florist needs to follow certain procedures in planning.

- Check local regulations on balloon releases. Some areas are restricted from releasing balloons outdoors.

- Make sure only 100 percent latex balloons are used. Balloons that are 100 percent latex are biodegradable.

- Make sure that the balloons are tied, not clipped, shut. When a balloon is sealed with a balloon clip or disc, it is not safe to be released outdoors.

Balloon Drops

Balloon drops occur when multiple latex balloons have been inflated with air, knotted, and stuffed into bags. These bags are suspended from the ceiling of the room. At a given cue, these bags are opened, dumping balloons from the ceiling onto the guests below.

On occasion a customer may request a balloon drop to highlight a specific announcement or time in the evening such as midnight on New Year's Eve. Other elements may also be added to the drop. Messages can be added inside the balloons or loose in the bag. Confetti can also be added to enhance the effect.

Balloon drops can be difficult to execute simply because of the location. Anytime the florist is asked to work with items suspended from the ceiling, the job becomes more difficult. When asked to provide a balloon drop, the florist needs to evaluate the situation. Unless the florist has experience in this area, he may be wiser to subcontract this service to a balloon decorator.

Balloon Drop Bag

Balloon drop bags are available from balloon distributors in different sizes and prices. However, it is possible for the florist to make his own bag using the following steps.

Figure 6.20e Constructing a Stuffed Wall Step 5

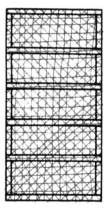

Figure 6.20f Constructing a Stuffed Wall Step 6

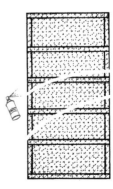

Figure 6.20g Constructing a Stuffed Wall Step 7

Figure 6.20h Constructing a Stuffed Wall Step 9

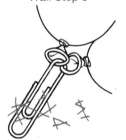

Figure 6.20i Constructing a Stuffed Wall Step 10

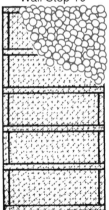

Figure 6.20j Constructing a Stuffed Wall Step 11

Figure 6.20k Constructing a Stuffed Wall Step 12

Materials Needed

- Roll of plastic wide enough to fold over to create a large tube

- Heavy string

- Grommets (These are small metal rings pressed into material to allow cording or ribbon to be inserted. They are available at fabric stores and usually come with a special tool that secures them into the fabric.)

- Grommet tool

Construction Steps

1. Roll out the plastic, cut it to the desired length, and fold it open. *(Figure 6.21a on page 170)*

2. Starting at the edge of the plastic, use a grommet tool to add a grommet every 12 inches on one of the long sides of the plastic. *(Figure 6.21b on page 170)*

3. On the opposite side, start by adding the first grommet 6 inches from the end and then every 12 inches for the rest of the length. *(Figure 6.21c on page 170)*

4. Add a grommet every 12 inches lengthwise down the center of the plastic. *(Figure 6.21d on page 170)*

5. Thread a heavy cord in and out of the grommet in the middle of the bag. This will become the top and what the bag will be hung by. *(Figure 6.21e on page 170)*

6. Fold the plastic over so that the grommets on one side meet the grommets on the other side. *(Figure 6.21f on page 171)*

7. Fold over each of the short ends about 2 inches and staple to seal them closed. *(Figure 6.21g on page 171)*

8. Thread the string through the grommets stitching three-quarters of the opening shut. Leave a long string

on one end to be used as a rip-cord. This cord will be pulled at the appropriate time to release all the balloons from the bag. *(Figure 6.21h on page 171)*

9. Fill the bag with balloons.

10. Stitch the remainder of the bag shut leaving the end of the cord free, **not** tied.

11. The filled bag is then hung in place and the rip-cord placed for easy pulling. *(Figure 6.21i on page 171)*

Ceiling Walkers

Ceiling walkers are a very simple effect. They are made with a 16-inch helium inflated latex balloon released to float on the ceiling with a ribbon or fishing line hanging down, holding an air-filled mylar balloon or other light-weight item. For instance, a party with a romantic theme can be enhanced with ceiling walkers using air-filled mylar heart balloons floating above the guests. (Clear latex balloons are recommended for the top balloons so they blend into the ceiling.) A 16-inch balloon is recommended, due to the amount of helium required. Smaller balloons can be used, but often more than one is required to hold the floating object.

Other objects can be used to hang from the balloons as long as they are very light-weight. Small pieces of foam board or paper cut outs, such as snowflakes can also be used.

The ceiling walkers are designed to float with the air current and should be designed so that the objects float a safe distance above the guests. *(Figure 6.22 on page 171)*

Ceiling Treatments

A special ceiling effect can be created over a dance floor or any part of the room by filling the area with helium balloons with ribbon streamers hanging down. This can be very effective when lights are set up to shine through the streamers. The main problem is keeping the balloons corralled in a specific area. Depending upon the type of ceiling at the site, plexiglass pedestals, such as Lomey® Pedestal Dividers, can be inverted and attached to the ceiling. If the ceiling is a dropped acoustical tile, the pedestals can be slipped in between the tile and frame. *(Figure 6.23a on page 172)* Once the pedestals are in place, outlining the area, monofilament

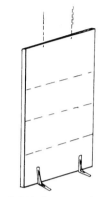

Figure 6.20l Constructing a Stuffed Wall Step 13

Figure 6.21a Creating a Balloon Drop Bag Step 1

Figure 6.21b Creating a Balloon Drop Bag Step 2

Figure 6.21c Creating a Balloon Drop Bag Step 3

Figure 6.21d Creating a Balloon Drop Bag Step 4

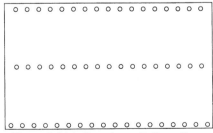

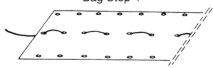

Figure 6.21e Creating a Balloon Drop Bag Step 5

Figure 6.21f Creating a Balloon Drop Bag Step 6

Figure 6.21g Creating a Balloon Drop Bag Step 7

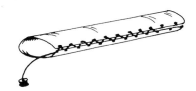

Figure 6.21h Creating a Balloon Drop Bag Step 8

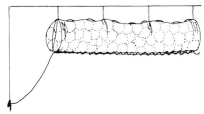

Figure 6.21i Creating a Balloon Drop Bag Step 11

Figure 6.22 Ceiling Walkers

line can be tied from one pedestal to another forming a corral. *(Figure 6.23b on page 172)* Once this is done there will be a fence effect hanging from the ceiling to corral the balloons. *(Figure 6.23c on page 172)*

Fruit Trees

For parties with country or outdoorsy themes, balloons can be used to turn ficus trees or other tree-like plants into apple trees. Underinflated 5-inch red latex balloons can be inflated to apple size and tied off. One or two small artificial corsage leaves can be glued on to add authenticity. The "apples" can then be attached to the ficus tree with paper clips or small spots of pan melt glue.

Any type of fruit tree can be made by changing the color of balloons, such as orange for an orange tree, yellow for lemon or grapefruit, or green for limes. The balloons can be shaped to resemble a more oblong look like that of a lemon. The balloon is simply inflated and tied off. The balloon can then be squeezed at the widest part, forcing the air into the top and bottom. This will give the elongated look desired for certain fruits.

Christmas Ornament

For a Christmas party, an interesting effect can be achieved by using balloons to create oversized ornaments. The ornaments can either be used as ceiling walkers, used on a large evergreen tree, or scaled down for table decorations. Both latex and mylar balloons can be used for ornaments.

Materials Needed

- One 40-inch paddle balloon for each ornament

- One Giant Quickie Clip® clip for each balloon

- Eight-inch by 8-inch by 3/16-inch foam board (available at art supply stores)

- Five-inch by 26-inch poster board

- Scissors

- Graphic arts knife (X-ACTO® knife)

- Stapler and staples

- Double and single-sided cellophane tape

- Cold glue gun (optional)

- Silver spray paint

Construction Steps

1. Using the pattern *(Figure 6.24a)* as a guide, draw an 8-inch diameter circle on the foam board. Draw a 3 3/4-inch diameter circle in the center of that circle. Using the graphic arts knife, cut out the interior and exterior circles. This piece is the top of the ornament cap.

2. Using the pattern *(Figure 6.24b)* as a guide, draw the cap's side and hanging loop on the poster board. Using the graphic arts knife, cut out the side and loop.

3. Apply double-sided cellophane tape around the outer edge of the top. Fit the side around the top. *(Figure 6.24c)* Staple the ends of the side together, then tape the seam.

4. To reinforce the top/side attachment, tape around the inside edge where top and side meet. *(Figure 6.24d on page 173)*

5. Insert the hanging loop through the interior circle. Tape each end of the loop to the underside of the top. *(Figure 6.24e on page 173)*

6. Spray paint the completed cap with two or three coats of silver paint. Allow to dry.

7. Inflate the balloon. Close with the Giant Quickie Clip®. *(Figure 6.24f on page 173)*

8. Bend the cap's tabs toward the inside. Position the cap directly over the neck of the balloon. Attach the tabs to the balloon, using either double-sided tape or a cold glue gun. *(Figure 6.24g on page 173)*

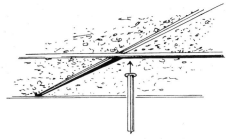

Figure 6.23a Creating Ceiling Treatments

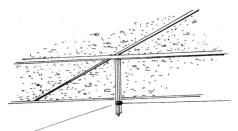

Figure 6.23b Creating Ceiling Treatments

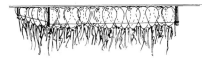

Figure 6.23c Creating Ceiling Treatments

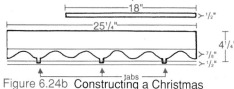

Figure 6.24a Constructing a Christmas Ornament Step 1

Figure 6.24b Constructing a Christmas Ornament Step 2

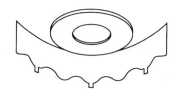

Figure 6.24c Constructing a Christmas Ornament Step 3

Figure 6.24d Constructing a Christmas
Ornament Step 4

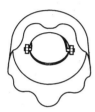

Figure 6.24e Constructing a Christmas
Ornament Step 5

Figure 6.24f Constructing a Christmas
Ornament Step 7

Figure 6.24g Constructing a Christmas
Ornament Step 8

Figure 6.25 Balloon Stuffed Plant

Balloon Stuffed Plant

At some parties, there may be green floor plants on site. Color can be added to these existing plants with air-filled balloons. Latex balloons to match the color scheme can be inflated and tied together and then gently wedged between the stems to hold them in place. If the stem structure of the plant is sturdy enough, a balloon cluster can be wrapped around the stem. However, care must be taken not to damage the plant. Depending on the type of the plant structure, the balloons can be added in and around the foliage like a scarf. *(Figure 6.25)* Balloons can also be added at the base of the plant to cover the soil area.

The wide variety of looks that can be achieved with balloons make them the perfect complement to party flowers. Whether used on the tables or throughout the room, balloons create an instant party atmosphere. When designing for parties, the addition of balloons can expand the decoration possibilities of the florist. Balloons can add that hard-to-achieve color, fill large voids of space, and offer a unique texture contrast to the flowers. Many balloon designs and structures are easy to create. Others require complicated mechanics and hours of labor. Florists need to keep in mind their capabilities and not commit themselves to more than they can realistically handle. If a florist intends to design elaborate balloon decorations on a regular basis, he should invest in the tools and supplies needed to create professional looks. He must also make time to practice and experiment with new ideas for constructing balloon structures. He must strive for a balance between the floral materials and the balloons used to accessorize them. No matter what decorations are created and no matter how extensively balloons are incorporated, the designs in total should be masterful complements to the party theme and setting.

Note: The specific designs and instructions for the balloon spiral, square garland, candy cane, puffed balls (small, medium, and large), heart arch, puffed heart, stuffed wall, and Christmas ornament are reprinted from the Decorator Series published by Pioneer® Balloon Company, Wichita, Kansas.

Notes, Photographs, Sketches, etc.

Notes, Photographs, Sketches, etc.

Table Settings

Chapter

7

*F*loral designers enjoy creating arrangements that are festive, decorative, beautiful, and fun. Though many events call for traditional table designs, which may limit a florist's creativity, parties often provide opportunities for designers to interpret the unique ideas and preferences of a diverse customer base. Whether the client is entertaining the town mayor, professional associates, or friends and family, flowers are the key to fabulous, memorable tables at parties.

This chapter is dedicated to providing florists with practical ideas for creative table settings. Included is information on etiquette, table sizes, skirtings, and chair treatments. Sample arrangement styles, located at the end of the chapter, provide complete instructions to facilitate construction. Knowledge of such techniques should free florists to expand the creative principles of floral design.

Table Guide

It is important for florists to be familiar with the sizes and shapes of common special event tables, as well as the number of people normally seated at each. This knowledge allows proper coordination, so that florists can plan tablecloth sizes, arrangement styles, and comfortable seating for guests. This section will focus on table shapes, sizes, and seating.

Round Tables

Round tables are readily available in a variety of sizes. More brides and party planners are opting for the use of "rounds," as they are commonly called. At a party they afford good communication where all the seated guests may participate in the conversation. The general rule-of-thumb is to

177

allow 15 to 20 inches of table space from the edge of the table inward and an 18-inch to 20-inch width per person. *(Figure 7.1)* Formality often determines the amount of space needed. For a seven-course dinner, the full 20 inches of space will be needed. The height of most tables is usually 30 inches; however, the diameter varies. Table 3 lists typical table diameters and the number of people which may be seated for dinner or served at a buffet. It should be kept in mind that the type and size of chairs used will affect the number of guests a table will seat.

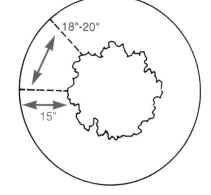

Figure 7.1 Round Tables

TABLE 3

ROUND TABLE DIAMETERS AND SEATING CAPACITY

Table Diameter	Seating Capacity
24 inches	2
30 inches	4
36 inches	4
42 inches	6
48 inches	6
54 inches	6 to 8
60 inches	8
66 inches	8 to 10
72 inches	10 to 12

Rectangular Tables

Traditionally, rectangular tables have been used for weddings and parties. While many people are opting for rounds, if space is limited and there are a lot of people to be seated, rectangular tables will take up less space than their round counterparts. For rectangular tables, allow 2 to 2 1/2 feet of table space per person. It should be kept in mind that the seating capacity of rectangular tables is decreased when tables are positioned end to end, eliminating seating on the ends of the tables. Seating capacity is cut in half when all guests are seated on one side of the table (as in the case of a head table). Table 4 on page 179 lists standard rectangular table sizes and the number of guests they typically seat. (Florists' Review, March 1991, 67-68.)

Figure 7.2a Decorations for a Round
Table

Figure 7.2b Decorations for a Round
Table

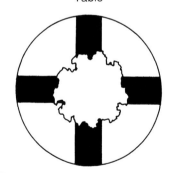

Figure 7.2c Decorations for a Round
Table

Figure 7.2d Decorations for a Round
Table

TABLE 4

RECTANGULAR TABLE SIZES AND SEATING CAPACITY

Size	Seating Capacity
8 feet by 30 inches	8 to 10
6 feet by 30 or 36 inches	6 to 10

Decorating Round and Rectangular Tables

With round tables, the center area of the table that requires decorations increases proportionately as the table becomes larger. For example, for a small table that is 24 to 30 inches round, there is room for only a bud vase. However, the same bud vase may appear insignificant on a larger table of 60 to 72 inches. *(Figures 7.2a and 7.2b)*

Excess area of the center of large round tables may need to be incorporated into the center floral arrangement. This can be done inexpensively by crisscrossing ribbons in the center of the table and filling in with foliage. *(Figure 7.2c)* Another idea is to place tall tapers in candlesticks and clustered votives around the central centerpiece to fill space attractively. *(Figure 7.2d)*

Floral decorations for rectangular tables are usually one-third the length of the table. *(Figure 7.3 on page 180)* For example, if there is a head table that is 30 feet long, a florist would need approximately 10 feet of floral arrangements. Three 3-foot pieces with space in between them would suit such a space nicely.

Rectangular tables for seating or buffet may be decorated with runners of lace, tulle, or fabric, or they can be draped with garlands of fresh foliage and flowers, tied together with flowing ribbons.

Buffet Tables

More than a hybrid of the sit-down meal, the buffet is a movable feast. Because it is a fast way to serve many people, it is often used for large parties. Buffet decorations can easily be adapted to the tastes, desires, and pocketbooks of the different clients by creatively incorporating party themes and floral designs. Buffet tables are often arranged in patterns. These patterns should facilitate the guests serving themselves. (See Appendix E.)

To facilitate movement, buffet tables are arranged in the following configurations.

- *Serpentine* - A snake-like formation. ***(Figure 7.4a)***

- *Multiple Stations* - Tables in different locations throughout the room. ***(Figure 7.4b)***

- *Straightway* - Having no twists or bends. ***(Figure 7.4c)***

- *Integrated* - Combining different configurations and shapes. ***(Figure 7.4d)***

Buffet tablecloths should hang to the floor. Since the table height of most buffet tables is about 30 inches, 60 inches should be added to both the length and width of the tablecloth in order to reach the floor. In a pinch, a king-sized sheet can be used under a cloth that is not long enough. Having the cloth meet the floor is important so that additional items can be stored under the table.

Table Linens

Generally owned, rented from linen companies, or provided by the hotel, table linens are used to cover the table completely and surround the outside of the table. Linens are valuable as the florist unifies the tables, flower colors, and additional accessories in order to coordinate the overall effect of the decor.

When linens are rented, each cloth and napkin should be checked for stains before it is put on the table. Over cloths or fabric squares should be used to cover spots and holes.

Linen Sizes

Linens are available in an infinite number of possible sizes. Rented linens usually come in standard sizes. Table 5 on page 181 lists general linen sizes and applications for each size.

There are times when it becomes necessary to customize table coverings to accommodate a variety of table shapes and sizes. Florists may use this as a guideline while keeping in mind the following techniques for measuring tables.

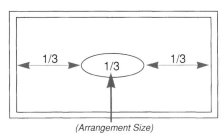
(Arrangement Size)

Figure 7.3 Rectangular Tables

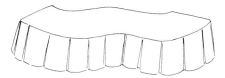

Figure 7.4a Buffet Tables

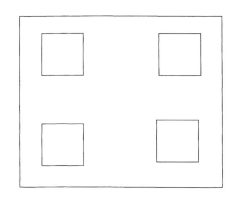

Figure 7.4b Buffet Tables

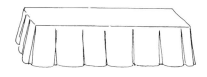

Buffet Tables

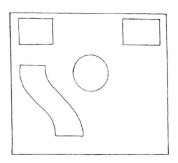

Figure 7.4d Buffet Tables

TABLE 5

LINEN SIZES AND APPLICATIONS

Linen Sizes	Applications
85-inch round	72-inch table and smaller
102-inch round	42-inch and 48-inch table liner
120-inch round	60-inch, 66-inch, and 72-inch table liner
60-inch square	24-inch and 48-inch table overlays
21 1/2-foot skirt	8-foot by 30-inch table perfect fit
120-inch by 54-inch rectangle	8-foot by 30-inch rectangular,
	6-foot by 30-inch rectangular, or
	6-foot by 36-inch rectangular

Figure 7.5 Measuring the Table

Measuring the Table

Table coverings are usually measured to cover the table and evenly touch the floor. As with the skirt of a long dress, the edge of the covering needs to brush the floor but push easily out of the way with the touch of a toe.

Measuring accurately is not difficult but should be done carefully to get the desired length. Following is a procedure that can be used to simplify measuring. *(Figure 7.5)*

1. Measure the diameter of the table.

2. Measure the distance from the top of the table to the floor or other desired length.

3. For the full working diameter, add the diameter to twice the length.

4. Add 3/4 inch for seam allowance all around.

5. If the cloth is to drape onto the floor, add 2 to 4 inches.

6. Subtract the length of any fringe or border.

Fabrics

Some florists invest in a supply of fabric tablecloths for professional use. Others make their own from inexpensive fabrics.

There is an infinite variety of fabrics and colors available, ranging from pink moiré to opalescent satin. Solids and prints can be mixed and matched to provide excellent color and theme coordination for parties.

Bed sheets have become a common source of interesting fabric, due to the wide variety of colors and patterns available. These can easily be crafted onto tablecloths. Table 6 provides standard measurements for different sheet sizes to help estimate the number of sheets needed in order to create a table cloth of a particular size.

TABLE 6

STANDARD MEASUREMENTS FOR SHEET SIZES

	Conventional Measurements		Metric Measurements	
Flat Sheets	Finished Size	Approximate Yardage	Finished Size	Approximate Yardage
Twin	66" x 96"	4 yards	167 cm x 243 cm	3.7 m
Double	81" x 96"	5 yards	205 cm x 243 cm	4.6 m
Queen	90" x 102"	6 yards	228 cm x 259 cm	5.5 m
King	108" x 102"	7 yards	274 cm x 259 cm	6.4 m
Pillowcase, Standard	20" x 30"	2/3 yard	51 cm x 76 cm	0.7 m
Pillowcase, King	20" x 40"	1 yard	51 cm x 101 cm	0.9 m
Fabric-by-the-Yard	66" x 108"	3 yards	167 cm x 274 cm	2.8 m

Linen Treatments

Ordinarily, tablecloths are simply laid over the table and left to hang straight over the sides. Creative linen treatments can be used to give party tables a more unique look. For example, the corners of a square tablecloth can be knotted or tied with ribbon. *(Figure 7.6a)*

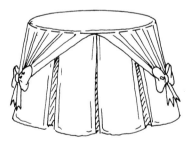

Figure 7.6a Linen Treatments

An alternate style that can be used with fabric coverings is a tablecloth with a gathered bottom. This is done by gathering the fabric of an oversized tablecloth around the bottom. It can be tied with a ribbon or braid to give the table a sculptured look. *(Figure 7.6b)*

Table skirts add drama and formality to a table setting. A new woven paper or plastic aisle runner may be used for table skirting. It is disposable and moderately priced; it is normally available in

Figure 7.6b Linen Treatments

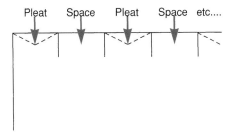

Figure 7.7a Creating a Pinch Pleated
Skirt Step 3

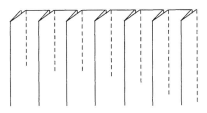

Figure 7.7b Creating a Pinch Pleated
Skirt Step 5

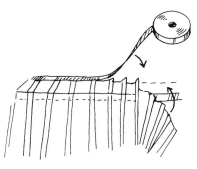

Figure 7.7c Creating a Pinch Pleated
Skirt Step 6

lengths of 50 to 300 feet. This may be wrapped smoothly around a table for a functional tailored look or more decoratively pinch or box pleated. It should be noted that pleating takes more fabric than straight wrapping and needs to be planned accordingly. When using an aisle runner as a table skirting, whether box or pinch pleated, it should be attached to the table with masking tape and the edges covered with a fabric overlay.

Pinch Pleated Skirt

Pinch pleats require a piece of fabric one and one-half to two times the length of fabric needed when straight wrapping. The cloth can be created by folding and stapling before attaching it to the table. Following are instructions for creating a pinch pleated skirt.

1. Determine the desired width of the pleats. (One inch, 2 inches, and 3 inches are common widths.)

2. Lay the aisle runner on a clean, smooth surface.

3. Using a ruler, thumb, or other consistent measurement tool, beginning on the leading edge of the wrong side, mark the pleats and spaces along the runner. *(Figure 7.7a)*

4. Bring the lines of each pleat section together and staple with a traditional stapler.

5. Leaving the space section between pleats, continue folding and stapling each pleat section until finished. *(Figure 7.7b)*

6. Secure the top edge of the skirting to the table using 2-inch to 4-inch masking tape. *(Figure 7.7c)*

Box Pleated Skirt

Box pleating takes approximately three times the amount of fabric as pinch pleating. Following are instructions for making a box pleated skirt.

1. Lay the aisle runner on a clean, smooth surface.

2. Mark the aisle runner with alternating 2-inch and 4-inch marks. Continue through the fabric, ending with two 2-inch marks.

3. Beginning with the first 2-inch mark, label the marks with an *A-B-B-A, A-B-B-A* pattern. *(Figure 7.8a)*

4. Placing the *A* marks together with *B* marks in front, staple in the back and fold the *B* marks so that a 4-inch, flat surface is formed. Continue through fabric. *(Figure 7.8b)*

5. Secure the top edge of the skirting to the table using 2 to 4-inch masking tape. *(Figure 7.8c)*

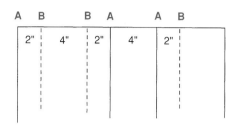

Pattern = A - B - B - A - A - B - B - A - etc...

Figure 7.8a Creating a Box Pleated Skirt Step 3

Napkins

Whether formal or informal, napkins are an indispensable part of the table setting. Even limited expertise in napkin folding can enable a designer to create exciting table settings. Techniques for utilizing napkins can be learned from books and articles, but the contribution of learning by observing styles and traditions passed from families and used in professional food establishments can be beneficial.

Napkins are available in a variety of colors, fabrics, and textures. They usually range in size from 12 to 24 inches square. Smaller napkins are usually used for informal events, such as luncheons, while larger napkins are reserved for formal affairs, such as a sit-down evening dinner or a black tie social. Whatever the personal choice of napkins may be, it is essential that they be meticulously clean and neatly presented.

There may be an occasion where the right napkins are difficult to obtain. For instance, for a country dance, blue and white gingham napkins would be perfect but may be hard to find. Since napkins are not difficult to construct, the party florist should be familiar with the process, should the need arise.

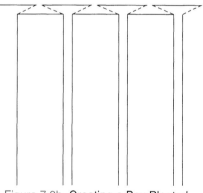

Figure 7.8b Creating a Box Pleated Skirt Step 4

How to Make Customized Napkins

1. Fold the desired fabric in half with right sides together; this will allow cutting more than one napkin at a time.

2. To make a pattern, draw a perfect square the desired napkin size on a piece of sturdy construction paper. Use a ruler and a pencil in this process.

3. After the pattern has been drawn, place the paper on the fabric, pin it in place, and cut out the square with fabric shears. Each pattern will cut two napkins.

4. Carefully fold the napkin edge under 1/8 inch, pin it, and press it flat with an iron. Remove the pins.

Figure 7.8c Creating a Box Pleated Skirt Step 5

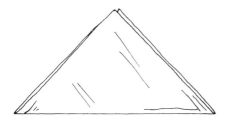

Figure 7.9a Folding a Flower Pot
Napkin Step 2

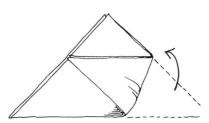

Figure 7.9b Folding a Flower Pot
Napkin Step 3

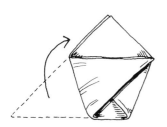

Figure 7.9c Folding a Flower Pot
Napkin Step 4

Figure 7.9d Folding a Flower Pot
Napkin Step 6

5. Fold under once more, pin, press flat, and stitch 1/8 inch from edge. Trim excess threads.

6. As an extra touch, lace, braids, ribbon, or other trims may be stitched to the edges.

Napkin Folds

There may be times when a florist wants to coordinate napkins with a table design. A florist can increase sales by adding a flower to the creases of a folded napkin. If provided from an outside source, the napkins may be picked up and folded to the desired shape in advance so a flower may be dropped in at the last moment.

Ironed napkins are best stored flat to keep them free of creases and ready to fold. Lightly-starched napkins work best for folding. Napkins folded into the flower pot, lotus, fleur-de-lys, palm leaf, and iris styles are particularly suitable for enhancement with flowers. Cut flowers or small corsages may simply be tucked into the decorative folds. Following are instructions for folding napkins in these styles.

Flower Pot

Silverware or a flower may be tucked in the "flower pot" for a unique look.

1. Lay the napkin flat, with the points facing top and bottom.

2. Fold the napkin in half from bottom to top. *(Figure 7.9a)*

3. Fold the right corner to the center of the left side. *(Figure 7.9b)*

4. Fold the left corner to the top edge of the right fold. *(Figure 7.9c)*

5. Fold the top layer of the point down to create the flower pot.

6. Fill the flower pot with tiny stems of branched material, such as spirea or heather. *(Figure 7.9d)* (Neff, 1990)

Lotus

This procedure for folding napkins would be ideal for napkins at a bridesmaids' luncheon or Christmas dinner when a tiny gift may be presented to each guest. The gifts are placed in the center of the folded napkins.

1. Lay the napkin flat and fold all four corners to meet in the center. *(Figure 7.10a)*

2. Turn the four corners in once again. *(Figure 7.10b)*

3. Carefully turn the folded napkin over. Fold all four corners to meet in the center once again. *(Figure 7.10c)*

4. Put one finger on the center to hold the corners in place. Reach under each corner and pull out a petal. Shape the flower.

5. Place a flower in full bloom, such as an opened rose, in the center. *(Figure 7.10d)* (Neff, 1990)

Fleur-de-Lys

The fleur-de-lys folded napkin provides a classic appearance for a place setting. The pleats in this stuffer make it look quite formal.

1. Lay the napkin flat, points facing top and bottom. Fold in half from bottom to top. *(Figure 7.11a on page 187)*

2. Fold the bottom edge toward the top of the triangle, leaving 2 to 3 inches between the top point and the folded edge. *(Figure 7.11b on page 187)*

3. Pleat the napkin, accordion style, in 1-inch folds from left to right. *(Figure 7.11c on page 187)*

4. Carefully pinch the pleats together and insert the napkin in a glass. Fan out the top and drape the sides over the edges of the glass.

5. Use floral tape to cluster three to five stems of delicate flowers (lily of the valley, wood hyacinth, etc.) together. *(Figure 7.11d on page 187)*

6. Place the floral clusters between the folds of the napkin. *(Figure 7.11e on page 187)* (Neff, 1990)

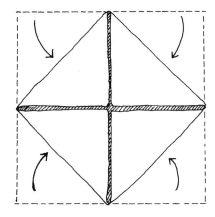

Figure 7.10a Folding a Lotus Napkin
Step 1

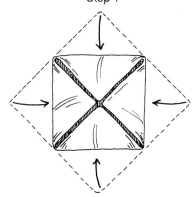

Figure 7.10b Folding a Lotus Napkin
Step 2

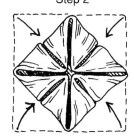

Figure 7.10c Folding a Lotus Napkin
Step 3

Figure 7.10d Folding a Lotus Napkin
Step 5

Figure 7.11a Folding a Fleur-de-Lys Napkin Step 1

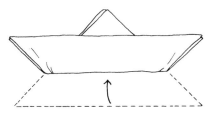

Figure 7.11b Folding a Fleur-de-Lys Napkin Step 2

Figure 7.11c Folding a Fleur-de-Lys Napkin Step 3

Figure 7.11d Folding a Fleur-de-Lys Napkin Step 5

Figure 7.11e Folding a Fleur-de-Lys Napkin Step 6

Palm Leaf

This attractive napkin fold style is ideal when time may be short but the host's desire to impress the guests is still present.

1. Lay the napkin square and fold it in half to form a rectangle. *(Figure 7.12a on page 188)*

2. Fold the top left corner down to the center of the rectangle bottom. Repeat by folding the top right corner down to the bottom. *(Figure 7.12b on page 188)*

3. Turn the napkin over. Grasp the top left and top right corners and fold down to the bottom edge of the napkin. *(Figure 7.12c on page 188)*

4. Fold the lower left corner up. Repeat with the right corner. *(Figure 7.12d on page 188)*

5. Carefully pleat the napkin from left to right in 1-inch accordion folds. Secure by sliding the bottom into a napkin ring, then spread out the leaf. *(Figure 7.12e on page 188)*

6. Tuck flowers into the napkin folds and through the napkin ring. *(Figure 7.12f on page 189)* (Neff, 1990)

Iris

The iris napkin fold technique incorporates the use of a fresh flower into the center of the flower created by the folds of the napkin.

1. Lay the napkin flat with corners facing top and bottom. Fold it in half from bottom to top to form a triangle. *(Figure 7.13a on page 189)*

2. Fold the left corner up to meet the top point. Repeat with the right corner. *(Figure 7.13b on page 189)*

3. Fold the bottom point up to meet the top point, creating a smaller triangle. *(Figure 7.13c on page 189)*

4. Fold the left and right bottom corners in to the center, tucking one inside the other. *(Figure 7.13d on page 189)*

5. Turn the napkin over and stand it up. Pull the first two points down. *(Figure 7.13e on page 190)* Pull the remaining two points to left and right.

6. Place a single showy flower, such as a gardenia, into the center of the iris. *(Figure 7.13f on page 190)* (Neff, 1990)

Place Setting Etiquette

While the strict rules of designing and creating table settings have relaxed, it is still necessary for the florist to be familiar with the different types of flatware, plates, and stemware used for different dining situations, as well as basic fundamental place setting arrangements. This knowledge is useful when a place setting must be rearranged after the placement of flowers. Knowing current place setting etiquette may also provide a foundation for a designer to tastefully expand basic principles.

Flatware

Whether the setting style is to be Oriental, Colonial, or Modern, there are utensils used for specific dining purposes. Regardless of the style of flatware or the creativity of the designer, there remain some appropriate and inappropriate uses. For example, it is inappropriate to use a cocktail fork for dessert or a condiment spoon for soup. Some misuses of flatware are obvious while others are less easily avoided. It is important for those setting the tables to familiarize themselves with the identification of flatware and its uses. Appendix E shows a wide range of common, as well as less frequently used flatware.

Informal Place Settings

Informal settings are basically used everyday or in a casual dining situation. The informal setting usually includes a dinner plate, salad or dessert plate, bread and butter plate, cup and saucer, two forks, a knife, and two spoons. (See Appendix E.) Experimenting and modifying is acceptable. Making the most of the utensils is the key. Following are some points to remember.

- Forks are on the left; knife and spoons on the right.

- Utensils are positioned so the diner uses those on the outside first and works in toward the center.

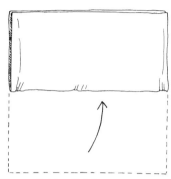

Figure 7.12a Folding a Palm Leaf Napkin Step 1

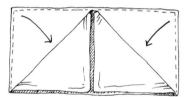

Figure 7.12b Folding a Palm Leaf Napkin Step 2

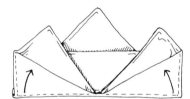

Figure 7.12c Folding a Palm Leaf Napkin Step 3

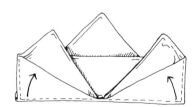

Figure 7.12d Folding a Palm Leaf Napkin Step 4

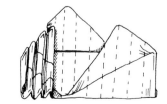

Figure 7.12e Folding a Palm Leaf Napkin Step 5

Figure 7.12f Folding a Palm Leaf
Napkin Step 6

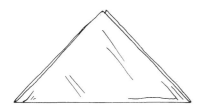

Figure 7.13a Folding an Iris Napkin
Step 1

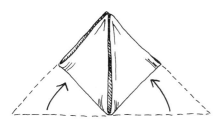

Figure 7.13b Folding an Iris Napkin
Step 2

Figure 7.13c Folding an Iris Napkin
Step 3

Figure 7.13d Folding an Iris Napkin
Step 4

- The knife is turned in toward the plate.

- The glassware is generally above the knife and spoon.

- There is always a napkin included or available.

Formal Place Settings

Formal place settings often use stemware rather than the more informal tumblers. (See Appendix E.) Cups and saucers are not part of a formal place setting because coffee is often served after dinner with dessert. Place card holders, menu stands, and napkin rings are part of formal settings but are certainly optional. A florist might provide samples of place cards as an option in a design package. These cards might be tastefully designed on available enclosure cards. A formal place setting is an expansion of the informal setting. Additions of specialty plates or goblets and stemware for flavored wines can be included. (See Appendix E.) As formal place settings expand, it becomes more manageable if ingenuity and logic are used in the format. A table and the placement of setting pieces can be an expression of hospitality. Following are important points to remember.

- Formal settings are expansions of the basic principles of informal settings.

- Formal settings never use paper napkins.

- Formal meals include three or more separate courses.

Glass and Plate Decorations

An occasion, such as a shower, birthday party, or a holiday, may inspire the hostess to decorate each glass or wine goblet or even the plates with flowers. These decorations may be as simple as embellishing the guests' plates with a few flowers to the construction of more complicated corsage-like designs.

Mini-Decos™, developed by the Smithers-Oasis Company, are perfect for plate decorations. Once soaked in water, these small, 1 1/2 inch diameter pads of floral foam have a peel-off sticker on the bottom that will gently adhere to a dinner plate. Once secured on the plate, the designer may insert a few leaves and flowers, giving each setting an individual accent. *(Figure 7.14 on page 190)*

The mechanics for complicated decorations are similar to the construction of a corsage, with one exception; instead of the design being pinned to a dress or purse, it is tied to a glass with ribbon or a complete bow.

Elaborate decorations are not always necessary. A quick and simple way to decorate a wine glass or water goblet is to construct a bow, leaving the tie ends 2 1/2 inches long. Then, using the tie ends of the newly-constructed bow, the bow is tied to the stem of the glass. Flowers, foliage, and filler should be glued to the bow using OASIS® Floral Adhesive. Care should be taken to prevent the adhesive from dripping. *(Figure 7.15)*

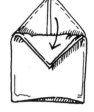

Figure 7.13e Folding an Iris Napkin
Step 5

Table Cover Treatments

Once the table is covered with a cloth, a florist may incorporate a simple or elaborate covering. Mirror, fabric, sod, and foliage are a few of the possible coverings that can be used to tie a table setting together. Caterers or hotels may have linens that the florist could creatively use, deferring the cost of renting or purchasing. Table coverings cloak the table but usually do not mask the table underneath. If a florist does not want to invest in expensive table linens, creative use of coverings is a way to achieve or enhance the desired look.

Mirrors

Mirrors are excellent coverings due to their reflective qualities. Flowers, candles, and greenery can be highlighted by the strategic placement of mirrors. An initial investment for a florist, mirrors can be kept for years and rented for special events of many kinds. Mirrors can be cut to almost any size and are most long lasting when mounted on a thin piece of wood. The cost of the mirrors should be included in the cost of the table setting. As with preparations of any table setting, a florist needs to know the exact measurements of the tables being used in order to appropriately plan the use of mirrors.

Figure 7.13f Folding an Iris Napkin
Step 6

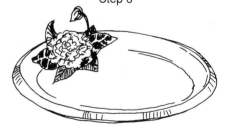

Figure 7.14 Plate Decorations

Fabrics

Experimenting with a variety of colors, textures, and combinations can stimulate creativity and propel the table setting onto another level of individuality. Some specific combinations might include denim and multicolored bandanna fabric for a casual or outdoor mood, and peach moiré and burgundy velvet tied with gold cording could be used for a more formal or evening event.

Figure 7.15 Glass Decorations

Figure 7.16a Fabrics

Figure 7.16b Fabrics

Originality is often a question of overturning convention. Tradition being set aside for the unexpected can be effective and stimulating. Perhaps the florist should expose the reverse side of a fabric or exploit the ridged pattern of seams instead of carefully hiding them. For example, linings that are usually unseen can be exposed, giving a table an unexpected texture and variance in color.

The character of a fabric can be altered simply by layering or bunching other fabrics over the top. In addition to combining colors and fabric texture, techniques, such as gathering, folding, or twisting fabric on a tabletop, can further enhance the desired look. Allowing a flowing fabric to drift naturally into position and utilizing the soft folds can form a foundation for an alluring table setting. Loose fabric can also be knotted and twisted at the ends to add variety. **(Figures 7.16a and 7.16b)**

Fabric overlays are only limited by creativity. In addition to combining fabrics, special effects can be achieved inexpensively with techniques such as tie-dyeing and paint spattering. The following techniques can turn an inexpensive sheet or piece of fabric into something unique and individual.

Tie-Dyed Overlay

Unique overlays can be created by tie-dyeing fabric. Following are instructions for creating such overlays.

1. Using the appropriately sized sheet or fabric, gather a handful and tie a string or rubber band around it.

2. The center can be poked into the banded section and tied again to add additional circles to the pattern.

3. Repeat this procedure as many times as desired to add pattern.

4. Place the fabric into fabric dye that has been properly mixed until the desired color is achieved.

5. Remove the fabric from the dye and allow it to dry.

6. When the fabric is dry, remove the ties or bands and iron flat.

Spattered Paint Overlay

Spattered paint overlays can help create a casual or impressionistic effect. They are relatively inexpensive and simple to make. Following are instructions for creating a spattered paint overlay. *(Figure 7.17)*

1. Spread the appropriately sized sheet or fabric flat onto a clean, dry surface.

2. Using three or four different colors of paint, one at a time, dip a paint brush into the paint and shake the brush over the fabric. Increasing the amount of force used when shaking the brush determines the size of the paint droplets. The harder the force, the smaller the drops.

3. Allow the paint to dry before use.

Figure 7.17 Spattered Paint Overlay

Fresh Plant Materials

Using fresh plant materials as covers can be an interesting way to accent a tabletop. By strategically placing dried flowers, gourds, and twisted vines, a table may evoke an autumnal feeling. On the other hand, a tabletop covering of fresh grass (sod) can change the atmosphere of a table setting, giving a spring or summer effect. Since nature has few limits, there are infinite possibilities. Some ideas for using plant material and flowers are provided here but are intended to rouse innate creativity rather than limiting the designer to the ideas included.

Sod Table Cover

A naturalistic or rural theme can be enhanced with sod table coverings. Following is a method for constructing a sod table cover.

1. Lay fresh sod stripes (20 to 24 inches wide) on a flat surface, side by side. Water well and provide plenty of sunshine. *(Figure 7.18a)* The sod should be an even, thick, green texture, before cutting.

2. Carefully measure the diameter of each table and cut several paper templates, each in perfect circles. *(Figure 7.18b)*

3. Position the templates as closely as possible on the sod strips, utilizing as much sod as possible.

4. Cut the sod strips with a sharp knife and roll the units together to avoid confusion when assembling on the tables.

Figure 7.18a Creating a Sod Table Cover Step 1

Figure 7.18b Creating a Sod Table Cover Step 2

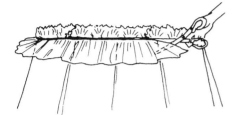

Figure 7.18c Creating a Sod Table Cover Step 7

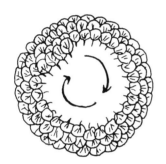

Figure 7.19a Creating a Galax Table Cover Step 6

Figure 7.19b Creating a Galax Table Cover Step 7

Figure 7.19c Creating a Galax Table Cover Step 8

5. Before the sod is placed on the tables, make certain the tables have been skirted and a piece of heavy plastic has been laid on the surface to protect from the moisture in the soil.

6. Place the sod on the protective plastic.

7. Trim the excess plastic, keeping it even with the edge of the table. **(Figure 7.18c)**

Galax Table Cover

Table coverings of burlap and greenery are easy to construct. Following are instructions for creating a galax cover.

1. Determine the size of the cover, using the method described in "Measuring the Table" on page 181.

2. Cut a tablecloth of the desired size and shape from a piece of burlap.

3. Completely remove the stems from the galax leaves.

4. Placing the galax leaves face down, apply either OASIS® Floral Adhesive or spray glue to the back side of each leaf. (Melted pan glue may also be used, but it tends to discolor the leaves and peel away after hardening.)

5. After applying the glue, adhere each leaf to the burlap tablecloth, beginning with a ring along the outer hem.

6. Continue placing leaves in concentric rings around the cloth, overlapping the galax stem ends and working from the outside of the cloth toward the center. **(Figure 7.19a)**

7. Finish by overlapping leaves in the center of the cloth. **(Figure 7.19b)**

8. Place the galax overlay on top of a floor-length tablecloth. **(Figure 7.19c)**

Flax Table Cover

The flax table cover would be an ideal way to decorate a table at a party with an environmental or natural theme.

Following are instructions for creating the woven look of a flax table cover.

1. Determine the size of the cover by checking the diameter of the tables involved.

2. Lay the vertical sections of the flax weave evenly on the table.

3. Starting in one corner, carefully weave the horizontal flax over and under the vertical flax. *(Figure 7.20a)*

4. Using OASIS® Floral Adhesive, carefully glue the outermost flax pieces to secure the structure.

5. Trim the ends of the flax and place the cover on the table. *(Figure 7.20b)*

   Note: As an alternative, ribbon may be used in place of flax for a colorful, woven table cover.

Tabletop Accessories

Accessories other than flowers that are used on the table to carry out the theme can be a source of additional sales, as well as enhancing the look of the place settings. Items such as candles, small figurines, braids, beads, or decorative ornaments can contribute to the personalizing of the settings.

Christmas Ornament Place Card Holder

A decorative Christmas ornament may be used as a place card holder and taken home after dinner. To construct a decorative Christmas ornament, follow the steps outlined below.

1. Using a glue gun, secure silk leaves to an ornament of the appropriate size. *(Figure 7.21a)*

2. Using a glue gun, attach ribbon and add larger silk floral materials to establish a center of interest on both sides of the ornament. *(Figure 7.21b)*

3. Fill with bits of twigs, moss, cones, tiny pearls, or beads.

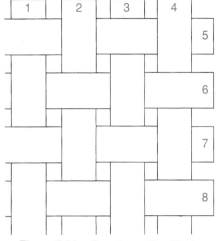

Figure 7.20a Creating a Flax Table Cover Step 3

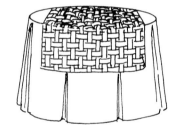

Figure 7.20b Creating a Flax Table Cover Step 5

Figure 7.21a Constructing a Christmas Ornament Place Card Holder Step 2

Figure 7.21b Constructing a Christmas Ornament Place Card Holder Step 4

Figure 7.21c Constructing a Christmas Ornament Place Card Holder Step 4

Figure 7.21d Constructing a Christmas Ornament Place Card Holder Step 5

Figure 7.22a Creating a Ribbon Braid Step 2

Figure 7.22b Creating a Ribbon Braid Step 4

Figure 7.22c Creating a Ribbon Braid Step 7

4. To create a stand, glue a piece of ribbon to an empty floral tape roll. *(Figure 7.21c)*

5. Place the decorated ornament on the ribbon-covered roll. Make a hole in the place card and tie it to the ribbon. *(Figure 7.21d)*

Ribbon Braids

Another method of accenting a table is to braid ribbon, and then drape the braid over the table, incorporating the floral design. Braids can be made from a variety of colorful, textured fabrics. Fabrics or rags tied together can make interesting braids and table accents. The following procedure is a simple method of traditional braiding.

1. Cut three strands of ribbon to the desired length, keeping in mind that the finished tie will be shorter than the original length.

2. Tie the three pieces of ribbon together with a small piece of the same ribbon. *(Figure 7.22a)*

3. Starting on the left, bring the outermost ribbon over and across the center and position it between the center and the ribbon on the far right. The left ribbon is now in the center. (The position of each ribbon shifts when a ribbon is crossed.)

4. Bring the far right ribbon over the new center and position it between the center and the left ribbon. *(Figure 7.22b)*

5. Continue to alternate the outer ribbon strand, bringing it over the middle.

6. Continue through the length of the ribbon strands and tie off at the end.

7. Drape the braid through the table centerpiece and over the sides of the table. *(Figure 7.22c)*

Candles

Romantic by nature, mysterious by effect, candles and candlelight are universally accepted as providing an alluring atmosphere. The soft light provided by candles contributes a warmth and glow to a room that cannot be simulated electrically. People, as well as settings, look better in candlelight; however, it is inappropriate to light candles on a table before sunset. Candles can make an informal event special and memorable, as well as providing additional sales when provided by the florist. Following are descriptions of types of candles commonly used by florists. (See Appendix E for diagrams of each type of candle.)

- *Taper* - Usually tall (8, 10, 12, 15, 18, 20, 22, or 25 inches) and narrow (1/4 to 1 inch in diameter)

- *Designer Candles* - Vary in thickness and can be 36 to 48 inches in height.

- *Pillar* - Cylindrically-shaped candles that are seldom taller than 22 inches and vary in diameter from 2 inches up.

- *Votive* - Small, cylindrically-shaped candles that are 2 1/2 to 3 inches tall.

- *Egg, Ball, or Sphere* - Usually a small, round candle 2 to 3 inches in diameter.

- *Floating* - Low, flat candle, often measuring 3 to 4 inches in diameter and 1 inch thick, which can be floated in water.

Safety must always be the primary concern when dealing with candles. Proper knowledge regarding the care and handling of candles may reduce risks and provide more satisfaction. Below is a list of care and handling considerations.

Candle Care and Handling

- Review laws governing the use of candles in the city and state. Most large cities require the candle to be enclosed in a glass covering.

- Check the burning time of each type of candle used. The diameter of the candle will determine how long the flame will last. This can be of particular importance when candles are used in a wedding or party. The florist can predict how long the candles will last and whether or not a possible safety hazard exists.

Notes

- When grouping candles together in an arrangement, it is important to leave space for three fingers between each candle placement. This allows each candle sufficient space and keeps the candles from simultaneously melting each other.

- Extremely tall designer candles may be secured by taping three 4-inch picks to the base with waterproof tape before inserting them into floral foam. Standard candle caddies are not recommended for this purpose because they are too shallow to support the height.

- Votive candles should always have a little water placed in the bottom of the cup. Water adds a safety measure and facilitates cleanup, as the wax is easily removed.

- Dripless candles remain as such when drafts and overheating are avoided. Candles of this kind must be inserted vertically into designs.

- Thin candles may be secured in a candle holder by placing sticky wax on the bottom or dropping liquid wax into the holder before positioning the candle.

- Candles light more easily once they have been burned. To assist in lighting, candles may be lit, then extinguished. Thick candles must burn at least until the top surface of the candle is filled with liquid wax.

- Thick candles may be shaved with a knife or held under hot water and then reshaped with the hands in order to make them fit into slightly smaller candle holders.

- If candles are smoking, trim the wicks, check for a draft, or release wax that may be too high in the rim.

- A flame that is too small may be the result of a wick that is too thin or dye from a color-dipped candle that has clogged the wick.

- Dusty candles may be cleaned by wiping up and down with a cloth that has been moistened with alcohol or with clean floral waxed tissue.

- To straighten a crooked candle, hold it near a heat source or place it in hot water, reshape it, and then allow it to cool before use.

- Freezing candles makes them last longer.

- Because of flammability, care should be taken when using any kind of moss around or near candles of any type.

- Beeswax candles may turn gray if stored for a long period of time. This gray covering is a sign of the material purity.

- To remove wax from clothes, place fabric between two pieces of blotting paper or a paper towel. Using a hot iron, go over the spot until the wax is absorbed. Often remaining wax can be removed by dry cleaning.

Figure 7.23a Creating an Artichoke Candle Step 1

Creative Candle Uses

Designers frequently seek unusual ways to incorporate candles into theme-oriented table settings. Candles can be modified and/or decorated in a variety of ways to make them more distinctive or useful in party designs. Following are two methods for using votive candles creatively.

Artichoke Candle Votive

Figure 7.23b Creating an Artichoke Candle Step 2

Table centerpieces for parties often incorporate different types of fruits and vegetables together with natural floral materials. Regular glass votives do not always look appropriate with such a natural look. Instead, they can be tucked inside artichokes (or other fruits and vegetables of similar shapes) to help them blend into the setting.

1. With a sharp knife, flatten the bottom of a fresh artichoke. *(Figure 7.23a)*

2. Using a glass votive as a size guide, remove the center of the artichoke with a sharp knife. *(Figure 7.23b)*

3. Carefully rinse the inside of the artichoke with water and then lemon juice. (Lemon juice keeps the artichoke from turning brown.)

Figure 7.23c Creating an Artichoke Candle Step 4

Figure 7.24a Constructing a Wire
Votive Holder Step 2

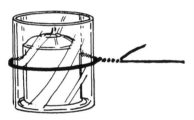

Figure 7.24b Constructing a Wire
Votive Holder Step 3

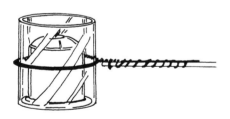

Figure 7.24c Constructing a Wire
Votive Holder Step 4

Figure 7.25a Creating an Aisle Runner
Chair Back Step 3

4. Place the glass votive inside the artichoke and place the candle into the glass votive. *(**Figure 7.23c on page 198**)*

Wire Votive Holder

Occasionally, the florist may need votive light within a design, such as a topiary tree or wall piece. This requires the attachment of a glass votive to the design, using a wire and wooden pick mechanism.

1. Tape a #18 gauge wire with floral tape. Choose a color that will be easily hidden in the design. The best color is often light green because it mimics the foliage.

2. Gently fold the wire into a hairpin shape. *(**Figure 7.24a**)*

3. Place the votive into the curved section of the hairpin and twist the wire to secure it around the votive. *(**Figure 7.24b**)*

    Note: A cylindrical-shaped votive is better for this method than a round votive.

4. When positioning the votive into the design, attach a wooden pick for extra security. *(**Figure 7.24c**)*

Chair Decorations

Chairs offer many design possibilities, whether rented, provided by the customer, or available at the party location. They range in style from white, green, and black wooden folding chairs to clear, lucite chairs to gilded, white, natural, or black bamboo opera chairs. Whatever the style, all may be enhanced with flowers. Following are several possibilities.

Aisle Runner Chair Back

A lace aisle runner makes a good, sturdy fabric for covering chair backs for parties. A floral bouquet may be attached to each chair to give extra drama.

1. Measure the width and length of the chair back.

2. Cut a rectangular piece of aisle runner to generously fit around each chair.

3. Place the aisle runner over the upper part of the chair and position it so all four corners can easily be joined at the back. *(Figure 7.25a on page 199)*

4. From the back of the chair, tie and knot the ends to secure. *(Figure 7.25b)*

5. The aisle runner may also be stapled with a hand-held stapler. To conceal the stapled section, attach a large bow or small floral piece, using corsage pins. *(Figure 7.25c)*

6. For safety, make certain the tips of the pins are not exposed.

Hand-Tied Chair Bouquet

Petite hand-tied bouquets can be made for attachment to chair backs. These can be designed in a neutral style and used on all of the chairs, or they can be given a more feminine look and be used on every other chair for female guests only.

1. Using one hand to hold the flowers and the other to place and arrange, position the bouquet's vertical lines with several pieces of foliage. *(Figure 7.26a)*

2. Add focal flowers. *(Figure 7.26b)*

3. To increase length, add cascading material, such as ivy. *(Figure 7.26c on page 201)*

4. Secure the bouquet at the joining point by tying with waxed string. *(Figure 7.26d on page 201)*

5. To avoid unattractive separations, wrap string at least five or six times around the joining point before tying off.

6. Attach the bouquet to the back of the chair with corsage pins inserted through the knot or stapled section of an aisle runner chair cover or by tying around the chair with ribbon or cording.

Figure 7.25b Creating an Aisle Runner Chair Back Step 4

Figure 7.25c Creating an Aisle Runner Chair Back Step 5

Figure 7.26a Creating a Hand-Tied Chair Bouquet Step 1

Figure 7.26b Creating a Hand-Tied Chair Bouquet Step 2

Figure 7.26c Creating a Hand-Tied
Chair Bouquet Step 3

Figure 7.26d Creating a Hand-Tied
Chair Bouquet Step 4

Figure 7.27a Creating a Fabric Chair
Cover Step 3

Figure 7.27b Creating a Fabric Chair
Cover Step 5

Fabric Chair Cover

Ordinary straight chairs can be given a formal and elegant look by covering them completely with fabric. Although aisle runners can be used for this purpose, soft, flowing fabrics in prints or solids can be shaped around the chairs more easily.

1. The length and width of the runner is determined by the height and width of each chair. Usually a piece of fabric 2 to 5 yards long by 24 inches wide will suffice.

2. Place the right sides of two identical lengths of fabric together.

3. Stitch the two pieces of fabric together with a 5/8-inch seam, leaving a section of about 5 inches open. *(Figure 7.27a)*

4. Turn the fabric to the right side by pulling it through the section that has not been stitched and carefully press seams until smooth.

5. Using a needle and thread, hand stitch the 5-inch section closed. *(Figure 7.27b)*

6. Carefully press the runner flat.

7. Drape the fabric runner over the desired chair and secure it with ribbon at the back of the chair and around the front legs. *(Figures 7.27c through 7.27e on page 202)*

Rose Chair Garland

A garland draped over the back of guests' chairs and secured with ribbon or cording adds a regal look to a formal party setting. Alternative flowers, such as daisies or baby's breath, can be used instead for a more casual setting.

1. Using one spool of wire as the lead wire and another as the wrapping wire, attach three or four roses to the end of the lead wire by securing the stems with the wrapping wire. Neither wire should be cut until the design is completed. *(Figure 7.28a on page 202)*

2. Continue to place small bunches of roses along the lead wire with other filler in between. Secure by wiring with the wrapping wire. When positioning the flowers, always overlap the previous stem ends.

3. Once the desired garland length is reached, finish by placing roses and foliage in the reverse direction at the end of the design. Secure with wire. *(Figure 7.28b on page 203)*

4. Attach the garland to chair backs by tying both ends with a piece of ribbon or a bow. *(Figure 7.28c on page 203)*

Table Centerpieces

Customers often desire creative and highly individualized arrangements for their parties. It is, therefore, important that designers constantly maintain a cache of fresh ideas. In this section, a collection of party designs is shown, complete with instructions, designed to inspire and encourage each florist to develop his own unique party style.

Bird's Nest Arrangement on a Branch

This arrangement of man-made bird's nests is constructed on a sturdy piece of wood, such as manzanita. Each nest contains a small floral design or votive candle.

Materials Needed

- Large manzanita branch

- Two to four bird's nests

- Number 18 to 20 gauge wire

- Sheet moss

- Glue gun and glue sticks

- Two to four plastic liners (or sheets of plastic)

- Floral foam

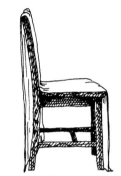

Figure 7.27c Creating a Fabric Chair Cover Step 7

Figure 7.27d Creating a Fabric Chair Cover Step 7

Figure 7.27e Creating a Fabric Chair Cover Step 7

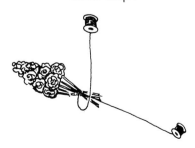

Figure 7.28a Creating a Rose Chair Garland Step 1

Figure 7.28b Creating a Rose Chair Garland Step 3

Figure 7.28c Creating a Rose Chair Garland Step 4

Figure 7.29a Constructing a Bird's Nest Arrangement on a Branch Step 2

Figure 7.29b Constructing a Bird's Nest Arrangement on a Branch Step 6

- Chenille stems

- Flowers and foliage

- Votives and candles

Construction Steps

1. To allow the branch to rest comfortably on the table, flatten the bottom of the branch limbs in several sections, using a sharp knife or, if necessary, a small table saw.

2. Attach the bird's nests by bending an #18 to #20 gauge wire into a hairpin shape. Insert the hairpin wire into the center of the nest. *(Figure 7.29a)*

3. Fasten nests to crooks in branch limbs by placing wire ends around the limb and twisting. Make certain each limb where a nest is attached can support not only the weight of the nest, but also the soaked floral foam and flowers.

4. Trim excess wire under each nest and conceal with moss glued over the mechanics.

5. Once the nests are secure, line them with small, plastic liners or layers of heavy plastic.

6. Place wet floral foam in the liners and fasten with chenille stems threaded through one side of the bird's nest, over the top of the foam, and through the other side. Twist the chenille ends to secure. (Chenille stems will not cut through foam and they adhere to the nest better than waterproof tape.) *(Figure 7.29b)*

7. Arrange foliage, moss, and flowers in soft, natural groups. *(Figure 7.29c on page 204)*

8. To further accent the arrangement, votive candles in glass holders may be placed in the nests and used as indirect lighting.

Spiral of Tulips

This design is a spiralled, hand-tied bouquet of tulips with the bulbs still attached. The design is tied and finished with decorative

French-wired ribbon. Following are instructions for creating a spiral of tulips.

Materials Needed

- Potted tulips

- Raffia

- Wired ribbon

- Shallow container

- Mood moss

Figure 7.29c Constructing a Bird's Nest Arrangement on a Branch Step 7

Construction Steps

1. Remove at least eight tulips of the same size from their pots. Carefully wash and rinse the soil from the roots. **(Figure 7.30a)**

Figure 7.30a Designing a Spiral of Tulips Step 1

2. Holding the tulips in one hand and positioning them with the other, arrange the tulips in a spiral by placing one stem over the other, always adding stems in the same direction. **(Figure 7.30b)**

3. Secure the design at the joining point by wrapping at least five or six times with raffia.

4. Position a tied, French-wired bow over the joining point, fastening tied ends to conceal the raffia bind. .

Figure 7.30b Designing a Spiral of Tulips Step 2

5. Add a second, matching bow on the opposite side of the bouquet.

6. Fluff the ribbon and place the design in a shallow container filled with dampened mood moss. **(Figure 7.30c)**

Tomato Vine Frame Centerpiece

This design is constructed on a galvanized tomato vine frame. Clear glass water tubes are attached and then filled with flowers. The entire design is accented with silver or gray French-wired

Figure 7.30c Designing a Spiral of Tulips Step 6

garlands of ribbon. It is appropriate as a centerpiece for guest or buffet tables.

Materials Needed

- Number 18 to #20 gauge wire

- Gray floral tape

- Large, clear water tubes

- Tomato vine frame

- Wired ribbon

- Flowers and foliage

- Round mirror

- Votives and candles

Construction Steps

1. Wrap about six #18 or #20 gauge wires with gray floral tape for each frame used as a centerpiece. More may be needed if the frame is large or if the design is for a buffet table.

2. Twist the taped wires around large, clear glass, orchid-type water tubes. Discard the rubber or plastic tops. **(Figure 7.31a)**

3. Evenly position the water tubes on the tomato vine frame and twist the wires to secure them in place. **(Figure 7.31b)**

4. Make a garland of French-wired ribbon and bows around the frame. Usually 2 to 3 yards of garland per frame is sufficient. **(Figure 7.31c)**

5. Fill the water tubes with water and add flowers, foliage, and filler as if creating small bud vases. **(Figure 7.31d on page 206)**

6. Position the completed frame in the center of a round mirror with several lighted votives in glass holders.

Figure 7.31a Constructing a Tomato Vine Frame Centerpiece Step 2

Figure 7.31b Constructing a Tomato Vine Frame Centerpiece Step 3

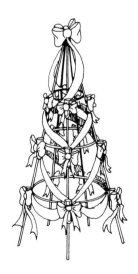
Figure 7.31c Constructing a Tomato Vine Frame Centerpiece Step 4

Petaled Collection

This party table setting features a tabletop accented with tall, clear glass bud vases filled with one or two stems of special flowers. In addition, the entire surface of the table is covered with petals removed from fresh flowers.

<u>Materials Needed</u>

- Three to seven tall, clear glass bud vases

- Glass votives

- Flower petals

- Flowers and foliage

<u>Construction Steps</u>

1. For a buffet centerpiece, puddle petals on the table in some areas. Petal puddles will indicate where bud vases are to be positioned.

2. Fill various sizes of bud vases with one or two special flowers, such as rubrum lilies or gerbera daisies. **(Figure 7.32a)**

3. Fill glass votives halfway with water and float small individual flower blossoms in each. **(Figure 7.32b)**

4. Place flower-filled bud vases and votives in mounded or puddled sections of petal-covered tables. **(Figure 7.32c)**

   Note: If the table is for a sit-down dinner, place bud vases and petals only in the center section.

Bamboo Frame for Amaryllis Bulbs

With the bulbs still attached, amaryllis are removed from their pots and placed in a grass-filled container. The amaryllis are secured to bamboo stakes that have been inserted into wet floral foam.

Figure 7.31d Constructing a Tomato Vine Frame Centerpiece Step 5

Figure 7.32a Creating a Petaled Collection Step 2

Figure 7.32b Creating a Petaled Collection Step 3

Figure 7.32c Creating a Petaled Collection Step 4

Figure 7.33a Constructing a Bamboo
Frame for Amaryllis Bulbs Step 1

Figure 7.33b Constructing a Bamboo
Frame for Amaryllis Bulbs Step 3

Figure 7.33c Constructing a Bamboo
Frame for Amaryllis Bulbs Step 4

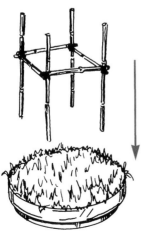

Figure 7.33d Constructing a Bamboo
Frame for Amaryllis Bulbs Step 6

Materials Needed

- Four bamboo poles - 24 to 30 inches in length

- Four bamboo poles - 8 to 12 inches in length

- Number 24 gauge wire

- Raffia

- Low, flat dish

- Floral foam

- Sod

- Four amaryllis plants

- Eight wooden picks

- Corkscrew willow

- Flowers and foliage

Construction Steps

1. Using wire, lash four vertical and four horizontal bamboo poles together to create a square frame. *(Figure 7.33a)*

2. Cover the wire by wrapping raffia around the joined sections of the frame. Set the frame aside.

3. Place soaked floral foam in a low, flat dish and secure with waterproof tape. *(Figure 7.33b)*

4. Cover the foam with a piece of sod. Tuck the edges of the sod inside the container. *(Figure 7.33c)* (Sod may be obtained from a garden or landscape center and should be allowed to green-up in the sun before being used in the design.)

5. Set the bamboo frame on top of the sod container.

6. Using a knife, cut four sections in the sod so the bamboo can penetrate and embed in the foam. *(Figure 7.33d on page 207)*

7. Push the bamboo frame into the foam.

8. Gently remove four opened amaryllis from their pots.

9. Rinse the soil from their roots. *(Figure 7.33e)*

10. Insert two wooden picks into one side of each exposed amaryllis bulb. *(Figure 7.33f)*

11. Push the wooden picks into the floral foam so that two or three amaryllis bulbs rest against the sod on the outside of the bamboo frame and at least one rests inside the frame.

12. Fasten the amaryllis to the bamboo with raffia. *(Figure 7.33g)*

13. If needed, add twisted branch material, such as corkscrew willow, for movement.

14. Additional flowers or foliage may be added to the design between the amaryllis, if desired. *(Figure 7.33h)*

Statue with Garland

This design uses an ornamental garden statue with a floral garland draped over the shoulders. Small flowers may also float in the shallow container at the base of the design. *(Figure 7.34 on page 209)*

Note: An arrangement such as this can be heavy; therefore, it is best if constructed on location.

Materials Needed

- Decorative statue

- Shallow container

- Spool wire

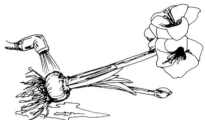
Figure 7.33e Constructing a Bamboo Frame for Amaryllis Bulbs Step 9

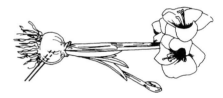
Figure 7.33f Constructing a Bamboo Frame for Amaryllis Bulbs Step 10

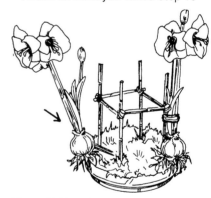
Figure 7.33g Constructing a Bamboo Frame for Amaryllis Bulbs Step 12

Figure 7.33h Constructing a Bamboo Frame for Amaryllis Bulbs Step 14

Figure 7.34 Statue with Garland

- Flowers and foliage

- Marbles or glass chips (optional)

Construction Steps

1. Place a decorative statue in the center or to one side of a shallow container.

2. Construct a flower and foliage garland, using the steps explained for the Rose Chair Garland (pages 201-202). The garland may be constructed of all roses or a combination of small flowers.

3. Drape the garland over the shoulder of the statue.

4. Pour 1/2 to 1 inch of water into the container.

5. Float three or four individual blossoms in the water or scatter marbles or glass in the base.

Cone-Shaped Floral Centerpiece

Constructed out of fresh flowers, this cone-shaped design, accented with moss and vines, makes an impressive table centerpiece. Several whimsical cones lined up along a rectangular buffet or guest table have an appealing look. Ribbons can be swagged from one cone to the next or fabric can be draped along the bases to unify the table setting.

Materials Needed

- Floral foam

- Low, flat container

- Wooden dowel

- Waterproof tape

- Sheet moss

- Greening pins

- Flowers and foliage

- Wired ribbon

Construction Steps

1. Place a large piece of soaked floral foam into a low, flat container.

2. Position a wooden dowel in the center of the foam.

3. Using the lasso method, tape from one edge of the container, around the dowel, and across to the opposite side of the container. Repeat on the other two sides of the container. *(Figure 7.35a)*

Figure 7.35a Creating a Cone-Shaped Floral Centerpiece Step 3

4. Impale and stack soaked pieces of floral foam, decreasing in size, onto the dowel until reaching the top.

5. Carve the foam to form a cone shape. *(Figure 7.35b)*

Figure 7.35b Creating a Cone-Shaped Floral Centerpiece Step 5

6. Secure the foam in place with waterproof tape, crisscrossing the tape from one side of the container, over the top of the cone, to the other side.

7. Lightly cover the foam cone with moistened sheet moss and secure with greening pins. *(Figure 7.35c)*

8. Insert fresh flowers, foliage, and filler into the cone. Continue placement until the cone is covered with the desired density of floral material.

   Note: Some areas may be left open with only moss visible for a lighter effect.

Figure 7.35c Creating a Cone-Shaped Floral Centerpiece Step 7

9. As an accent, swirl French-wired ribbon or vines around the cone. *(Figure 7.35d)*

Note: For a simple variation, the cone can be covered with boxwood instead of moss as a base.

Asparagus-Trimmed Poppy Arrangement

This arrangement consists of a shallow container, filled with poppies and trimmed with asparagus. Rich, green moss and bear

Figure 7.35d Creating a Cone-Shaped Floral Centerpiece Step 9

grass are used to unify the design. The look is fresh and natural and suitable for casual indoor or outdoor events.

Materials Needed

- Floral foam

- Rectangular or square shallow container

- Waterproof tape

- Asparagus

- Wooden picks

- Bear grass

- Poppies

- Mood moss

Construction Steps

Figure 7.36a Designing an Asparagus-Trimmed Poppy Arrangement Step 1

1. Place soaked floral foam into a rectangular or square-shaped container to a height of 1 inch above the sides. *(Figure 7.36a)* The sides of the container must be straight, with no curves. Secure foam with waterproof tape.

2. Lay asparagus on a flat surface with the tips nearly even.

3. Trim the bottom ends of the asparagus so they are all about the same size.

4. Insert a wooden pick horizontally into each stem of asparagus 1/2 inch higher than the height of the container edge. (For example, if the container has 1 1/2-inch sides, insert the wooden picks 2 inches from the base of the asparagus stems.)

   Note: For thin stems of asparagus, two toothpicks can be used instead of wooden picks. *(Figure 7.36b)*

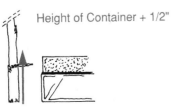

Height of Container + 1/2"

Figure 7.36b Designing an Asparagus-Trimmed Poppy Arrangement Step 4

5. Keeping the stem ends on the outside of the container, insert the picked asparagus in a parallel fashion into

the foam. The stem ends should rest flat against the tabletop. Keep the asparagus as close together as possible. *(Figure 7.36c)* Cluster several strands of bear grass into groups and knot the groups together to create one long rope-like unit. *(Figure 7.36d)*

6. Tie the bear grass rope around the outside of the container to secure the asparagus in place.

7. Position multiple stems of poppies freely in the top of the foam to a height several inches above the asparagus. *(Figure 7.36e)*

8. Add thick clumps of mood moss around the poppy stems to cover the foam.

Fresh Fruit Topiary

This classic topiary tree is placed in a white, square, wooden container and decorated with citrus fruit and white flowers. Its appearance is reminiscent of a summer garden, making it great for patio parties or indoor luncheons.

Materials Needed

- Plaster of Paris

- Wooden dowel or sturdy branch

- Plastic flower pot

- Decorative container

- Styrofoam™

- Floral foam cage

- Moss

- Wooden picks

- Assorted fruits (lemons, limes, peaches, etc.)

- Aerosol floral adhesive

- Flowers and foliage

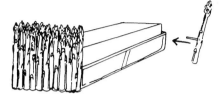

Figure 7.36c Designing an Asparagus-Trimmed Poppy Arrangement Step 5

Figure 7.36d Designing an Asparagus-Trimmed Poppy Arrangement Step 5

Figure 7.36e Designing an Asparagus-Trimmed Poppy Arrangement Step 7

Figure 7.37a Creating a Fresh Fruit Topiary Step 3

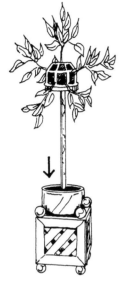

Figure 7.37b Creating a Fresh Fruit
Topiary Step 4

Figure 7.37c Creating a Fresh Fruit
Topiary Step 6

Figure 7.37d Creating a Fresh Fruit
Topiary Step 7

Construction Steps

1. Using plaster of Paris, secure a wooden dowel or sturdy branch in the center of a plastic flower pot. The flower pot must be plastic, because a terracotta or ceramic container will crack when the plaster of Paris expands during the hardening process.

2. Once the branch is stable, place the pot into a decorative holder. If the pot is loose inside the container, wedge pieces of Styrofoam™ around it to stabilize.

3. Attach a floral foam cage to the top of the central stem or branch. *(Figure 7.37a on page 212)*

4. Green the floral foam cage lightly with foliage and moss. *(Figure 7.37b)*

5. Using the pointed end of a wooden pick, pierce each piece of fruit.

6. Spray floral adhesive to the picked section of the fruit. *(Figure 7.37c)* This aids in securing the fruit and sealing the wounds.

7. Insert the picked fruit into the floral foam cage so the base of the fruit rests against the foam. Add fruit to all sides of the foam cage. *(Figure 7.37d)*

8. Fill in between the fruit with flowers and foliage to create an open, round form. *(Figure 7.37e on page 214)*

9. Add trailing foliage, such as ivy, to the base of the cage and wind it around the central pole.

10. Cover the base of the container with moss.

11. Place additional fruit in the base of the container and on the tabletop, if desired. For a creative touch, cut a wedge out of a piece of fruit and fill it with flowers. *(Figure 7.37f on page 214)*

Moss Globe with Spray Orchids

This arrangement is designed to hang over the top of each table. It is constructed of a 9-inch Styrofoam™ ball with water tubes inserted into the top. It is important to check the location of the party to see if there are ceiling hooks or railings that would facilitate such a design. In addition, the florist must coordinate the setup of all tables, so they will be positioned under the moss globes. Florists should not nail, drill, or place hooks into any surface without prior written permission.

Figure 7.37e **Creating a Fresh Fruit Topiary Step 8**

Materials Needed

- Nine-inch Styrofoam™ ball

- Water tubes

- Narrow cording

- Curtain rod ring

- Spray glue

- OASIS® Floral Adhesive

- Galax

- Moss

- Corkscrew willow

- Wooden picks

- Orchid sprays

Figure 7.37f **Creating a Fresh Fruit Topiary Step 11**

Construction Steps

1. Using a 9-inch Styrofoam™ ball, carve holes the size of water tubes into the top section. **(Figure 7.38a)**

2. Place water tubes into the newly cut holes.

3. Tie a strong, narrow cording around the globe so the knot is at the top of the ball.

Figure 7.38a **Creating a Moss Globe with Spray Orchids Step 1**

Figure 7.38b Creating a Moss Globe with Spray Orchids Step 4

Figure 7.38c Creating a Moss Globe with Spray Orchids Step 5

Figure 7.38d Creating a Moss Globe with Spray Orchids Step 6

Figure 7.38e Creating a Moss Globe with Spray Orchids Step 8

4. Tie a small curtain rod ring to the joining point of the cord. The ring will allow future cords, or cords of different lengths to be attached. *(Figure 7.38b)*

5. Using spray glue, as well as OASIS® Floral Adhesive, layer galax leaves *(Figure 7.38c)* and glue moss in groups to completely cover the globe. (See "Galax Table Cover" on page 193.)

6. Cut a sharp angle at the base of a piece of corkscrew willow and insert it into the globe. Wind the willow loosely around the globe and insert the opposite end on a wooden pick into the globe. *(Figure 7.38d)* Use several pieces, if needed.

7. Syringe water or use a narrow watering can to fill the water tubes. Cap the tubes with rubber tops.

8. Place orchid sprays or other cascading flowers in the water tubes. *(Figure 7.38e)*

Note: As a variation, the globe may sit directly on the table. Construction is the same, except the bottom of the globe is flattened to allow stability. *(Figure 7.39 on page 216)*

Composite Buffet Arrangement

This arrangement is a series of small designs, positioned along gently curving and rolled metal flashing. Flashing is an aluminum-type material that is available from hardware stores, traditionally used as a roofing product. For additional effect, place the flashing and its floral components on a large mirror, positioned flat on the table. Votives in glass holders will create a beautiful effect at night.

Materials Needed

- Aluminum flashing

- Mirror

- Three to seven small, shallow containers

- Floral foam

- Galax

- Moss

- Flowers

- Votives and candles

Construction Steps

1. Using shears that will cut metal, cut the desired length of aluminum flashing from the roll. When unrolling the aluminum flashing, take special care. Flashing is tightly wound and may jump and flip when released.

2. Arrange the flashing on a mirror. When arranging the flashing, allow for loops and folds to add interest. Use care; flashing can be sharp.

3. Place small, shallow containers filled with soaked floral foam in and out, as well as along the interesting configuration of the metal flashing. *(Figure 7.40a)*

4. Cover the floral foam in each container with layered galax leaves and moss.

5. Position flowers so they appear to be growing along the lines of the flashing. *(Figure 7.40b)*

6. Add votives in glass holders for evening sparkle.

Figure 7.39 Moss Globe with Spray Orchids Sitting Directly on a Table

Figure 7.40a Creating a Composite Buffet Arrangement Step 3

Figure 7.40b Creating a Composite Buffet Arrangement Step 5

Table settings for modern parties take on many styles and forms. Traditional rules of etiquette, although sometimes followed, no longer dictate the manner in which tables are arranged. Linens, china, crystal, and silver may all be displayed in creative ways to enhance a setting or develop a theme. Flowers may be creatively combined, as well. There are as many good formulas for table settings as there are personalities and client tastes. The table is essentially a stage where the florist has the opportunity to interpret the customer's preferences in flowers.

Table Settings

Notes, Photographs, Sketches, etc.

Notes, Photographs, Sketches, etc.

Table Settings

Notes, Photographs, Sketches, etc.

Room Decor

*W*hen planning decorations for a party, social function, or other special occasion, table settings are often the first item of discussion. Room decorations, however, are also important for carrying out the party theme and creating the desired atmosphere. Party guests often expect to see flowers used on the tables, but are frequently surprised and delighted by the use of floral decorations in other areas of the party setting. Site analysis will provide a comprehensive list of the areas suitable for floral enhancement. It is of the utmost importance that the facility be checked to assure that the necessary space and equipment are available before planning extensive decorations. (See Chapter 3 for information on conducting a site analysis.)

Floral designs and room decorations can be used to enhance or disguise incompatible or underside elements of the room. Customized floral designs built on site create a wonderful sense of refinement and attention to detail. Since many party room decorations are large, they require special construction and installation techniques. This chapter is devoted to providing explanations for creating room decorations of many kinds. The ideas presented are a creative starting point, intended to catch the imagination of the floral designer who wants to make every party a very special event.

Elements for Decoration

The physical elements of a room will dictate the possibilities for decoration, while the budget will dictate the realities. Clients are usually unaware of the ways in which decorations can be used to create the best visual impact for the money allocated. The florist can guide the customer by presenting a limited number of options for consideration. It is easy to present additional ideas, but when too many are tossed out at once, the client is often overwhelmed. The decision making process should be simplified as much as possible. It should be determined whether the client can visualize the ideas presented, and the presentation should be adapted accordingly.

The florist may request a floor plan of the room from the manager of the party site. This will allow additional details and information to be added. All pertinent measurements should be double checked. The scale of the room and the decorative elements in relation to the way it will look when filled with guests should be considered. This will dictate the areas which will require decorative emphasis.

Doorways

The entrance to a party site requires special attention. Is it important to immediately surround the guests with a sense of ambiance and mood, or is it preferable to leave the entrance undecorated in order to heighten the surprise when guests enter the decorated area? Decorating doorways with fabric, foam board, garlands, pillars, or pedestals of flowers should be considered. The doorway will establish the mood of the affair and can create an air of excitement, romance, or classical beauty.

Art Deco Entrance

Foam board is an indispensable material for creating customized party props. The art deco entrance utilizes foam board to create a stunning doorway that is appropriate as a grand entrance to a party with an art deco theme. *(Figure 8.1)*

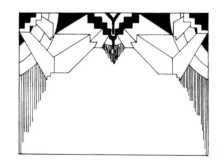

Figure 8.1 Art Deco Entrance

Materials Needed

- Foam board (if possible, use pre-colored pink board)

- Graphic arts knife and extra blades

- Opaque projector or Episcope™ (optional)

- Pink and black broad-tipped, felt marking pens

- Eight-foot pink mylar shimmer curtain

Construction Steps

1. Make a scale drawing of the desired design for the doorway.

2. Measure the doorway.

3. Use the opaque projector or Episcope™ to project the desired image onto the foam board. (If this is not possible, draw the pattern onto the board very lightly.) Trace the design in pink and black (or any desired color combination) with broad-tipped, felt markers.

4. Use the graphic arts knife to score the outline of the design in the foam board. Re-score the outline to cut all the way through the board. Change the knife blades often to ensure clean cutting.

5. To hang the archway, attach small tacks into the top edge of the door molding at the outer edges and center of the doorway. Be sure to obtain permission from the management in advance.

6. Run wire from the tacks, through the outer edges and center of the foam board, and tie off.

7. Cut two sections of 8-foot pink, mylar, shimmer curtain to be used to accent the ends of the design.

8. Pin or glue a shimmer curtain section behind the foam board at each end, and allow it to cascade to the floor.

9. Add a shortened accent of shimmer curtain to the center of the doorway design.

Stairs

The staircase is often used for a rather grand entrance by the guest of honor. As a bride sweeps down the stairs with her groom, the flashbulbs pop and the decorations, or lack thereof, are forever immortalized in photographs. Staircases are a natural location for formal photography. When this is the case, the florist should explain the importance of the area to the client.

Safety is a major consideration when decorating a staircase. It should be kept in mind that the handrails must be able to support the weight and lurch of festive guests. As much of the surface of the railing as possible should be left unobstructed. Fabric and garlands should be attached to the posts just above rails with waxed floral string or taped wires to blend in with the color of the banister. Any ends of wires should be buried so that they cannot injure the hand of a guest. An investment in fabric should be in colors that the florist is likely to be able to reuse for future events.

A colorful, yet inexpensive stair treatment is to wrap the entire railing in ribbon and tie it off at the ends with simple bows and streamers. The streamers should be short enough to avoid being a trip hazard.

Fabric-Swagged Staircase

Fabric is a relatively inexpensive material with which to create dramatic stairway decorations. It is also extremely versatile because it is available in nearly every color of the rainbow, as well as a multitude of prints and weaves. The following instructions are for a simple fabric-swagged staircase that can be enhanced as desired with flowers and ribbons.

Materials Needed

- Fabric (preferably finished on both sides)

- Lining fabric (if one-sided fabric is used)

- Chenille stems or wires and floral tape in a color that blends with the staircase railing

- Ribbon

- Fresh Flowers

- Water Tubes

Construction Steps

1. The depth of a swag will determine how much yardage is needed. The minimum yardage is usually one and a half times the length of the railing. For example a 10-foot railing would need at least 15 feet of garland or fabric.

2. When using fabric on a staircase, it will usually be seen from both sides. When the fabric is one-sided, it may be necessary to line the unfinished side. For example, a floral print cotton chintz may be lined with an inexpensive nylon chiffon in a coordinating color. Alternatively, the yardage may be doubled so that both sides are finished in the same print.

3. Use chenille stems or taped wires to secure the gathered end of the fabric and attach it to the railing.

4. Drape the fabric to create the desired length of swagging and secure the gathered fabric to the next railing with another chenille stem or taped wire.

5. Measure the lowest point of a swag from the stair tread and use that measurement to guide the installation of additional swags. *(Figure 8.2)*

6. Tie a small knot (or use a thin wire) to bunch the fabric in the top center of each swag. This will make the fabric drape properly. Use safety pins to make any adjustments in the fabric.

7. Finish with bows and fresh flowers in water tubes to accent the banister. Use chenille stems to secure each in the desired location.

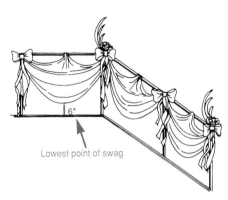

Figure 8.2 Fabric Swagged Staircase

Ceilings

Wonderful fantasy effects may be achieved with the unexpected treatment of a ceiling. The entire ceiling may be covered or intermittent accents may be used. Treatments may incorporate fabric, foliage, foam board mobiles, mylar, wind socks, dryer ducts, shimmer curtains, lattice (to lower the ceiling and hide ducts), fiberfill clouds, etc.

Local officials should be contacted regarding any fire-retardancy standards that must be met. Some, but not all fabrics, may be treated with flame-retardant chemicals. Treated fabric is sold with a flame proof verification tag or certificate. (These tags should be kept in case it is necessary to verify the flame retardancy to fire inspectors.) All ceiling decorations must be a safe distance from any source of extreme heat or other possible hazard. Another safety requirement is that no emergency exit signs be visually blocked.

A discussion with the site management regarding the method of hanging any special decorations should be held and permission granted for using any nails, screws, etc. (Often this can be done inconspicuously into ceiling and door moldings.) Arrangements should be made in advance with management to have the room cleared of tables and chairs during the installation. This will substantially affect the amount of labor for the project. The ceiling should be finished by the time the tables are to be set up.

It needs to kept in mind that installation at ceiling height will be 10 to 20 degrees hotter than at floor level. This is exaggerated when workers are closer to a light source. This will affect the number of crew members needed to complete the job.

When using a scissor lift or a one-man genie lift, the wheels should be wrapped in duct tape to protect the carpet. Wire or heavy monofilament (fishing line) can be used to attach decorations to the ceiling. When hanging props, the strength per inch of the wire or monofilament needs to be checked. It must be very secure. String should not be used because it can slip or stretch.

Usually, it is most effective during an event if the overhead lights are dimmed or turned off. The lighting can be especially effective from spotlights below or from string lights interwoven in the ceiling. The effect of lighting will drastically change in accordance with the reflective qualities of other props and room decorations. Lighting should be experimented with ahead of time.

When using dryer duct for a science fiction or futuristic look, the tubes should be filled with miniature white lights or well vented spotlights should be directed into the ends of the tubes to create an eerie glow.

Shimmer curtains are very effective with minimal lighting, and several sizes are available. Larger curtains may take more time to install because they tend to tangle easily; smaller sections are more efficient to install.

Fabric Ceiling Treatment

By swagging fabric, mylar, or aisle runners at regular intervals from the ceiling, a dramatic effect can be created in a large ballroom or party hall where the ceiling is high. This can be done in a solid, two-tone, or multicolor scheme. Overhead fans will help provide a billowing effect to lighter weight fabrics.

Materials Needed

- Fabric, mylar, or aisle runner

- Eight-foot to 10-foot sections of PVC pipe or inflexible metal tubing

- Number 20 gauge spool wire

- Ceiling clips for an acoustical ceiling

Construction Steps

1. For each strip of fabric, measure the width of the ceiling. Add 50 percent more to allow for draping. If the fabric is to extend down the sides of the walls, add to this subtotal the distance from the floor to the ceiling. Double the floor to ceiling measurement to allow yardage to cover both of the walls. Cut only one strip of fabric first so that the measurements may be adjusted if necessary.

2. Drill holes in the PVC pipe or tubing and add wire to facilitate hanging the supports.

3. Installation requires at least two people and two ladders. If acoustical ceilings are in the room, attach ceiling clips to the grid and suspend the PVC or tubing from the clips. Check with site management regarding alternate methods of hanging the supports.

4. Run sections of PVC pipe or inflexible metal tubing from the back of the room to the front. Space the bars approximately 10 to 12 feet apart. Use at least three sections of piping in the center and one on each side to create the woven effect pictured. *(Figure 8.3)*

5. If the fabric is especially slippery, use double-faced tape between the fabric and the piping.

6. Drape the first length of fabric over the first bar and under the second. Continue to alternate until the opposite side of the room is reached. Repeat this process, allowing some open space between each strip of fabric. *(Figure 8.3)*

Figure 8.3 Fabric Ceiling Treatment

Dance Floors

The dance floor should be decorated with an awareness of the density of the crowd using it. When it is likely to be very crowded, it is important that the decorations allow wide open areas for people entering and leaving the dance floor. For example, a garden under the stars can be created by clustering trees and banks of flowers around the dance floor. Garden benches and ornaments can be tucked in between the plants. Visually, this is effective, yet it is an impediment to traffic flow. Alternatively, weighted, fiberglass Roman columns may be used every 10 feet with massive arrangements on top. (See instructions for pillars on pages 230 through 232.) This is visually dynamic from any point in the room and allows ample access to the dance floor.

Dance Floor Festoons

A simple method of highlighting the dance floor is to suspend long lengths of fabric in swags above the area. Intermittently, a long cascade of fabric can tumble to the floor. Spotlights will travel further when focused on lighter colors, metallics, and vertical pleats. *(Figure 8.4)*

Figure 8.4 Dance Floor Festoons

Materials Needed

- Fabric, finished on both sides

- Number 20 gauge spool wire cut into lengths so that the festoon will hang at the desired height after being secured

- Ceiling clips for acoustical ceilings

Construction Steps

1. Calculate the perimeter of the area to be festooned. Multiply the perimeter by at least one and one-half times to allow for swagging. If fabric is to cascade to the floor, measure the distance from the top of the festoons to the floor. Multiply that number by the number of cascades. Always allow extra yardage in case it is needed.

2. Install ceiling clips to acoustical grids wherever a swag is to be gathered.

3. Cut the spool wire into the lengths needed to hang the festoons from the ceiling to the desired height. Suspend pre-measured wires from the ceiling clips.

4. Attach the fabric to the wires, and knot the center of each swag to control the way the fabric drapes.

5. Hang the fabric cascades and secure them to the carpet with 2-inch T-pins (available from office supply stores). On a smooth surface, use duct tape to secure a 1-inch by 2-inch wooden board to the floor and staple the fabric directly onto it.

Stages

The stage must be considered in light of how it will be used during the party. It may look wonderful to place lighted Roman columns in the corners of the stage; however, when the band arrives, their needs may require changes in placement and use of the nearest outlets. Inquiries about any way in which the stage is to be used should be made in advance. It should be made clear to the client how the space is to be filled.

On occasion, a stage will have a grand piano that is not moved, even when unused. A candelabra and lush flowers look wonderful gracing the piano top; however, within the music world, etiquette dictates that nothing be placed upon the top of a grand piano. The lid may be opened and a large arrangement may be placed on a pedestal in the curve of the piano, and lush fabric can flow through the design and cascade onto the floor.

Fabric can be used to visually lower the ceiling when swagged across the stage. Floral foam cages may be used at the corners to hold large arrangements of foliage or flowers.

Foam Board Stage Decoration

The following instructions are for creating a simple, yet inexpensive and profitable, stage decoration using foam board. The plan can be scaled up or down, according to the space available. Party theme accents and a flourish of balloons, together with a few well-placed spotlights, make this an exciting stage backdrop.

Materials Needed

- Four-foot by 8-foot foam boards (Use one board for approximately every 3 feet of stage to be decorated. Allow an extra board to make the musical accents.)

- Duct tape (or any strong, wide tape)

- Banking or straight pins

- Balloons

- Spotlights

- Plastic, Styrofoam™, or mylar letters

Construction Steps

1. Score the boards vertically down the center. Do not cut all the way through. Bend the boards to make sections of the screen.

2. From behind, tape the screens together at the party site. They should zigzag across the stage.

3. For a teenager's party, make oversized records out of foam board and spell out the name of the guest of honor on the labels, using the plastic, Styrofoam™, or mylar letters.

4. Use straight pins to secure these letters onto the screens.

6. Finish the screen with musical notes and scales made of foam board and interspersed throughout.

7. Add latex balloon columns to each end of the screen. (See Chapter 6.)

8. Place a floor standing spotlight behind the balloons to provide a dramatic glow. *(Figure 8.5)*

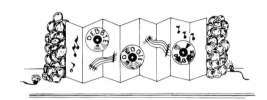

Figure 8.5 Foam Board Stage Decorations

Pillars

There are three basic types of pillars used as room decorations. First, the most common are structural pillars that are part of the room. When pillars exist in a room, they may be highlighted as important architectural elements. This can be achieved by using large floral foam cages at the top of the columns to hold fresh arrangements. The air temperature at ceiling level is hotter and drier than in the rest of the room, so highly perishable materials should not be used. Another way of arranging flowers at the top of a structural pillar is to take a length of chicken wire and wrap it lengthwise around the desired number of presoaked floral foam blocks. *(Figure 8.6a)* Small tacks can be hammered into the top of the column and the elongated floral cage hooked on, or chenille stems can be used to secure the cage from the ceiling. After letting excess water drip out, the arrangement may be completed. *(Figure 8.6b)*

The second type of pillars are movable columns that are often made of fiberglass, foam board, wood, PVC pipe, or sonotubes. *(Figure 8.7 on page 231)* The florist may purchase, construct, or

Figure 8.6a Decorating a Structural Pillar

Figure 8.6b Decorating a Structural Pillar

Figure 8.7 Portable Columns

rent them. They may be covered with fabric, twigs, melaleuca bark, wallpaper, or photocopied pictures for special effects. When storage space is at a premium, the decision to rent pillars may be especially advantageous. They should be break resistant and light enough to move easily. Upon installation, it may be necessary to weight them with bags of sand or gravel. When additional stability is necessary, a wire may be run from the top of the pillar to the ceiling. A stabilizing wire should not be run from the pillar to the floor because it can be a trip hazard. Flower arrangements or foliage plants may be placed on top of the stabilized pillars. This creates a dramatic formal effect with minimal expense. Lighting can be done from above, below, behind, or within the pillars.

The third type of pillars are freestanding floral pillars that may be made entirely out of flowers and foliage. They serve as room dividers or to create a formal linear accent throughout a room. They are very effective when used to guide traffic flow or to frame a focal area. Instructions for a freestanding pillar follow.

Floral Pillar

The mechanics for this floral pillar are easy to assemble. Once constructed, the base may be used repeatedly to create either one-sided or all-around flower or foliage-covered pillars.

Materials Needed

- Eight-foot long, 2-inch by 2-inch wooden board

- Bucket or large papier-mâché container

- Plaster of Paris

- Six presoaked floral foam cages with handles

- Six nails

- Two or three blocks of floral foam

- Flowers and foliage, as desired

Construction Steps

Figure 8.8a Constructing a Floral Pillar
Step 1

1. On opposite sides of the 2-inch by 2-inch board, attach the nails, starting at the top and then repeating this at 18 to 24-inch intervals. **(Figure 8.8a)**

2. Fill the container with plaster of Paris and insert the 2-inch by 2-inch piece of wood vertically into the container until the board rests on the bottom. Make sure the board is straight. Allow the plaster of Paris to set.

3. Hang a presoaked floral foam cage on each nail. Presoaked floral foam may be added to the base of the arrangement and secured with floral tape. *(Figure 8.8b)*

4. Use mixed foliage to create a dense green covering. Insert flowers horizontally to fill in. Taper the length of the stems at the top if a cone shape is desired. *(Figure 8.8c)* Non-tapered stem lengths will result in a straight architectural-looking column. *(Figure 8.8d)*

5. This floral pillar may be installed on top of tall pedestals for even greater impact. When this is the case, consider the perspective from which the design will be viewed. If it is above eye level, it will be necessary to arrange the flowers so that they show best from the underside.

Bars

The bar provides an area visually suited for floral accents. It is imperative that any decorations be structured, bearing in mind that this is an extremely busy work space. It is inconsiderate to create a floral extravaganza that aggravates the bartenders and guests all night. Usually tall, slender, well-balanced arrangements work best. They require a minimum of counter space and provide an area of beauty that soars over the heads of the guests. Suspended designs or wall hangings are creative alternatives. If the front of the bar is small, placing the arrangement behind the bar should be considered. If this is done, absolutely nothing should extend forward enough to catch on the clothing of a passing bartender. Large, bold flower forms will stand out in this busy area. Dramatic designs can also serve as conversation pieces that in turn may lead to additional business opportunities.

Tropical Bar Arrangement

The bar arrangement described here utilizes tropical flowers for an exotic look appropriate for a Hawaiian luau or other tropical party themes. For different themes, the flowers may be changed within the same design style.

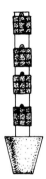

Figure 8.8b Constructing a Floral Pillar
Step 3

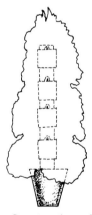

Figure 8.8c Constructing a Floral Pillar
Step 4

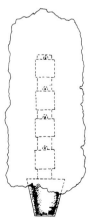

Figure 8.8d Constructing a Floral Pillar
Step 4

Notes

Materials Needed

- Cylinder vase

- Three anthuriums

- Two small to medium protea

- Bear grass

- Flat leaf eucalyptus

- One large monstera leaf

- Statice

- Miniature bananas from a banana flower (optional)

- Sheet moss

Construction Steps

1. Fill the cylinder so that the presoaked floral foam extends 2 inches over the lip of the container. Wedge the foam securely into place.

2. Contour the corners of the foam.

3. Cover the foam with a light layer of sheet moss.

4. Place the three anthuriums in a staggered line in the back left corner of the arrangement.

5. Place the single monstera leaf horizontally to the right of the cylinder.

6. Add the two protea low within the focal area.

7. Make a loop of bear grass, attach it to a wooden pick, and insert it to the left of the anthuriums. Attach a fountain-like collection of bear grass to another wooden pick and insert it at the same point as the loop so that it flows to the left of the design.

8. Cover the exposed foam by terracing the leaves of the eucalyptus and clustering the statice and bananas at the base. *(Figure 8.9)*

Note: As shown, this design would be most appropriate on the left side of the bar to prevent the bear grass from interfering with the passage of drinks across the bar.

Windows

Windows may be used as frames for floral decorations. An inexpensive ledge treatment is to design foliage arrangements in rectangular dishes and add two or three candles that are approximately 24 to 30 inches tall. *(Figure 8.10)* The soft glow of candles provides a gracious atmosphere.

When the windows are large and unobstructed by curtains, it is especially effective to use floral cages that have a suction cup on the back, such as Place-It™ containers manufactured by the Smithers-Oasis company. This allows the illusion of the flowers emerging from the glass. Instructions for this technique follow.

Paired Window Arrangements

This design features two crescent-shaped arrangements in the corners of a large picture window. Each design can be made as much as 5 feet in diameter as long as lightweight flowers and foliage are used. A modified version of this design can be created in smaller windows by using only a single crescent in one corner.

Materials Needed

- Presoaked floral cage with a suction cup attached

- Glass cleaner or vinegar

- Sheet moss

- Greening pins

- Lightweight flowers and foliage, such as anthurium, freesia, larkspur, plumosus, bear grass, and equisetum

Figure 8.9 Tropical Bar Arrangement

Figure 8.10 Window Decorations

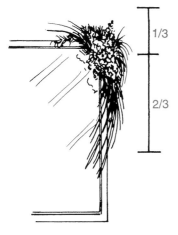

Figure 8.11a Creating Paired Window Arrangements Step 4

Figure 8.11b Creating Paired Window Arrangements Step 7

Construction Steps

1. It is important to follow the manufacturer's instructions carefully to ensure a secure installation of the floral cage. The glass must be very clean. Glass cleaner or vinegar can be used as a cleaner.

2. Following the manufacturer's instructions, attach the floral cage to the upper corner of the glass. Once the cage is on the glass, do not attempt to reposition it.

3. Cover the cage with a light layer of moistened sheet moss and secure it in place with greening pins.

4. Use line materials, such as larkspur, to establish the crescent outline. The upper portion of the crescent should be one-third of the total crescent length. *(Figure 8.11a)*

5. Establish the focal area near the foam cage, using moss or focal flowers.

6. Fill in the crescent shape with additional flowers and foliage. Be sure to trim the stem ends before insertion to reduce bulk within the foam cage.

7. Repeat Steps 2 through 6 in the opposite upper corner of the window, creating a crescent that is a mirror image of the other design. *(Figure 8.11b)*

Mirrors

When decorating mirrors, it is important to remember that any image is double in reflection. If the surface of the mirror is totally covered, this is not as important. More often, the accent is in one area of the mirror and a simplistic design works best. Mechanics show from behind, so they need to be covered completely.

The arrangement may be hung from a floral cage that is wired from behind and over the top of the mirror. Caution must be exercised to avoid damaging the frame. The same type of suction-backed floral foam cage used for window decorations can be used. Mirrors can be decorated by lacing the edges of the frame with foliage or tucking them behind the top. Instructions for this technique follow. Care should be taken with any plant materials that have sap, such as pine, which may mark the walls or frame.

Mirror Frame Decoration

This simple mirror decoration can be assembled on site within minutes. It can be scaled up or down to suit the size of the mirror. An ornate mirror in a foyer or entryway is an appropriate location for a more elaborate floral enhancement.

Materials Needed

- Assorted fresh flowers, including showy form flowers, such as cattleya orchids or gloriosa lilies

- Arching foliage, such as Italian ruscus or sprengeri

- Floral tape

- Water tubes

- Wired ribbon

Figure 8.12a Creating Mirror Frame Decorations Step 2

Construction Steps

1. Fill water tubes and insert stems of flowers approximately 6 inches long. Make sure that the tubes do no leak.

2. Insert long, arching stems of foliage into water tubes. Crisscross the water tubes and tape them together with floral tape to create a single crescent line. *(Figure 8.12a)*

3. Wedge the foliage tubes behind the top of the mirror so that the tips arch over the top edges of the frame.

4. Tuck the tubes of flowers into the foliage stems.

5. Finish with a wired ribbon bow at the center of the spray. The attachment wire can be wound around a water tube or taped to the back of the mirror. *(Figure 8.12b)*

Figure 8.12b Creating Mirror Frame Decorations Step 5

Chandeliers

The chandeliers in a room can be beautifully enhanced when they are bedecked with the season's most beautiful blossoms. This may be done using garlands, ribbons, or floral foam cages bursting with flowers. Care must be exercised to avoid any possible contact between decorations in water and the electrical current. It takes considerably more time and risk to install anything on a light fixture that is predominantly glass or crystal. Florists should determine liability in advance and be prepared to allow for it in determining the cost of the job.

For a very festive look, a multitude of ribbons that can be easily stapled around the arms of the chandelier and allowed to flow to a few inches above the floor can be used. People seem to love to play with the myriad of ribbon streamers by waving their arms through them. When mylar ribbons are used, it creates an interplay of light and reflection that shimmers in the night.

An inexpensive way to create a dramatic effect is to tie long pieces of #9 ribbon to a chandelier, unroll them to the edges of the room, and tack them into place on the walls or ceiling. In a large room, #40 ribbon is appropriate. When it is not possible to use thumbtacks, a wire should be run from one corner to the next and the ends of the ribbon fastened to the wire. *(Figure 8.13)* When planning this job, the ribbon should not be pre-cut because the length needed is greater from the chandelier to the corners than from the chandelier to the center of the wall. At Christmas, this treatment is especially festive when ribbon and bells are suspended from the chandelier.

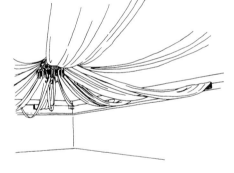

Figure 8.13 Decorated Chandeliers

Chandelier Arrangement

Floral arrangements in chandeliers are an unexpected surprise. They are a simple way to use flowers that are well lit and highly visible from most of the room. A variety of combinations of flowers, foliage, and ribbons can be used to enhance chandeliers. This design features flowering branches as the dominant floral material for a formal, elegant focal point within the party room.

Materials Needed

- Two medium-sized, presoaked floral cages

- Chenille stems

- Flowering branches

- Assorted flowers and foliage

Construction Steps

1. Allow excess water to drip from the presoaked floral cage overnight. When working, be very careful to avoid any contact with electrical current. Ideally, shut off the current to the fixture first. Make sure that no water drips into the wiring during installation. Work with a towel or bucket below the foam cage to catch any drips.

2. Secure two or three cages to the chandelier, depending on the size of the design. *(Figure 8.14a)* Attachment methods will vary, depending on the configuration of the chandelier; however, chenille stems work well in most situations.

3. Cover the floral cages with a light base of foliage.

4. Add long, whimsically placed flowering branches, such as dogwood and forsythia.

5. Tuck an elegant combination of flowers, such as peonies and spray roses, into the center of the design. *(Figure 8.14b)*

6. For a more abundant look, add more branches and flowers out the top of the chandelier until the fixture is completely encased in blossoms.

Figure 8.14a Creating a Chandelier Arrangement Step 2

Figure 8.14b Creating a Chandelier Arrangement Step 5

Mantles

Many party rooms include fireplaces and even those that do not sometimes include a mantle area on one or more of the walls. Mantles are a natural area for floral decorations. The width of the mantle, as well as existing decorations on or above it, will affect the type of floral arrangement that can be used.

Simple mantle decorations could include a bed of foliage or flowering branches casually laid in place. Flowers in water tubes could be added, if desired. Alternatively, a foliage garland could be swagged along the front edge of the mantle with ribbons intertwined. Plants can be grouped along the mantle as well, with moss, fabric, or mylar used to cover the pots.

Floral arrangements of many kinds can be designed for mantles, including low centerpieces and paired vertical designs. An important consideration when creating mantle arrangements is whether or not a fire will be lit at the time of the party. If so, wilt-sensitive flowers should be avoided in the mantle decorations since the heat of the fire will likely cause more rapid wilting. Cascading arrangements should also be avoided when the fireplace will be lit to eliminate a fire hazard.

Mantle Landscape

A fireplace mantle may be decorated in a variety of ways, yet the naturalistic landscape style always seems to be a favorite. It can be very showy with flowers being used at maximum height. It is suitable year round for any special occasion, as well as for holiday decoration. *(Figure 8.15)*

Figure 8.15 Mantle Landscape

Materials Needed

- Rectangular, utility containers or OASIS RAQUETTES®

- Heavy, black plastic trash bag or green polyfoil

- Sheet moss

- Greening pins

- Assorted flowers and foliage

- Pods and mosses

Construction Steps

1. Line the mantle top with the plastic from a heavyweight, black plastic bag.

2. Start with a series of design dishes, running the length of the mantle, end to end. Alternatively, OASIS RAQUETTES® may be used. Make sure that no water can drip out of any container or mechanic. When in doubt, use floral polyfoil under the foam to form a shallow tray.

3. Secure sheet moss to the front edges of the floral foam with greening pins.

4. Insert vertical clusters of flowers and branches in naturalistic patterns. Contrast materials of varied heights and textures. Make sure that the arrangement is not front-heavy or it might topple over. If a mirror is behind the mantle, the effect of any flower is doubled in the reflection.

5. Finish the base with foliage, pods, and mosses.

Versatile Room Decorations

While many party decorations are designed on, in, or around existing fixtures in a room, other decorations are often needed to enhance the room's atmosphere. Versatile designs that can be utilized in a variety of locations throughout a room and to suit a variety of purposes are especially useful. The arrangements in this segment are versatile designs specifically intended for party work. They are designed to provide the most impact possible in relation to the amount of time and money invested in their productions. The combination of flowers, foliage, and accessories used can help create the desired atmosphere or restate the theme of the festivity.

Massive Arrangements

These types of arrangements are designed to tower 10 to 15 feet in the air and are usually intended to be viewed from all sides. They may be used as a grand entry decoration, to flank a head table, in four corners of a large ballroom, or as a focal point within the party setting. The weight and stability of these arrangements sometimes makes them a challenge to construct. On-site design is recommended. Alternatively, each arrangement may be designed in sections in advance and have assembly completed on the job site. The arrangements cannot be readily moved after construction.

Materials Needed

- Large urn

- Bucket to be used as a liner for the urn

- Two-inch thick Styrofoam™ sheet

- Presoaked floral foam

- Chicken wire

- Spool wire

- One or two 15-inch round utility dishes or plastic saucers

Figure 8.16a Creating a Massive Arrangement Step 1

Constructions Steps

1. Build up the bottom of the urn approximately one-half the way, with 2-inch thick sheet Styrofoam™. *(Figure 8.16a)*

2. Fill the large bucket liner with presoaked floral foam that extends 4 inches beyond the top edge of the bucket.

Figure 8.16b Creating a Massive Arrangement Step 3

3. Cover the foam with chicken wire and extend it about 3 inches below the edge of the bucket. *(Figure 8.16b)*

4. Use spool wire to "sew" the chicken wire securely around the perimeter of the bucket.

5. Use a 15-inch plastic design dish and fill it with three layers of presoaked floral foam. Either standard floral foam bricks or extra large designer floral foam blocks may be used for additional stability.

Figure 8.16c Creating a Massive Arrangement Step 6

6. Wrap the dish entirely in chicken wire so that the top, sides, and bottom are covered. *(Figure 8.16c)* This method allows the mechanics to be set up in advance and transported to the site in segments that are somewhat manageable.

7. Upon arrival at the party site, place the bucket into the urn. It is extremely important to securely pack the space between the urn and the bucket with Styrofoam™. This will keep the entire design from shifting. *(Figure 8.16d)*

8. Move the urn to its final position in the room. A strong, draped table can be used to elevate the design.

Figure 8.16d Creating a Massive Arrangement Step 7

9. Place the foam-filled plastic dish on top of the foam in the bucket. The chicken wire on the bottom of the dish

and the top of the bucket will act to prevent the top layers from shifting.

10. Use spool wire to "sew" the two layers together.

11. Add broad-leaved foliage to cover the foam.

12. Insert very tall, flowering branches into the top layers. If necessary, cut open a single section of the chicken wire at a time to accommodate large branches. Do not twist the branches once they are inserted into the foam or they will create holes. In extreme emergencies, pan melt glue can be poured in to fill a gap around a heavy branch.

13. Add flowers in groupings for maximum visual impact. *(Figure 8.16e)* A variety of shapes may be designed within the established framework, including columnar, rounded, oval, and arching styles. *(Figures 8.16f through 8.16i on pages 242 and 243)*

14. At the end of the party, the client may appreciate having an appropriately dressed assistant come in and distribute the flowers in the arrangement to the departing guests.

Floral Garlands

Floral garlands may be designed for many price levels. The abundance and types of flowers used will be a major factor in determining the price. If the garland is made with hardy flowers, sprayed thoroughly with a surface sealer, and kept under refrigeration, it can be designed 1 or 2 days in advance. Water tubes are recommended in order to provide the flowers with an adequate water supply.

The garland may be made in sections and joined on site, or it may be made in one long unit; however, such a design is sometimes awkward to handle and transport. Following is a simple method that will help ensure that the garlands have a uniform look when more than one person is making them.

Materials Needed

• Eight-foot length of heavy green cord or 4-foot to 8-foot pieces of waxed floral string that are twisted together

Figure 8.16e Creating a Massive Arrangement Step 13

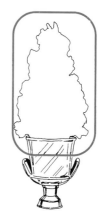

Figure 8.16f Creating a Massive Arrangement Step 13 - Columnar

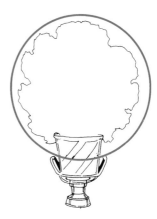

Figure 8.16g Creating a Massive Arrangement Step 13 - Round

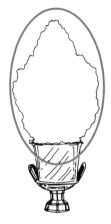

Figure 8.16h Creating a Massive
Arrangement Step 13 - Oval

Figure 8.16i Creating a Massive
Arrangement Step 13 - Massive

Incorrect   Correct

Figure 8.17a Creating a Floral
Garlands Step 1

- Number 28 gauge green spool wire

- Assorted flowers and foliage

Construction Steps

1. Cut the greens into 4-inch sections. Make sure that no bare tips of the stem protrude from the tips of the cut sections. *(Figure 8.17a)*

2. Cut a piece of heavy green cord or four pieces of waxed floral string to a length of 8 feet.

3. Use #28 gauge green spool wire and start to bind the pieces of foliage to the main string (or strings).

4. Fold about 2 inches of the end of the wire, and bind it securely with the spool wire to the cord. *(Figure 8.17b on page 244)*

5. Bind foliage and flowers into the garland by always holding the spool within a few inches of the cord and keeping it very tight. This garland is meant to be viewed from all sides, so be careful not to create a flat back. Right-handed people may find it easier to work tugging the wire away from themselves, then under the cord and back toward themselves. The opposite might be tried by left-handed people. All materials must be bound onto the previous stem, not just onto the cord, or it will collapse. Working on a table will allow ease in checking the roundness of the piece. *(Figure 8.17c on page 244)*

6. Keep the stem ends trimmed short to enhance flexibility.

7. Approximately 12 inches before the end of the garland, knot the wire and cut it. Then reverse the direction of the materials to be added from the bare end and work them toward the main part of the garland.

8. Use extra wire to reinforce the area where the foliage meets.

9. Securely add a wire loop to each end to facilitate hanging.

10. If desired, the foliage may be constructed days ahead and fresh flowers added just prior to the event.

Islands

Independent, freestanding clusters of plants or props can be used to emphasize a party theme or to camouflage an unattractive area within a party setting. For example, it is illegal to block a fire door, but a freestanding, naturalistic garden standing 10 feet in front of the doors can allow the overhead exit sign to be seen, while visually hiding the utilitarian fire doors. The doors are fully accessible by going behind the island in case of an emergency. Local fire regulations should be checked to assure compliance. Service areas, such as the kitchen entrance, may also be disguised in this way. The plans should be reviewed with the catering manager so that his staff is not impeded.

Woodland Island

A woodland island can easily be created to enhance many party themes. Following are instructions for constructing a woodland island. *(Figure 8.18)*

Materials Needed

- Heavy gauge plastic (drop cloth or from a roll)

- Large plastic saucers

- Floral foam

- Potted plants and trees

- Branches, hedges, etc.

- Flat or Western fern

- Assorted flowers

- Sheet moss

Construction Steps

1. Lay down plastic in the shape and size of the finished island. Trim as needed. This will minimize the chance of any spilled water affecting the carpet or flooring.

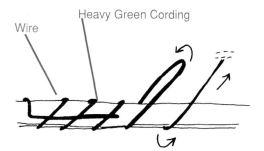

Wire
Heavy Green Cording

Figure 8.17b Creating a Floral Garland
Step 4

Figure 8.17c Creating a Floral Garland
Step 5

Figure 8.18 Woodland Island

Notes

2. Fill large plastic saucers with presoaked floral foam. Fill them with tall foliage, branches, clusters of flowers, etc.

3. Add some potted plants and trees for variation.

4. Use fern to cover as much of the bases as possible.

5. Use moss to finish the island and create a border.

When working on the special needs of customized room decorations, attention to detail is of the utmost importance. To ensure that the decorations are perfect, the florist should always walk out of the finished room for a moment and re-enter, looking at the room through the eyes of a guest. Any last minute adjustments can be made before the first guests arrive and the night magic begins.

With so many florists competing for the same customers, it is important to make clients feel as if they are getting the very best in value and quality for their investment. Merge this with imagination and genuine caring and the combination is sure to help make the reputation of the florist and his business grow and flourish.

Notes, Photographs, Sketches, etc.

Room Decor

Notes, Photographs, Sketches, etc.

Outdoor Settings

*T*he natural beauty of the outdoors can be utilized and enhanced by the professional party planner to create a variety of atmospheres for many types of parties. The challenge for the florist is to combine props with outdoor settings to create a beautiful scene or backdrop for the social event.

Unpredictable weather conditions can offer special challenges in outdoor settings. Floral designs and groupings must be designed to withstand rain, heat, and wind, as well as the uneven ground surfaces.

This chapter explores a variety of ways to create attractive outdoor party settings. The chapter opens with a discussion of general guidelines, such as consideration of scale, setup, appropriate flowers and plants, rental, and area definition. A variety of settings and props will be discussed, along with tent decorations and table treatments.

General Guidelines

Some basic guidelines can be applied to parties in outdoor settings. Scale relationships, defining specific areas, and suggestions about setup and rental are important considerations. Careful selection of long-lasting flowers is also a critical factor for designing arrangements for outdoor settings.

Scale

An on-site survey will reveal valuable information for considering the proper scale relationships of flowers and props to a specific site. When surveying the party site, existing plantings, the type of home or other structures near the site, and the overall lawn or patio area should be noted. Inquiries should be made as to whether guests will be dining under a tent or out-of-doors. The use of a tent will alter the scale of the required floral pieces; designing within a confined area of a tent rather than in an open outdoor setting will create a more intimate setting and less need for large-scale floral pieces.

Keeping the decorations and props in scale with the rest of the surroundings is very important. A key rule of thumb for designing in outdoor settings is to make everything larger and on a grander scale, with more eye-catching elements within the designs. A large backyard party site could visually support tall entry pieces, such as a gazebo with floral adornments, topiary trees on the buffet tables, and large showy table centerpieces. Even for a small patio area, designs, such as a small pool with tropical accent designs around it, should be larger than for areas of the same size indoors.

Defining Areas

For an outdoor party, defining areas and directing the traffic flow can be very helpful and necessary for both the client and guests. A detailed discussion must be held with the customer regarding the desired pattern of traffic flow. Both entrances and directional pathways leading to the dining or dancing areas need to be considered.

Entrances

Entrances can be emphasized so that guests will be easily directed to the party scene. Decorating an existing structure, such as a garden gate or lamppost, or an existing planting, such as a tree, shrub, or hedge, is one solution. Colorful ribbons and flower clusters could be tied to any garden structure or onto shrubs and trees. Flowering hanging baskets or decorated bird cages would look festive suspended from the branches of a tree. Potted flowering plants or tropical green plants could be grouped near an entry gate or fence or at the base of a tree. Door badges of flowers adorning a gate or patio door would announce in a grand way that "This is the party entrance!"

If suitable plantings do not exist at the entry site, potted rental plants and/or floral designs would also create a showy entryway. A grouping of potted fig trees with colorful crotons or prayer plants placed around the base would direct attention to the entry area. Cut palms in stands with tropical floral designs at the base to mask the stands would create a tropical paradise entrance.

Notes

Topiary trees bedecked with colorful ribbons would call attention to an entrance of an elegant garden party.

Lighting is another way to highlight an entrance. Spotlighting or pin lighting plants or garden structures will clearly mark an entrance, as well as provide additional atmosphere and visibility.

Utilizing both commercially available and custom-built arches and trellises create a grand entrance. Following are instructions for constructing several types of arches.

Commercial Entrance Arch

A rounded arch, sometimes used in wedding ceremonies, will transform a barren entry into a memorable one.

Materials Needed

- Rounded arch

- Stakes or sandbags

- Eight to ten foliage/flowering plants

- Spray bar or floral foam

- Foil

- Chicken wire

- Chenille stems

- Sprengeri

- Spool wire

- Liatris and gladiolus

- Scotch broom

- Yarrow

- Drumstick allium

- Carnations

- Galax leaves

- Sheet moss

Construction Steps

1. Position the arch on the site, ensuring that the ground is level and that the arch does not wobble. Anchor with stakes or bolster with sandbags. *(Figure 9.1a)* Position ferns or other foliage plants to conceal the anchoring. *(Figure 9.1b)*

2. Using chenille stems, attach a saturated spray bar or a block of saturated floral foam wrapped in foil and chicken wire to the top of the arch. *(Figure 9.1b)*

3. Create two sprengeri garlands by overlapping and wiring pieces of sprengeri together with spool wire. Loosely entwine the sprengeri garlands around the arch with ends meeting at the top. *(Figure 9.1b)*

4. Position the gladiolus, liatris, and Scotch broom in the spray bar at the top of the arch to create a crescent shape, repeating the gentle curve of the arch. *(Figure 9.1c)*

5. Choose flowers, such as allium, yarrow, and carnations, to fill in the crescent shape. Cover the mechanics with galax leaves and sheet moss. Repeat the foliage of the garland and let some sprigs cascade from the floral design. *(Figure 9.1d)*

Naturalistic Entrance Arch

A naturalistic entrance arch will look perfectly in place as an outdoor entryway. Since this arch is designed with dried flowers, it lends itself well to storage and reuse.

Materials Needed

- Four to six branches 7 to 8 feet in length

- Four to six branches 3 to 4 feet in length

Figure 9.1a Creating a Commercial Entrance Arch Step 1

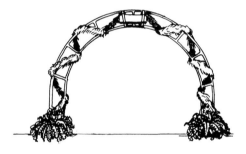

Figure 9.1b Creating a Commercial Entrance Arch Steps 1 - 3

Figure 9.1c Creating a Commercial Entrance Arch Step 4

Figure 9.1d Creating a Commercial Entrance Arch Step 5

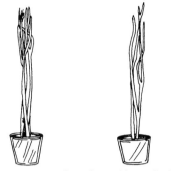

Figure 9.2a Creating a Naturalistic
Entrance Arch Step 1

Figure 9.2b Creating a Naturalistic
Entrance Arch Step 3

Figure 9.2c Creating a Naturalistic
Entrance Arch Step 5

- Two large papier-mâché liners

- Plaster of Paris

- String or small nails

- Moss

- Smilax garland

- Fully opened dried roses

- Dried baby's breath

Construction Steps

1. Using plaster of Paris that is available from hardware stores, cement two or three 7-foot and 8-foot upright branches into two large papier-mâché liners. Position the branches to suggest entwining and intergrowth. *(Figure 9.2a)* Allow adequate time for drying.

2. Place the liners into baskets or terra-cotta or stone pots.

3. Build the top of the arch by joining uneven lengths of 3-foot and 4-foot branches with string or small nails. The length of the top branches will depend upon the desired width of the entrance. Nestle the top branches into the top of the upright branches. Select long enough branch lengths so that the branches will overlap on the sides and at the top of the arch for a more natural look. Bind in sheet or Spanish moss with string to cover the joining points. *(Figure 9.2b)*

4. Purchase a smilax garland or create a smilax garland by overlapping the ends and wiring them together. Wire in additional smilax pieces to create sufficient fullness.

5. Wind the smilax garland around the arch framework, leaving additional garland at the base to cover any anchoring devices. *(Figure 9.2c)*

6. Tuck in clusters of fully opened dried roses and baby's breath. Secure the clusters by wedging the stems in between the moss and string. Use hot glue when necessary. *(Figure 9.2d)*

7. Position this entrance arch on the site and anchor well, if needed, using tree stumps or decorative logs, if available. If these are not available, use sandbags. Drape smilax garland to soften the logs or to mask the sandbags. Tuck in a few roses and baby's breath sprigs. Scatter rose petals and sprigs of baby's breath on the lawn near the arch.

Commercial Entrance Trellis

A garden trellis, such as those available from garden centers or hardware stores, made of wood or metal can transform an open area into the focal entryway of a party. For a Southern look of old New Orleans, a black wrought-iron trellis can be beautifully decorated with rambling branches and old-fashioned flowers.

Materials Needed

- Black wrought-iron trellis

- Stakes and/or sandbags

- Two OASIS RAQUETTES®

- Waxed string

- Stakes

- Wisteria branches (substitute with grapevine and curly willow)

- Hydrangea flowers

- Wisteria blossoms (silk optional)

- Spanish moss

- Leatherleaf

- Flat fern

Figure 9.2d Creating a Naturalistic Entrance Arch Step 6

Figure 9.3a Constructing a Commercial Entrance Trellis Step 1

Figure 9.3b Constructing a Commercial
Entrance Trellis Step 3

Figure 9.3c Constructing a Commercial
Entrance Trellis Step 4

Figure 9.3d Constructing a Commercial
Entrance Trellis Step 5

Construction Steps

1. Position a black, decorative, wrought iron trellis at the desired entryway. Secure well with stakes and/or sandbags or bags filled with gravel for added weight. *(Figure 9.3a on page 254)*

2. Securely fasten an OASIS RAQUETTES® Holder with waxed string to the upper left corner of the trellis. Position a second RAQUETTES® Holder at the base of the trellis on the right side. Attach with stakes or heavy gauge wire bent into a hook to secure all sides.

3. Insert wisteria branches into the RAQUETTES® Holder, creating a vining effect. *(Figure 9.3b)* Grapevine branches and curly willow could be used as a substitute.

4. Position hydrangea blossoms to create a focal area. *(Figure 9.3c)*

5. Add wisteria blossoms for a cascading accent and feeling of a Southern garden. *(Figure 9.3d)* Cover the RAQUETTES® Holder with Spanish moss and fern fronds.

Custom-Built Entrance Trellis

A simple and pleasing garden trellis can be created with materials from a lumberyard or hardware store. This design captures a summer feeling with the use of summer flowers on a garden trellis.

Materials Needed

- Two redwood planter boxes, 4 feet in length

- Three sections of crisscrossed lath with wood borders

- Quick-setting cement

- String

- Floral foam

- Garden netting or chicken wire

- Staple gun

- Corkscrew willow

- Lilies

- Phlox

- Purple coneflowers

- Daisies

- Equisetum

- Ivy

- Sheet moss

- Fungi and/or mushrooms

Construction Steps

1. Cement a lath section in an upright position into each planter box. *(Figure 9.4a)*

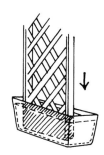

Figure 9.4a Constructing a Custom-Built Entrance Trellis Step 1

2. Position the upright sections at the site and securely tie the third lath section across the top with string. Allow for some overlap of the lath, extending beyond the upright sections. *(Figure 9.4b)* Provide additional anchoring of the trellis, if necessary.

3. Cover floral foam bricks with garden netting or chicken wire and use a staple gun to secure the netting to the horizontal lath section. OASIS RAQUETTES® can also be hot glued, pan glued, or taped to the horizontal lath piece with waterproof tape. The foam mechanic should extend across most of the top lath section. *(Figure 9.4b)*

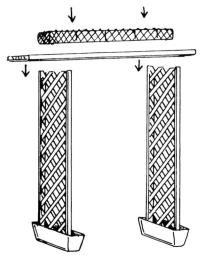

Figure 9.4b Constructing a Custom-Built Entrance Trellis Steps 2 & 3

4. To create a natural garden look on the trellis top, position garden phlox, lilies (two or three colors), and

Figure 9.4c Constructing a Custom-Built Entrance Trellis Step 4

Figure 9.5 Entrance Columns

Figure 9.6 Single Entrance Column

equisetum in groupings. Add corkscrew willow on the sides to frame the garden scene and in small groupings between the phlox and lilies. *(Figure 9.4c)*

5. Insert additional groupings of purple coneflowers, daisies, and fungi and/or mushrooms. Complete the picture with draping ivy and mosses.

Note: The trellis is easy to disassemble (remove the top lath section) and store until the next use.

Entrance Columns

Floral-decorated columns are another eye-catching entryway. Columns can be rented from party supply companies or purchased from architectural salvage firms. Columns of any height can be well incorporated into a special party theme or look. Columns could be made from sonotubes or empty floral preservative cylinders. Sprays or faux finishes could be used to transform these items to the desired look. For complete instructions, refer to Chapter 5.

A simple, yet beautiful, look can be created by placing ferns atop the column with the fronds draping down and softening the column top. Urns of lavish mixed flowers look impressive when placed upon columns on either side of an entryway. *(Figure 9.5)* Garlands or ribbons can also be added to soften the look.

A single column can also make an entrance look impressive. *(Figure 9.6)* Securely attach a RAQUETTES® Holder to the top and design an "arbor look" with draping vines, twigs, ferns, and a mix of colorful flowers. Wisteria (fresh or silk), grapes, and grapevine would be appropriate additions.

Anchor the plants or designs securely with double-sided tape and/or waterproof tape placed across the container base. A draping of tulle will cover the tape and provide aesthetic appeal. Position one or two ferns at the base of the column and place two or three more ferns 4 to 5 feet to one side of the column to create a defined entryway for guests.

Directional Pathways

Guests can be subtly led or directed in the most appropriate traffic flow pattern by creating pathways. Corners and edges of a party site can also be marked, using some of the techniques described in this section. Potted plants, both green and blooming, can be positioned in twos or threes at intervals along a pathway. Ribbon can be laid along the pathway first with the plants placed upon the ribbon. RAQUETTES® can be positioned along a pathway or near the corner edge of a party site and designed with a variety of plant combinations as follows:

Figure 9.7 Stanchions Decorated with Ribbons and Flowers

- Flowers
- Flowers and potted plants
- Branches and evergreens
- All foliage
    - Tropical foliage
    - Boxwood hedge
    - Vines and ferns

Figure 9.8 Stanchions Decorated with Tulle or Fabric

Using stanchions or aisle markers with posts is an easy way to direct traffic flow. The posts, which can be rented or purchased, may or may not have attached self-supporting bases. Posts without the base can be positioned directly into the ground. The most appropriate type should be determined before renting. *(Figures 9.7 and 9.8)*

To decorate the aisle markers, ribbons or small clusters of flowers can be tied to each post. Pew clips can be used to design larger floral designs to attach to the stanchions. *(Figure 9.7)*

Another way to decorate stanchions for pathway markers is to drape tulle or fabric for added texture and color contrast. Flowers and foliage can be glued to the draping. *(Figure 9.8)* Blooming plants can be positioned at the base of the posts.

Depending upon the theme, short picket or iron fences can also be used to guide traffic flow. Fencing is readily available at lumber yards or lumber supply companies. A variety of sizes and styles can be purchased and stained or painted. The fences should be anchored directly into the ground with stakes, or cross-hatch pieces of wood can be nailed to create a base for the fencing. Sandbags and plants can be used for support at the base.

Potted Tree Pathway Markers

Potted dwarf Alberta spruce trees make delightful pathway markers. Other dwarf evergreens or boxwood trees also work well.

Figure 9.9a **Creating Potted Tree Pathway Markers Step 2**

Figure 9.9b **Creating Potted Tree Pathway Markers Step 5**

Materials Needed

- Dwarf Alberta spruce trees

- Baskets, terra-cotta, brass pots, or fabric with ribbon ties

- Gardenias

- Green chenille stems

- Ribbon

- Crowning Glory

- Paper ribbon, tulle, or cording

Construction Steps

1. Choose trees of uniform height. Taller specimens can be placed at the beginning and end of the path.

2. Mask the containers by placing each pot into a basket or terra-cotta or brass pot. Depending upon the party theme and look, gathered fabric or tulle will nicely cover the container. Tie the fabric or tulle with ribbons, cording, or raffia and let streamer ends flow onto the lawn. **(Figure 9.9a)**

3. Position the trees at 6-foot, 8-foot, or 10-foot intervals, depending upon the number and size of the trees and the size of the area to be covered.

4. Decorate the trees with gardenias and ribbons. Attach the gardenias to the tree branches with green chenille stems. Spray the gardenias with Crowning Glory.

5. Connect the trees with ribbons, paper ribbon, tulle, or cording. **(Figure 9.9b)**

Custom-Built Aisle Markers

For simple-to-make aisle markers, collect coffee cans and purchase broom handles from a local hardware store. These stanchions can be stored away and used repeatedly.

Materials Needed

- Coffee cans

- Broom handles

- Quick-setting cement

- Spray paint - white, black, silver, etc.

- Aisle runner, tablecloth, mylar, or fabric

- Eye screws

- Ribbon, raffia, or curling ribbon

- Votive candles (optional)

- IGLU® holders (optional)

Construction Steps

1. Saw off the rounded tip of the broom handle. Cement a broom handle into each coffee can. *(Figure 9.10a)*

2. After the cement is dry, spray paint the broom handle and coffee can either white, black, silver, or another desired color that suits the party color scheme.

3. Cover the coffee can with a portion of an aisle runner, colorful tablecloth, mylar, or fabric. Gather the material and tie with ribbon, raffia, or curling ribbon. *(Figure 9.10b)*

4. Secure an eye screw into the top or side of the broom stick. *(Figure 9.10c)*

5. Thread cording, ribbon (single, double, or braided), tulle, or paper ribbon through the eye screws to connect the stanchions. *(Figure 9.10d)*

6. Attach bows of matching ribbon or fabric to the eye screw atop each pole.

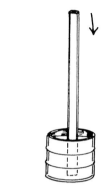

Figure 9.10a Creating Custom-Built Aisle Markers Step 1

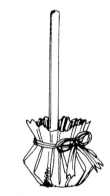

Figure 9.10b Creating Custom-Built Aisle Markers Step 3

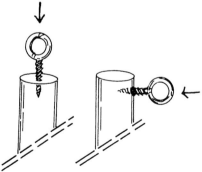

Figure 9.10c Creating Custom-Built Aisle Markers Step 4

Figure 9.10d Creating Custom-Built Aisle Markers Step 5

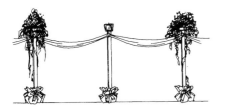

Figure 9.10e **Creating Custom-Built Aisle Markers Step 7**

7. For a more festive look, try the following variations.

- Hot glue a votive candle cup to the top of the broom handle.

- Nail an IGLU® to the broom handle and design an arrangement.

- Alternate votive candles and floral designs. *(Figure 9.10e)*

Large-Scale Aisle Marker Pillars

To design larger floral pieces atop directional pathway markers, make these pillars from readily available materials.

Materials Needed

- Empty Floralife® Preservative drums

- Two-inch by 4-inch wooden posts (one per pillar)

- Black garbage bags

- Metallic spray paint

- Fabric or paper ribbon

- O-bowls

- Hot glue and glue gun

- Floral foam

- Ting ting

- Miniature gladioli

- Drumstick allium

- Carnations

- Rubrum lilies

- Spanish moss

- Plumosus fern

- Monte casino

- Ribbon

Construction Steps

1. Cement a 2-inch by 4-inch wooden post (8 feet in length) into a Floralife® drum. *(Figure 9.11a)*

2. Cover the drum with a black garbage bag and paint with a metallic finish spray paint. Shape the bag before the paint dries. *(Figure 9.11b)*

3. Cover the 2-inch by 4-inch upright posts with fabric or paper ribbon. *(Figure 9.11b)*

4. Nail an O-bowl to the top of the 2-inch by 4-inch wooden post. Apply hot glue around the nail to water seal the O-bowl. *(Figure 9.11b)*

5. Secure a cylinder of saturated floral foam into the O-bowl. Add white ting ting, miniature gladioli, and drumstick allium for height. *(Figure 9.11c)*

6. Position pink carnations and rubrum lilies at the base. For filler, add plumosus, monte casino, and ribbon loops. Cover the mechanics with Spanish moss.

7. Add ribbon streamers and foliage, such as asparagus plumosus, to drape down the fabric-covered upright post. *(Figure 9.11d on page 263)*

Outdoor Rental Items

A party work florist needs to know the availability and costs of rental items to assist in the selling and planning of parties. Visiting and/or calling rental places is a good way to investigate the options. A complete inventory listing and pricing sheet for rental items should be kept on file. A myriad of items for outdoor parties can be rented, including the following.

Figure 9.11a Creating Large-Scale Aisle Marker Pillars Step 1

Figure 9.11b Creating Large-Scale Aisle Marker Pillars Steps 2 - 4

Figure 9.11c Creating Large-Scale Aisle Marker Pillars Step 5

Figure 9.11d Creating Large-Scale
Aisle Marker Pillars Step 7

- *Flooring* - Flooring in a variety of shapes and dimensions can be rented. Dance floor sections and complete flooring for sites are available. Artificial turf in any dimension can also be rented to cover a party site.

- *Lighting* - Many types of lights and lighting devices can be rented, such as spotlights for highlighting entrances or statuary, *pin lights* for creating a twinkling or starry effect in trees, *rotating lights* for a unique background effect, *globed street lamps* to create a formal setting, *neon lights* for an upbeat 50's look, *strobe lights* to liven up a dance floor, and both battery-operated and electrical *candles with hurricane lantern shades*.

- *Specialty Machines* - Machines can be rented that create special effects, such as a *snow machine* for a Christmas in July party, a *bubble machine* for a "bubbly" champagne brunch, a *fog machine* to create a Sherlock Holmes mystery setting, and *confetti cannons* to create a miniature "ticker tape" parade to celebrate a special milestone at a party.

- *Structures* - A wide array of structures, such as swings, benches, fencing, arches, trellises, columns, and even gazebos, can be rented.

- *Fountains and Pools* - For a water effect at a party and to enjoy the splashing sounds of water, fountains and pools can be rented and incorporated into the party theme, such as a Caribbean cruise theme and the Ol' Swimmin' Hole party.

- *Tables and Coverings* - All sizes, shapes, and styles of tables can be rented. Tablecloths and drapings, as well as napkins, can also be rented. Ask about colors and styles of cloths and drapings.

- *Musical Equipment* - Many types of speakers, stereos, compact disc players, tape players, and soundboards can be rented. Musical instruments, such as an organ, drums, etc., can also be rented. Consider hiring strolling minstrels or a three-piece band. Maintain a file of good musicians to hire.

- *Tents* - Check on prices and availability at firms that specialize in the rental, setup, and removal of tents of all sizes, shapes, and colors for any and all outdoor events.

- *Air Conditioning and Heating* - Tent companies and some rental companies can install units within tented areas to provide both cooling and heating. The tent dimensions and ceiling heights must be determined prior to ordering such units.

When renting items from a rental firm, ask about delivery. Also, determine who sets up the rental items on the site and who is responsible for operating any equipment required. Liability should be discussed in case anything breaks or malfunctions. Rental companies will provide contracts to sign; therefore, they should be read thoroughly and all of the provisions of the contract noted. For more information on rental props and equipment, see Chapter 5.

Setup Suggestions

Setup can proceed smoothly with proper selling, planning, and the utilization of a few helpful tips. Refer to Chapter 3 for additional information on efficient party installation.

Selling

Properly selling an outdoor party is an important first step in successful party planning. The use of good selling strategies can prevent many problems when setting up and implementing the event.

Arranging to go to the outdoor site at the same time of day that the party will be held is a good idea. Shaded areas, wind patterns, and "hot spots" should be noted. Utilizing the site's best features, as well as avoiding full sun and windy areas, requires strategic planning. During the site survey, the amount of outside lighting and electrical outlets should be checked. If the amount is inadequate, plans should be made to provide additional outside outlets (i.e., extension cords). Cords should be positioned and covered so that guests will not trip.

Flooring should be discussed with the client. Some customers may want a complete flooring laid, including a dance floor. If the client has no definite plans for the flooring, suggestions can be

Notes

made for laying artificial turf over the trafficked lawn area. The artificial turf protects the lawn from excess damage and helps level uneven surfaces. The turf can be positioned earlier in the day to allow the setup of tables and any other structures, such as arches, aisle markers, or benches.

Flowers that can withstand outdoor conditions should be suggested. Fragile flowers that wilt easily need to be avoided. The following list includes long-lasting flowers that are suitable for outdoor settings.

Long-Lasting Plant Materials for Outdoor Settings

Allium	Foliage - all types except ivy
Alstroemeria	Gladiolus
Anthurium	Heliconia
Aster	Kangaroo Paw
Astilbe	Liatris
Banksia Lily	
Bird of Paradise	Orchids - Cattleya
Carnation	Cymbidium
Chrysanthemum	Ornithogalum
Echinops	Protea - all types
Eryngium	Safflower
Fillers - Baby's Breath	Statice
German Statice	Vegetables and Mushrooms
Spray Asters	Yarrow

Also, highly visible colors should be sold for parties held at night. Booking a party of dark, receding color combinations for an evening event will have a disappointing effect.

Colors for Evening Events

Effective Colors:	Colors to Avoid:
White	Blue
Silver	Purple
Metallic	Burgundy
Warm Colors	
Yellow, Orange,	
Bright Red	
Hot Pink	
Turquoise	
High Contrast Color Combinations	
Black/White	
Black/Yellow	
Peach/Lime Green	
Silver/Hot Pink/Green	

Selling balloons for outdoor events should be discouraged. Air currents will tangle the lines outdoors. When used outdoors, balloons will quickly oxidize, a natural aging process that changes the look of clear balloons and turns them "milky." Because of environmental reasons, mylar balloons should **never** be used outside. The foil may get caught in electrical wires. If a customer must have some balloons for the party, choose opaque 100 percent latex balloons to inflate, knot, and tie with biodegradable string. The effect of oxidation on opaque balloons is less noticeable. It might be suggested that balloons be used within the tent area where air currents are decreased. Balloons are useful for decorating tent poles. Chapter 6 contains additional ideas on using balloons to decorate the tent area.

Outdoor Table Treatments

Attractive table treatments are a key component of an outdoor party setting. The types of tables chosen for an event should suit the site and the number of guests. A variety of table sizes in round and rectangular shapes is available and appropriate for use in outdoor, as well as indoor, party settings, as described in Chapter 7. Other suitable tables for outdoor settings include umbrella tables and picnic tables.

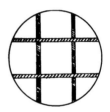

Figure 9.12a Ribbon Tie Table Covering - Round Table

Outdoor Table Coverings

Well-anchored, yet attractive, table coverings are a bonus for the florist who does outdoor parties, because the tables can be set up and covered well ahead of time. The tablecloths can be placed on the tables with clips to hold the cloths down in case of wind. The clips can be hidden with small bows and/or clusters of flowers tied to them.

Another table-covering technique is to ribbon-tie the cloth to the table. Both round and rectangular tables, including picnic tables, can be treated this way. *(Figures 9.12a and 9.12b)* Ribbon cording or tulle will work to hold the tablecloth in place. The tie and tablecloth should be tied securely to the undersides of the tables.

Tablecloths can be placed on a rectangular table or picnic table and tied with cording or ribbon at the four corners of the table. This method will give a festive, gathered effect to the table covering. *(Figure 9.13)*

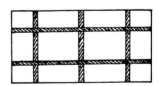

Figure 9.12b Ribbon Tie Table Covering - Rectangular Table

Figure 9.13 Table Covering with Gathered Corners

Figure 9.14 Round Table Covering with a Fabric Tie

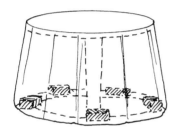

Figure 9.15 Weighted Table Covering

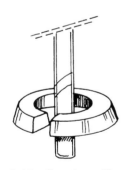

Figure 9.16a Creating a European Wreath Centerpiece for Umbrella Tables

Figure 9.16b Creating a European Wreath Centerpiece for Umbrella Tables

For a more formal look, long tablecloths to cover round tables may be selected. The tablecloth should be gathered around the middle with another piece of fabric. *(Figure 9.14)* The chairs would coordinate well if draped with matching cloths that were also tied with fabric.

Another covering of a round table with a full length tablecloth incorporates weighting the tablecloths. Position a longer than needed tablecloth over the round table. Turn the tablecloth ends inward toward the table legs and weight them down with bricks around the entire outside edge. *(Figure 9.15)*

Outdoor Table Centerpieces

The covering and decoration of tables for outdoor events should be slightly altered to take into consideration the effects of wind and weather. Centerpieces may need extra weight to prevent them from tipping over in the wind. Sand, gravel, rocks, cement, or plaster may be used, depending on the size of the container. Outdoor table centerpieces should be designed so that they are not too tall or top heavy. For the illusion of height, lightweight ting ting, miniature gladioli, or liatris should be used as the top flowers. For very windy sites or in extreme heat, centerpieces should be designed in bubble bowls, either placing floating flowers in the water or placing a small design inside the bowl. For an umbrella table, a design can be created on a European wreath form that has been cut through in one place. The wreath form will slip around the center pole of the umbrella. *(Figures 9.16a and 9.16b)*

Delivery

Before the day of delivery, the best place and the most effective method of unloading supplies, designs, and any large items should be determined. A delivery schedule with the order of delivery and the time to deliver specific items should be completed. (See the party delivery chart in Appendix A.) The client should be notified of early delivery plans.

Rented or purchased carts can be used to move supplies to areas where a vehicle cannot be used. Supplies and designs need to be packed in an efficient manner, and water sources should be located in advance.

Nonperishable, non-floral items should be delivered first. Floral designs and plants need to be delivered and positioned 1 to 2 hours prior to the start of a party. Fresh flowers should be kept in shaded areas as long as possible and then set out. For an evening party, it is advisable to place the floral pieces and plants on the site after the heat of the day, if possible. Likewise, it is best to inflate any balloons later in the day.

Notes

Garden Settings

Ideally, if the party site has a garden, the garden will be in peak bloom for the party. In the event that flowering occurs too early or late, the garden can be embellished with cut flowers inserted into water tubes and placed into the soil around existing plants. For a larger effect, a cemetery vase can be filled with flowers and inserted into the soil behind a cover of garden foliage. Potted blooming plants can also be added to the garden bed and the pots disguised by layers of sheet moss.

Creating a Flower Garden

Entire gardens of cut flowers and plants can be created in bare areas on the party site as follows.

Materials Needed

- Floral foam

- Hyacinth stakes

- Liatris

- Zinnias

- Marigolds

- Lilies

- Ferns

- Sheet moss

- Wood chips

- Stones, driftwood, or log sections

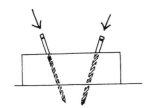

Figure 9.17a Creating a Flower Garden
Step 1

Figure 9.17b Creating a Flower Garden
Step 2

Construction Steps

1. Secure bricks of saturated floral foam to the ground by diagonally inserting two hyacinth stakes through the foam and into the ground at a 3-inch or 4-inch depth. OASIS RAQUETTES® can also be used and should be staked to secure them to the ground. *(Figure 9.17a)*

2. Create a garden look in the foam. Design in the way flowers and plants would grow with flowers grouped by like variety and uniform, appropriate heights. For example, liatris would be positioned in a tall, upright manner, while zinnias and marigolds would be grouped lower in a mounded fashion. Lilies would display a tall, vase-shaped growth pattern. Design with foliage also. Ferns can be designed in a rosette or whorled pattern with all the fronds emerging from a central point. *(Figure 9.17b)*

3. Cover any exposed foam with dampened sheet moss or wood chips to blend the design with the rest of the garden. The use of stones, driftwood, or sections of logs is also effective.

Note: A flower garden can be created in containers and transported to the site if installation time does not permit on-site construction.

Creating Flower Gardens in Baskets

Combining floral designs and potted plants within baskets or other large containers can create a beautiful flower garden effect. This look creates impact and textural contrasts and is easily delivered and set up.

Materials Needed

- Large baskets

- Green and blooming potted plants

- Sandbags or stones

- Newspaper, tissue, or floral foam pieces

- Utility containers

- Floral foam

- Lilies, orange and yellow

- Red gladioli

- Red kangaroo paws

- Red twig dogwood or bamboo

- Red ti leaves

- Galax leaves

- Spanish moss

Figure 9.18a Creating a Flower Garden
in a Basket Step 3

Construction Steps

1. Select large baskets and a variety of green and blooming potted plants, as well as fresh cut flowers.

2. Weight the base of the basket with one or two sandbags or some stones.

Figure 9.18b Creating a Flower Garden
in a Basket Step 4

3. First, position the plants, such as potted crotons, marigolds, and dracaenas, in the basket. Fill the empty spaces of the basket with floral foam pieces, crumpled newspaper, or tissue to bring the plants up to the desired placement level in the basket. *(Figure 9.18a)*

4. In the remaining open areas, tightly wedge in foam-filled utility containers or foiled, saturated floral foam bricks. *(Figure 9.18b)*

5. Design by grouping orange and yellow lilies, red gladioli, and red kangaroo paws. Add red twig dogwood branches or bamboo for height and red ti leaves and galax leaves for texture. *(Figure 9.18c)*

6. At the base of the baskets, place additional potted plants and some flower groupings in utility containers to provide transition to the lawn.

Figure 9.18c Creating a Flower Garden
in a Basket Step 5

Figure 9.19 Flower Gardens in Multiple Baskets

7. Cover all the containers and pots with Spanish moss. Drape some moss from the branches or bamboo and secure in place with hot glue.

Note: This garden look is effective when designed in multiple baskets. *(Figure 9.19)*

Creating a Complete Garden Landscape

To create a large-scale garden landscape, the florist can use trees, shrubs, flowers, and garden structures, such as a trellis, bench, gazebo, arch, swing, and even sod, to form a memorable scenic vista for an outdoor social event. This setting is attractive when placed in a corner area of a party site or designed on either side of a buffet table or gazebo. Depending upon the area to be embellished with plants, the size of this garden landscape can be increased by adding more trees or moveable hedges, as well as additional potted plant groupings.

Creating a complete landscape involves planning ahead so that high quality plant materials and garden structures can be located. Local garden centers, nurseries, and landscape firms often have these necessary materials. Purchase plants, such as shrubs and hedges, in planter boxes and rent them to customers.

Materials Needed

- Flowering tree in a container

- Dolly

- Shrubs (containerized)

- Potted plants

- Hedges in planter boxes

- OASIS RAQUETTES®

- Garden flowers

- Moss, stones, and/or driftwood

Construction Steps

1. Move a containerized tree on a dolly onto the site. Leave the tree on the dolly for ease in removal. *(Figure 9.20a)*

2. Position containerized shrubs to mask the tree container. *(Figure 9.20b)*

3. Group potted blooming plants near the shrubs to provide a colorful focal area. *(Figure 9.20c)*

4. To finish the front and sides, position both garden-look floral designs created in RAQUETTES® and small hedges in planter boxes in front of the blooming plants to mask the containers. Use mosses, driftwood, and stones to cover all mechanics and create a border. *(Figure 9.20d)*

Optional: If the surface of the garden landscape is concrete, gravel, or wood, consider laying sod to create a natural-looking lawn. The process of laying sod includes the following.

1. Purchase freshly-cut sod.

2. Lay the sod immediately and stagger the placement of the roll ends. *(Figure 9.21 on page 273)*

3. Allow time after laying for sod to "green up," several hours preferably.

4. After the party, the sod can be discounted and sold to a previously-arranged customer.

Garden Additions

Many types of garden structures can be added to the landscaped party scene to give character and personality to the site. These structures will also provide seating or a feeling of enclosure. Arches, trellises, gazebos, decorative swings, and benches, as well as statuary, bird baths, stepping stones, or decorative stones can be used to embellish and enhance the garden party scene.

Figure 9.20a Creating a Complete Garden Landscape Step 1

Figure 9.20b Creating a Complete Garden Landscape Step 2

Figure 9.20c Creating a Complete Garden Landscape Step 3

Figure 9.20d Creating a Complete Garden Landscape Step 4

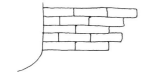

Figure 9.21 Sod Placement for a
Garden Landscape

Statuary

Statuary can add a lovely focal point to a garden setting. Existing statuary can be decorated on the party site or appropriate statuary provided to add a special touch and enhance a party theme. The possibility of renting statues or sculptures from rental or architectural salvage firms should be investigated.

Ways to adorn and enhance statues include placing a bouquet in the hand of a female figure, garlanding a statue or sculpture with flowers, foliage, and/or fruit, positioning garden-style floral designs at the base of both human or animal statues, and placing potted blooming plants or moveable hedge planters around the base.

Garlanding Statuary

This garland technique works well for large statues but can be adapted and scaled down for statues of any size. (Florists' Review, July 1991, 28, 34)

Materials Needed

- Statue

- Floral foam

- Chicken wire

- Wire

- Ribbon or string

- Moss

- Galax leaves

- Miniature carnations

- Roses and petals

- Astilbe

- Purple and green grapes

Construction Steps

1. Lay the desired length of soaked floral foam blocks along a rectangular piece of chicken wire. Roll the chicken wire around the foam and fasten securely with wire along the length and at the ends. Bend any exposed wires into the foam. *(Figure 9.22a)*

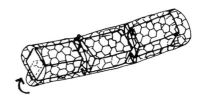

Figure 9.22a Garlanding Statuary Step 1

2. Tie the roll of foam to the statuary with ribbon or string.

3. Green the roll with mosses and galax leaves. Insert flower heads of miniature carnations, roses, and astilbe in groupings. Position purple and green grape clusters on wood picks within the design for textural contrast. *(Figure 9.22b)* Place some flower heads and petals at the base of the statue.

Swings and Benches

Other natural additions to a garden setting are swings and benches. These structures can create a beautiful focal point in the garden. Both of these structures can be rented if not available on the site. Benches can also be obtained from local park districts, whose personnel will often deliver to the site, as well as pick up the benches after the party.

Figure 9.22b Garlanding Statuary Step 3

Swings and benches can be designed into the setting for both functional and decorative uses. If a swing or bench is strictly decorative, be sure to position the structure well away from the traffic flow and place plants and floral designs in front of it, thereby discouraging guests from sitting upon it. On the other hand, sturdy and functional swings or benches can be utilized at a party for additional conversational seating areas. Traffic flow patterns can direct guests near these garden additions.

Benches and swings can be adorned with floral and/or foliage garlands. Pew clips can be used to design accent floral pieces on the back of benches or top of the swing's framework. *(Figures 9.23a and 9.23b)* A garden backdrop can be created on the sides and in the back of these structures by grouping potted plants and floral designs. The use of the swing should not be obstructed by plants.

Figure 9.23a Swing and Bench Decorations Using Pew Clips

Creating a Grape Arbor Swing

The garden swing can be transformed into a delightfully intimate seat within a grape arbor.

Figure 9.23b Swing and Bench Decorations Using Pew Clips

Materials Needed

- Grapevine branches

- Brown floral tape

- Wire - 18 inches in length

- Galax leaves and/or silk grape leaves

- Fresh or artificial grapes

Construction Steps

1. Attach grapevine branches to the swing framework with brown floral-taped, 18-inch wires. Curl excess wire ends around a finger to resemble grapevine tendrils. *(Figure 9.24a)*

2. Secure galax leaves and/or silk grapes by wiring them onto the branches. Curl taped wire ends to resemble tendrils.

3. Attach clusters of fresh or artificial grapes by wiring them onto the branches. Curl taped wire ends to resemble tendrils. *(Figure 9.24b)*

Figure 9.24a Creating a Grape Arbor Swing Step 1

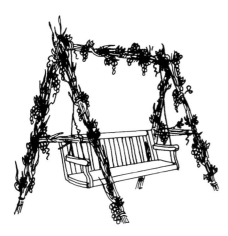

Figure 9.24b Creating a Grape Arbor Swing Step 3

Gazebo

A gazebo on a party site acts as an impressive focal point. If the site has a gazebo, it can be incorporated into the theme. For example, for a Southern cotillion, draping the gazebo with vines, Spanish moss, and gardenias would capture the Southern feeling. Gazebos can also be rented and constructed by the florist as a prop.

It should be determined if the gazebo is large and sturdy enough to be useful or decorative only. If the gazebo is decorative only, guests should be restricted from entering it by placing the gazebo back into the landscape setting with plants and flowers in front of it to frame it. The inside space can be filled visually by placing birds in decorated cages in the gazebo. Small colorful birds or talking parakeets could be rented and would be appropriate if the weather is moderate. A night event with parakeets should not be planned because these birds will not talk, preferring to quietly rest. Another idea incorporating birds for a spring or a farm theme is to place baby chicks in the gazebo. One-foot high pieces of Plexiglas™ or netting around the inside base of the gazebo will keep the chicks confined and allow the guests to view them. The chicks can be purchased by the flat from a poultry company. It should be arranged beforehand to give a 4-H or FFA student the chicks to use for a project afterward. The birds should be well cared for while in the florist's possession.

If the structure has large enough dimensions and is completely sturdy, an hors d'oeuvre or punch table can be placed inside the gazebo. Another idea is to construct a gazebo to gracefully cover the food tables and give a feeling of enclosure. *(Figure 9.25)* The gazebo could be made into an old-fashioned bandstand and the band could perform in it.

Decorating a Gazebo

Figure 9.25 Gazebo Framing a Buffet Table

Gazebos can be decorated in a multitude of ways from the most simple ribbon treatments to lavish floral-covered displays. The following steps are for a moderately decorated gazebo, featuring fresh flowers and blooming plants.

Materials Needed

- Four IGLU® Grande Cages

- Wire

- Fantail willow

- Cymbidium orchid sprays

- Salal

- Sheet moss

- Bear grass

- Two potted fig trees

- Four spider plants

- Six azaleas

- Baskets

Construction Steps

1. Attach four saturated IGLU® Grande Cages with wire to the gazebo railings and roof - two on either side of the entrance, one centered on the back railing, and one placed (with a ladder) at the center of the roof.

   Note: These designs can be created at the shop and quickly attached at the party site.

2. Position fantail willow in the designs for height and contour.

3. Add cymbidium orchid sprays. Green with salal and moss. Add bear grass tufts to drape and add space.

4. Outside the gazebo entrance, group a potted fig tree, two spider plants, and three azaleas on each side. Cover the pots with baskets. The fig trees and the ceiling of the gazebo can be lighted with pin lights. **(Figure 9.26)**

Figure 9.26 Decorated Gazebo

Constructing a Branch Gazebo

The florist can make a gazebo to fit the required dimensions and needs of a site and party theme. It can be stored for reuse by detaching the roof and storing the gazebo in sections.

Materials Needed

- Eight sturdy branches or tree limbs, each 7 to 8 feet tall

- Four large, sturdy pots or containers

- Quick-setting cement

- Waxed string or spool wire

- Moss

- Three to four bunches of birch branches

- Fresh flowers

- Sprengeri

- Ribbon

- Spray bar

Construction Steps

1. Cement four attractive and stable branches or tree limbs into four large containers. *(Figure 9.27a)*

2. Position the four upright branches at the site. Attach the four remaining large branches to create the horizontal roof line, allowing for overlap, and secure well with waxed string or spool wire. Bind moss into the string or wire to cover it. *(Figure 9.27b)*

3. Select branching twigs to complete the roof. Position the branched ends of the twigs onto the horizontal branches every 10 to 12 inches and secure with waxed string or spool wire (and moss to cover). Align the stem ends of the branches to angle upward and meet at the center of the roof. Securely fasten the stems together. *(Figure 9.27c)*

4. Decorate with flower clusters, sprengeri, and ribbons along the horizontal branches to form the base of the roof.

5. With wire, attach a floral design fashioned in a spray bar onto the joining point of the branches to form the top of the roof. *(Figure 9.27c)*

6. Enhance the pots with matching floral pieces or blooming potted plants of marguerite daisies.

Fountains and Pools

The bubbling, splashing sound of water is a compelling, delightful addition to a party event. Even the calm, reflective qualities of a quiet pool add a special touch.

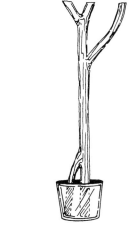

Figure 9.27a Constructing a Branch Gazebo Step 1

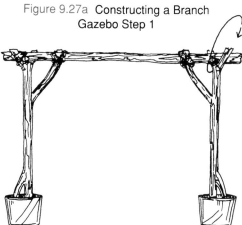

Figure 9.27b Constructing a Branch Gazebo Step 2

Figure 9.27c Constructing a Branch Gazebo Steps 3 & 5

Notes

To add a fountain to a party site, a lovely fountain statuary can be rented. These fountains cascade water into catch basins and then recirculate the water repeatedly for a lovely audible addition to a setting. An electrical outlet must be provided.

A fountain can be added to a pool by buying or renting a self-contained recycling pump. The pump should be immersed completely in the water and secured with rocks. The electrical cord must be carefully positioned and covered. The guests will enjoy the fountain effect and the splashing sounds.

Preformed Pool Water Feature

One method of adding a water feature on a site is to purchase, position, and design around a child's pool, a molded plastic form that holds water. Firms that supply water lilies and other water plants offer a wide array of pools in a variety of shapes in black or other muted colors. This pool will add a touch of the tropics to any party site.

Materials Needed

- Child's pool

- Black plastic liner (optional)

- Blue food coloring (optional)

- Potted plants - ferns, bromeliads, and orchids

- Floral foam

- Red ginger

- Heliconia

- Orchid flowers

Construction Steps

1. Purchase a preformed child's pool, selecting the appropriate size and color.

2. Place the pool in the desired location. If the pool's colors are distracting, plan to add blue food coloring to

the water or line the pool with a sheet of black plastic. Fold the black plastic ends up around the pool. *(Figure 9.28a)*

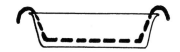

Figure 9.28a Constructing a Preformed Pool Water Feature Step 2

3. To mask the pool edges, surround the pool with a lush growth of plants and flowers, i.e., ferns, potted orchids, bromeliads, and floral designs of red ginger and heliconia. Fill the pool with water and float an orchid or two on the water's surface. Cover all containers and floral foam with moss. *(Figure 9.28b)*

Figure 9.28b Constructing a Preformed Pool Water Feature Step 3

Flexible Shaped Pool

Placing black plastic over floral foam and creating a water reservoir in the middle is an effective method of designing a pool of any shape and size.

Materials Needed

- Floral foam

- Hyacinth stakes

- Black plastic

- IGLU® Grande Cage

- Bags of stones

- Bird of paradise

- Red ginger

- Red ti leaves

- Croton foliage

- Umbrella papyrus

- Galax leaves

- Spanish moss

Figure 9.29a Constructing a Flexible Shaped Pool Step 1

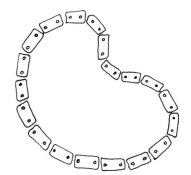

Figure 9.29b Constructing a Flexible Shaped Pool Step 2

Figure 9.29c Constructing a Flexible Shaped Pool Step 3

Figure 9.29d Constructing a Flexible Shaped Pool Step 5

Construction Steps

1. Position bricks of saturated floral foam in the outline of the desired shape and size of the pool. Anchor the foam with hyacinth stakes. **(Figure 9.29a)**

2. Lay a sheet of black plastic to cover the foam bricks. Tuck the plastic ends under the bricks, cutting off large excesses of plastic where necessary. **(Figure 9.29b)**

3. Poke the flower stems through the black plastic and into the foam underneath. Cut a small opening for individual flower stems with a knife, if necessary. **(Figure 9.29c)** Position groupings of birds of paradise and red ginger.

4. Design groupings of red ti leaves, croton foliage, and umbrella papyrus between the flower groupings. Design arrangements to completely cover the black plastic around the edges of the pool. Use Spanish moss and galax leaves to help cover the black plastic.

5. Place an IGLU® Grande Cage in the shallow pool just slightly off center and weight it with a couple of small plastic bags of stones. Design an "island" arrangement, repeating some of the perimeter flowers. **(Figure 9.29d)** Cover the mechanics with galax leaves. Do not use moss. Fill the pool.

Swimming Pools

A gala party event beside a pool has a special atmosphere, a special magic. Emphasize the pool with plants, floral designs, and floating pool decorations.

Live blooming and green plants make lovely decorations for around the pool. The plants should be grouped in large clusters at several poolside locations to add color and softness to the edges of the pool. Sparkly pin lights placed in the plants for a night event will add a special charm.

Pool Floats

A beautiful floating decoration in the pool can capture attention and captivate the party guests' imaginations. A pool float arrangement must have perfect balance and well-constructed mechanics to offer the best and most exciting illusion. Two types are frequently constructed: Styrofoam™ and acrylic.

Constructing a Styrofoam™ Pool Float

Styrofoam™ pool floats are constructed with a dense Styrofoam™ funeral wreath or a children's life preserver and a sheet of Styrofoam™. This type of float will support only a small amount of weight, approximately 15 pounds. However, variations will support 15 to 25 pounds. Following are instructions for constructing a Styrofoam™ pool float.

Materials Needed

- Two-inch sheet of Styrofoam™

- Child's life preserver ring

- Pan melt glue

- Design tray or utility container

- Waterproof tape

- Floral foam

- Fresh flowers and foliage

Construction Steps

1. Cut a piece of 2-inch sheet Styrofoam™ to fit over the top of a Styrofoam™ funeral wreath or a child's life preserver ring. (If the ring is 18 inches in diameter, cut out an 18-inch circle of foam.)

2. Attach the Styrofoam™ circle to the life preserver ring with pan melt glue. Be neat, but use plenty of glue to assure a good bond.

3. Attach a design tray to the center of the foam circle in the same manner. **(Figure 9.30a)**

4. Tape or glue soaked floral foam into the container.

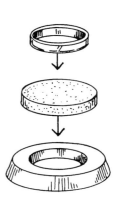

Figure 9.30a Constructing a Styrofoam™ Pool Float Step 3

Figure 9.30b Constructing a Styrofoam™ Pool Float Step 5

5. Create the desired arrangement, making sure to cover the exposed Styrofoam™ with flowers and foliage. Do not use foliage (sprengeri or asparagus fern, for example) or moss that will shed and make the pool look messy. Keep the design balanced during assembly. It is very important to test float the design in the floral shop before delivery! *(Figure 9.30b)*

Variations: To hold slightly heavier designs, make a pool float base, using either of the following methods.

- Sealing three 3-inch green Styrofoam™ sheets together with ample pan melt glue.

- Using a heavy foam, such as the type used for marine and insulation work. This commercial foam is available in 4-foot by 4-foot sections and is 4, 6, or 8 inches thick, which eliminates piecing and sealing thinner sheets together. Simply cut the sheet to size.

Constructing an Acrylic Pool Float

Acrylic pool floats are constructed with acrylic sheeting and bubbles. They can be designed to hold as much weight as desired and should be used as a rental item because of the cost of construction. Following are instructions for creating an acrylic pool float.

Materials Needed

- Three acrylic half bubbles

- One acrylic triangle, 3/8 inch thick

- Aquarium sealer

- Design tray or utility containers

- Pan melt glue

- Floral foam

- Waterproof tape

- Fresh flowers and foliage

Construction Steps

1. Have the following materials made by a plastics company.

   - Three 8-inch or 10-inch acrylic half bubbles with a 1-inch lip. This size bubble should support an arrangement weighing 35 to 65 pounds. Larger or smaller bubbles can be used, depending on the weight of the arrangement to be floated.

   - One piece of 3/8-inch acrylic sheeting cut into an equilateral triangle large enough to accommodate all three bubbles on its surface. Each of the three points of the triangle should have a hole drilled through it 3 inches from the edge. These will be used to anchor the float in the pool. All pieces should have their edges flamed for a smooth surface finish.

2. Seal the lips of the three half bubbles to one side of the triangle with clear aquarium sealer. Allow the sealer to dry for about 5 days. **(Figure 9.31a)**

3. Turn the float over and allow it to rest on the bubbles. Attach a design tray or a group of smaller trays to the triangle with pan melt glue or floral clay.

4. Secure the floral foam with tape or glue and create the arrangement. **(Figure 9.31b)**

5. Any type of structure can be created on this style float, as long as it is balanced.

Pool Float Installation

There are two methods used to secure a floating arrangement in a pool. The first method requires the florist to get into the pool.

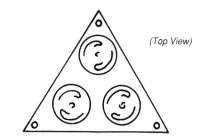

(Top View)

Figure 9.31a Constructing an Acrylic Pool Float Step 2

Figure 9.31b Constructing an Acrylic Pool Float Step 4

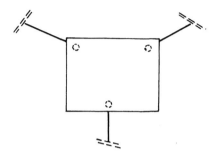

Figure 9.32a Constructing a Pool Float Installation, Method I Step 3

Figure 9.32b Constructing a Pool Float Installation, Method I Step 3

Figure 9.32c Constructing a Pool Float Installation, Method I Step 3

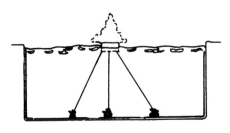

Figure 9.32d Constructing a Pool Float Installation, Method I Step 6

Although this may be an inconvenience, it is necessary when the anchoring lines must be out of sight or reach of the guests. The second method of installing a floating pool arrangement requires two people; however, neither person must get into the pool. Regardless of the method used, it is recommended that the pool filter be turned off to help stabilize the pool floats.

Method I

1. Fill a fine mesh bag with enough clear marbles to anchor the arrangement into position. For larger pool arrangements, paint concrete blocks the color of the bottom of the pool and use them for anchoring.

2. Tie the bag closed with nine pieces of 60-pound test fishing line measured to a length of about 1 foot longer than the depth of the pool.

3. Attach the nine pieces of fishing line to the float at three equidistant points. *(Figure 9.32a)* Three pieces of fishing line should be secured at each point by attaching the line to a 6-inch pick. From the underside of the Styrofoam™, thread the pick up through the Styrofoam™ and out the top. *(Figure 9.32b)* Then anchor the pick by inserting it diagonally into the top of the Styrofoam™. *(Figure 9.32c)*

4. Carefully place the pool float in the water with the anchor at the pool's edge.

5. Get in the pool and hold the anchor as the float is slowly pushed into the desired position.

6. Hold the fishing lines close to the top and release the anchor to the bottom of the pool. *(Figure 9.32d)*

Method II

1. Use 60-pound test fishing line in lengths that are 5 feet longer than the longest point across the pool. Use three lengths of line for each hole in the acrylic float or two lengths for the Styrofoam™ ring.

2. Attach the fishing line to the float at three equidistant points (either with wooden picks for the Styrofoam™ ring as described in Method I, Step 3, or by tying through the holes in the acrylic triangle).

3. Two people are required to complete the installation. Carefully place the pool float arrangement in the water from the side of the pool, while holding the lines. Pull the lines to position the arrangement.

4. Securely tie the lines to ladders, diving board supports, or any other fixed object that is secure and away from foot traffic around the pool. Alternatively, three concrete blocks can be wrapped with fabric or mylar and used as locations to tie down the pool float. These must be placed at the edge of the pool in three different locations. Potted plants will beautifully mask these blocks. *(Figure 9.33)*

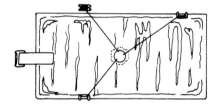

Figure 9.33 Pool Float Installation, Method II

Tent Decorations

Garden parties often include tents to provide protection from possible inclement weather. Tent rental companies prefer to se up the tents early, possibly on Thursday for a Friday night or Saturday event, due to staffing and timing considerations. The early setup is a positive aspect for the florist because this allows time to decorate the tent and allows the tented area to cool down.

Tent poles can be decorated with fabric festoons, balloons, or foliage garlands to create different looks. The poles can even be turned into large palm trees. The inner roof of the tent can be decorated with hanging plants or arrangements or covered with a layer of helium filled balloons. It is important to secure all hanging arrangements or plants with a #18 gauge taped wire to prevent them from falling if the wind begins to blow. When planning decorations for tent poles, the florist should contact the tent company to find out the diameter of the poles. Also, the use of fireproof or fire code approved materials is recommended when decorating a tent.

Festooning Tent Poles with Fabric

Fabric-covered tent poles help blend the hardware of the tent with the party atmosphere. Solid or print fabrics can be used to coordinate with the theme and/or color scheme of the party. The pole cover described here is easy to install and allows the fabric to be reused for other events.

Materials Needed

- Double-faced tape

- Fabric (one and one-half times pole length)

- Floral tape

- Number 18 gauge wire

Construction Steps

1. Apply strips of double-faced tape around the poles, beginning at the top and then at equal intervals, approximately every 2 feet. *(Figure 9.34a)*

2. Cut the fabric to a length about one and one-half times the length of the pole. (Plastic fabric that is fire code approved can be used to decorate a tent.)

3. Wrap the fabric around the top of the pole. Gather it evenly and secure it to the tape with a taped wire.

4. Pull up the fabric to create a puffy effect at the next taped location on the pole. Secure the fabric with a taped wire. Work in the same manner until the base of the pole is reached. *(Figure 9.34b)*

5. Finish the bottom with the balance of the fabric. Trim off any excess fabric to avoid having fabric lying on the ground.

<u>Attaching Garlands to Tent Poles</u>

Foliage garlands add a garden-like effect when wrapped around interior tent poles. The garlands may be spiralled like a barber pole or wrapped more thickly to cover the poles completely. Fresh flowers in water tubes may be tucked into the garlands for an added floral touch.

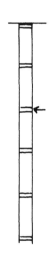

Figure 9.34a Festooning Tent Poles with Fabric Step 1

Figure 9.34b Festooning Tent Poles with Fabric Step 4

Materials Needed

- Foliage garland (smilax or self-made)

- Floral tape

- Number 18 gauge wire

Construction Steps

1. Securely attach the end of a smilax or self-made foliage garland to the top of the pole and cross frame, using a taped #18 gauge wire. Hide the point of attachment with a bow or similar treatment.

2. Wrap the garland around the pole to the base.

3. Attach the end of the garland to the base of the pole with another taped wire.

4. The length of the garland needed will depend on how closely together it will be wrapped. Generally, one and one-half times the length of the pole is sufficient for a barber pole effect. *(Figure 9.35a)* To fully wrap and cover a pole, a garland at least two times the length of the pole is needed. *(Figure 9.35b)*

Creating Palm Trees on Tent Poles

For tropical, beach, or safari party themes, palm trees are an appropriate room decoration. When the party is held under a tent, the tent poles can be enhanced to look like palm trees. Free-standing palm trees (as described in Chapter 5) can also be used to create a lush atmosphere.

Materials Needed

- Poly fiberfill

- Waxed string

- Paper ribbon

- Straight pins or raffia

Figure 9.35a Attaching Garlands to Tent Poles Step 4

Figure 9.35b Attaching Garlands to Tent Poles Step 4

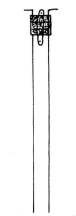

Figure 9.36b Creating a Palm Tree on a Tent Pole Step 2

Figure 9.36c Creating a Palm Tree on a Tent Pole Step 4

- One or two floral foam cages

- Moss

- One and one-half to three bunches of emerald fern

Construction Steps

1. Securely attach one or two floral foam cages to the top of the tent pole. Use the cross poles to help secure the cages in place so that they cannot slip down the pole. One cage is needed for a half or corner tree, and two cages are needed for an all around tree. *(Figure 9.36a)*

2. To create a trunk, wrap the poles from top to bottom with sheets of poly fiberfill from a fabric store. Use waxed string to secure the fiberfill in place. Then wrap natural-colored paper ribbon over the fiberfill. Straight pins or raffia may be used as needed to hold the paper ribbon in place. The overall effect should be that of a plump tree trunk. *(Figure 9.36b)*

3. Moss the floral foam cage to hide the mechanics.

4. Insert large fern or palm fronds (emerald fern works well) to create the treetop. The number of fronds needed will vary from thirty-five to seventy-five (one and one-half to three bunches), depending on the desired size of the tree. *(Figure 9.36c)*

Other Settings

While the majority of outdoor parties are staged in garden settings, some party themes dictate different uses of the outdoor environment. Following are suggested ways to enhance an outdoor setting for non-garden party themes.

Forest

Most guests would be surprised to walk through a forest entryway or to dine under a forest canopy at a party. A forest scene can be created on a small scale outside a home's front entrance, in a foyer, or on an outdoor patio area. It can be created on a large scale in a side lawn that opens onto a large back lawn area. Here, the forest may thin out somewhat, allowing guests to mingle and be seated.

Following are types of forests that could be created.

- All evergreens of various heights.

- A combination of evergreens and deciduous trees, either in leaf or with an open silhouette of branches.

- All deciduous trees, not in leaf, with a wildflower understory.

- A combination of deciduous trees with some in leaf, some in flower, and some not in leaf.

A simulated forest can be created by bringing cut trees or containerized trees to a site. Containerized trees will be heavier and may require more equipment plus wood chips for covering the containers. However, flowering trees should be handled only as container specimens for the lasting quality needed during a party. The weight of these trees should also be considered before placing any on an existing lawn or flooring.

The use of cut trees to create a forest is less labor intensive and more flexible. The challenge is to find a source of trees to cut and use for the party scene. Check with Christmas tree farms, nurseries, and garden centers. Trees that exhibit less than ideal shape are perfect for creating a forest and will be less expensive.

Figure 9.37a Creating a Forest Step 1

Creating a Forest

1. Locate the needed types and amounts of trees. Have the trees cut off with an even surface perpendicular to the trunk. Fashion stands of crossed 2-inch by 4-inch wooden posts and nail them to the cut ends of the trees. **(Figure 9.37a)**

2. When at the party site, position the trees and stabilize them with at least two sandbags placed on the stands. **(Figure 9.37b)**

Figure 9.37b Creating a Forest Step 2

Figure 9.37c Creating a Forest Step 3

3. Cover the stands and sandbags with natural burlap. Scatter pine needles, leaves, mosses, or wood chips across the burlap to soften it and provide a realistic forest floor appearance. *(Figure 9.37c)*

4. Additions to the forest scene could include a few wildflowers tucked in, fallen logs or stumps, recorded sounds of birds, a simulated stream with recorded splashing water sounds, and mosses and stones.

Light green and forest green tablecloths could be used. A woodland scene in a log, stump, or piece of driftwood can be fashioned for each table. Leaves, acorns, or mosses can be scattered near the centerpieces on each table.

Picnic

A fun theme for an outdoor party is a picnic theme. Quilts can be spread on the ground for a casual picnic lunch or they can be used as tablecloths or a combination of both styles can be used. Picnic tables covered with colorful quilts will be very appropriate.

A branch gazebo would provide a natural focal point. An old-fashioned picnic-in-the-park feeling can be created with a band in a bandstand. Period costumes for the band members and guests will add to the effect.

Picnic baskets overflowing with garden flowers should be positioned at the base of the gazebo. Flowers can be strewn on the path leading to the gazebo. Smaller baskets of mixed flowers can be placed on each tablecloth.

Games, such as horseshoes and croquet, can be provided. Attaching a small ribboned flower cluster to each croquet mallet and wicket is a good idea. Fashioning a ribbon net for a fun match of badminton would also be effective.

Farm Fun

Another party theme features farm fun and farm life. For the entryway, split-rail fencing and pots of garden flowers, such as marigolds, zinnias, petunias, and even sunflowers and corn, can be positioned. *(Figure 9.38)* A scarecrow seated upon a bale of straw will lead the eye and traffic flow to the serving tables. Repeat straw bales and sections of split-rail fencing throughout the party site.

Figure 9.38 Farm Fun Party Setting

Checked gingham cloth for a tablecloth or a runner in the center of the table would be ideal. Handkerchiefs of many colors could be used as napkins, while a ring of barbed wire could form the napkin ring.

Vegetables, fruits, and small pots of flowers might be grouped and placed on a layer of straw on each table and buffet table. Larger baskets filled with garden flowers and vegetables can be placed on the serving tables. A flat bed wagon would work well as a serving table.

There are countless ways to create decorations for parties in outdoor settings. Entrances and pathways are important areas to decorate in order to direct guests to the party site. Existing structures, such as gazebos, fences, fountains, and pools, are natural areas for floral accents. Instant gardens can be created to provide spatial definition and a feeling of enclosure within large outdoor areas. Tents, arches, and other rental structures can be decorated to enhance specific party themes. Tabletop decorations can range from simple to elaborate arrangements, but must be designed to withstand variable weather conditions.

Outdoor settings often provide greater decorating challenges due not only to weather factors, but also to limitations of electrical availability, uneven ground surfaces, lack of an overhead ceiling, and many others. Creative mechanics and structural engineering are often needed to design the desired floral enhancements. Advance planning and site analysis are the keys to successfully decorating outdoor party settings. When well prepared and carefully installed, outdoor party flowers are the perfect complement to nature's own beauty.

Outdoor Settings

Notes, Photographs, Sketches, etc.

Notes, Photographs, Sketches, etc.

Notes, Photographs, Sketches, etc.

Glossary

Balloon Drop - A special effect for parties in which multiple air inflated balloons are released from overhead and allowed to fall to the ground.

Balloon Release - A special effect for parties in which multiple helium-inflated balloons are released to rise into the atmosphere, typically outdoors.

Balloon Structures - Architectural objects made by attaching balloons together.

Bolt Cutters - Large wire cutters capable of cutting thick, heavy wire.

Canopy - An overhead covering, typically including four posts and a flat or peaked roof; used to bring attention to important areas within a party setting.

Ceiling Walkers - Helium balloons, which contain a light object, that float in the air.

Confetti Cannon - A specialty machine used at parties to shoot confetti into the room, creating a "ticker tape" parade effect.

Double Napkin - Two napkins, usually linen, decoratively folded, rolled, or tied together; one used for dinner, the other for dessert.

Escort Board - A decorative board diagramming the party floor plan with table numbers and seat assignments included. Used by formally attired escorts to locate seats for guests and escort them to their tables.

Foam Board (also called *Foam Centered Board*) - A lightweight board made of an extruded core of polystyrene with clay-coated paper bonded to both sides; frequently used to construct party props.

Favors - Token gifts given to party guests as mementos of an event.

Festoons - Fabric, ribbon, or other draping material gathered and swagged between or along posts, such as tent poles or staircase banisters.

Four Balloon Clusters - Four balloons tied together.

Garland - Air-filled balloons tied and wrapped to form a garland.

Grommet - A metal eyelet used on material to feed line through.

Integrated Buffet Table - A buffet table arrangement combining different table shapes and configurations.

Luminarias - Plain or decorative paper bags containing votive candles used to line driveways and sidewalks, creating a luminous pathway for party guests to follow.

Map Cards - Printed cards included with the party invitations to communicate to guests how to reach the party.

Monofilament - Fishing line.

Networking - Coordinating marketing efforts with professionals in related party businesses, such as caterers, bakers, and photographers.

Nipple - Plastic apparatus used to inflate balloons with either air or helium.

Opaque Projector - A machine that allows the user to project a picture or image onto another surface and simultaneously enlarge it so that it can be traced and reproduced accurately.

Oxidization - A natural process in which a latex balloon ages and dries out, causing a cloudy or powdery appearance on the surface of the balloon.

Paddle Balloon - A large balloon that is molded on a form shaped like a paddle.

Place Card Holder - Any of a variety of mechanisms designed to hold a place card; often decorative and sometimes incorporating a party favor.

Place Cards - Cards used to assign party guests to specific seats or tables.

Place Setting - The complete set of dishes, glasses, flatware, and linens displayed at each chair at a guest table.

Pool Float - A floral arrangement designed on a Styrofoam™ or acrylic base to float on water.

Response Card - Printed cards included with the party invitations requesting a response from the guests regarding acceptance or rejection of the invitation. A formal type of R.S.V.P.

Scissor Lift - A mechanical device that can be rented or purchased; it is intended to be used as an adjustable scaffold instead of a ladder.

Scoring - A technique in which one layer of paper and foam is cut through, leaving the second layer of paper intact; used to shape and bend foam board.

Shoji Screen - An Oriental-style divider with a wooden frame and paper or cotton muslin covering.

Space Enhancers - Free-standing screens, figures, or other props used to enhance or redefine the boundaries of a party setting.

Spiral Garland - A structure of balloons that have been tied to form a spiral, such as a barber pole.

Square Garland - Balloon structure that has been inflated and tied to form a square shape.

Stanchions - A set of upright posts to which ribbon, fabric, or roping is attached, creating a pathway or barrier.

Story Board - A board designed with a collage of party invitations, napkins, favors, ribbons, etc., as a means of presenting the colors, theme, and style of the party decor to a client during the selling process.

Subcontracting - Contracting jobs or projects out to specialty businesses, such as caterers, balloon artists, or lighting companies.

Taper - A tall, narrow candle, usually 8 inches tall or more and 1/4 to 1 inch in diameter.

Votive - A small, cylindrically-shaped candle, 2 1/2 to 3 inches tall, usually placed inside a glass cup rather than a candlestick.

Appendix A

Party Planner

GENERAL INFORMATION

Client _____

Billing Address _____

_____

Phone _____ Fax _____

Party Date _____ Time _____

Site _____

Consultant _____

Initial Consultation _____

2nd Consultation _____

Proposal Accepted _____

Contract Signed _____

Deposit Received _____

Balance Received _____

Address _____

Room Location _____

Caterer/Site Manager _____ Phone _____ Fax _____

Theme _____ Color Scheme _____

Number of Guests _____ Formality _____

Names of Main Function Rooms:

_____ Number of Guests _____

_____ Number of Guests _____

_____ Number of Guests _____

Number/Size/Shape of Tables _____ Number of Guests/Table _____

Head Table (yes/no?) _____ Number of Guests _____

Floral Style/Preferences _____

_____

FLORAL DECORATIONS

Table Centerpieces _____ $ _____

Sketch

Head Table _____ $ _____

Sketch

Food/Cocktail Tables _____ $ _____

Sketch

Entrance Decorations _____ $ _____

Sketch

$ [_____]

Room Decorations   PRICE

Walls _____ $ _____

Ceilings _____ _____

Stage _____ _____

Band Stand _____ _____

Dance Floor _____ _____

Bars _____ _____

Windows _____ _____

Chandeliers _____ _____

Mirrors _____

Additional Decorations $ _____

Rest Rooms _____ _____

Body Flowers for _____ _____

for _____ _____

for _____ _____

Tents _____ _____

Pool Floats _____ _____

_____

Other _____ _____

_____

_____

_____

$ _____

RENTAL ITEMS

Linens _____ $ _____

_____

Candelabra _____ _____

_____

Votives _____ _____

Mirrors _____ _____

Containers _____ _____

Plants _____ _____

_____

Props _____ _____

_____

_____

Other _____ _____

_____

$ _____

PRICE

Favors _____ $ [_____]

_____

_____

Special Effects _____ $ [_____]

_____

_____

PAYMENT INFORMATION

Subtotal	[_____]
Delivery Charge	$ _____
Installation Charge	_____
Removal Charge	_____
Tax	_____
TOTAL	[_____]
Deposit	$ _____
Balance Due	_____

Party Planners are available for purchase from
Redbook Florist Services.
1-800-643-0100

Party Site File

Site _____ Date _____

Address _____ Contact Person _____

_____ Phone _____ Ext. _____

Directions from Shop _____

Best Entryway or Loading Dock _____

Entry Restrictions _____ Fire Restrictions (Candles) _____

Lighting and Adjustability _____

Name(s) of Main Function Rooms: _____

_____ Maximum Number of Guests _____

_____ Maximum Number of Guests _____

_____ Maximum Number of Guests _____

_____ Maximum Number of Guests _____

_____ Maximum Number of Guests _____

Size/Shape of Dining Tables _____

Color of Carpeting _____ Colors of Walls _____

Color of Chairs _____ Color Selection of Linens _____

Special Areas of Decoration: _____

_____ Measurements _____

_____ Measurements _____

_____ Measurements _____

_____ Measurements _____

_____ Measurements _____

_____ Measurements _____

_____ Measurements _____

_____ Measurements _____

Event Site Checklist

Party Name:_____ Contact Person:_____

Location:_____ Phone Number: _____

Make a sketch of the room on the back of this sheet.

On the sketch, mark the following:
Entries, exits, windows, support pillars, band and dance floor locations,
location of electrical outlets (if applicable)

Make the Following Observations:

_____ Floor plan with measurement
including ceiling height

_____ Sizes/shapes of available tables

_____ Condition and colors of chairs

_____ Take photos of site, main rooms, etc.

_____ Present decoration colors

_____ Lighting and adjustability

_____ How to get there

_____ Best entry way or loading dock

_____ Electrical outlets

_____ Hills or valleys (if outdoors)

_____ Sources of water

_____ Available dollies/carts

Check the Following with Site Staff:

_____ Fire regulations

_____ Floral restrictions

_____ Entry restrictions

_____ Candle restrictions

_____ When area is available for
setup

_____ When props may/must be
picked up

_____ Events running concurrently

_____ Expected additional decorations
to site at event time

_____ Florist vehicle parking area

_____ Contact person at time of event

_____ Cleanup necessary

PARTY DELIVERY CHART

Vehicle #_____

Driver_____

Loading Time _____

Party Name _____ Party Date _____

Site _____ Contact Person _____

Address _____ Phone # _____ Site Phone # _____

Leave Shop Time _____ Party Room Access Time _____

Party Start Time _____ Best Entry to Site _____

Directions _____

Notes _____

Special Instructions _____

Party Finish Time _____ Pickups: Yes _____   No_____

Item to Load	Quantity	Loaded (✔)	Pickup (✔)	Done (✔)

Daily Event Schedule

Time	Procedure	Person Assigned
6:30 a.m.		
7:00		
7:30		
8:00		
8:30		
9:00		
9:30		
10:00		
10:30		
11:00		
11:30		
12:00 p.m.		
12:30		
1:00		
1:30		
2:00		
2:30		
3:00		
3:30		
4:00		
4:30		
5:00		
5:30		
6:00		
6:30		
7:00		
7:30		
8:00		
8:30		
9:00		
9:30		
10:00		
10:30		
11:00		
11:30		
12:00 a.m.		
12:30		
1:00		
1:30		
2:00		
2:30		
3:00		
3:30		
4:00		
4:30		
5:00		
5:30		
6:00		

Party Work Personnel Worksheet

Matching Key Employees with Specific Skills

SKILL/DUTY	EMPLOYEES		
	#1	#2	#3 or Trainee (T)
Selling			
Planning			
Design Work			
Designs			
Props			
Ordering			
Production			
Scheduling			
Site			
Staff			
Space			
Delivery			
Timing			

Designing Floral Props

Shop's Party Work Limitations	Strategy to Correct

Production Chart

Product _____ Party Name_____ Date _____

Design Segment	Order per Design	Other Items Needed	Construction Time	Shelf Life

PARTY PRODUCTION CALENDAR

Booking Date:	Party Name:		Party Date:
Segment of Party	Date to Order Parts	Date to Complete Segment	Done ✔

Party Purchasing Form

Party Name_____ Date _____

Flower	Variety/Color	Supplier	Quantity	Date Ordered	Date to Receive

Supply	Specifications	Supplier	Quantity	Date Ordered	Date to Receive

Prop Inventory Form

Prop _____ # in Stock _____ Storage Location _____

Party Name	Party Date	Site Location	Delivery Date/Time	Pickup Date/Time	Done ✔

Prop Resources

DISPLAY HOUSES:

Corman and Associates, Inc.
881 Floyd Drive
Lexington, Kentucky 40505
(606) 233-0544

David Sloan Creations, Inc.
Airport Industrial Office Park, Bldg. A-6
Valley Stream, New York 11581
(516) 561-1060

David Hamberger Inc.
410 Hicks St.
Brooklyn, New York 11201
(718) 852-7101

Garrison-Wagner, Co.
2020 Delmar
St. Louis, Missouri 63103
(800) 441-1819

Niedermaier Display Inc.
2828 N. Paulina Street
Chicago, Illinois 60657
(312) 528-8123

Prop Exchange, Inc.
451-A Broome Street
New York, New York 10013
(212) 274-1917

Robelan Display Inc.
395 Westbury Blvd.
Hempstead, New York 11550
(516) 564-8600

Superior Specialties, Inc.
2525 N. Cassaloma Drive
Appleton, Wisconsin 54915
(800) 666-2545

Susan Crane, Inc.
8107 Chancellor Row
Dallas, Texas 75247
(214) 631-6490

Trimco Corporation of America
459 West 15th Street
New York, New York
(212) 989-1616

TRADE JOURNAL:

Special Events
Miramar Publishing Company
6133 Bristol Parkway
Culver City, California 90230
(310) 337-9717

PROFESSIONAL ORGANIZATION:

International Special Events Society
8606 Allisonville Road, Suite 210
Indianapolis, Indiana 46250
(800) 344-4737

Appendix B

Subcontracting Agreement

This Contract and Agreement is made and entered into by and between
_____ , hereinafter called "Florist" and
_____ , hereinafter called "Subcontractor"
for services which will be rendered on _____
for _____ . The services to be rendered by
Subcontractor are as follows:

_____
_____
_____
_____
_____
_____
_____
_____
_____
_____
_____

For the performance of this service, Florist will pay Subcontractor the sum of $ _____.
A deposit of $ _____ equalling _____ % of the total price has been made to Subcontractor
by Florist on this day, leaving a balance due of $ _____ , which amount shall be paid by
Florist no later than ten (10) days after the even date stated above. In the event of a
cancellation of the need of services of Subcontractor described above, Subcontractor shall
retain the deposit as payment in full, and Florist shall have no further liability under this
Contract.

If Subcontractor requires services of other parties to complete the services specified above,
said services shall be the sole responsibility of Subcontractor and Subcontractor shall hold
Florist harmless from any claims asserted by said parties. The relationship of the parties hereto
shall be that of independent contractors and not that of principal/agent or employer/employee.

EXECUTED this _____ day of _____ , 19 _____ .

_____   _____
Florist   Subcontractor

By: _____   By: _____
Authorized Signature   Authorized Signature

Party Contract

This Contract and Agreement is made and entered into by and between _____

_____ , hereinafter called "Florist," and _____ ,

hereinafter called "Client," for services which will be rendered on _____

for _____ . The services to be rendered by Florist are as follows:

_____

_____

_____

_____

_____

For the performance of this service, Client will pay Florist the sum of $ _____

equalling _____ percent of the total price, thirty (30) days prior to the event, leaving a

balance of $ _____ , which is due two (2) weeks prior to the day of the event. In the

event of cancellation of the need for services, Florist shall retain the deposit as payment in full,

and Florist shall have no further liability under this Contract.

If Client requires services of other parties to complete the services specified above, said

services shall be the sole responsibility of Client and Client shall hold Florist harmless from any

claims asserted by said parties. The relationship of the parties hereto shall be that of

independent contractors and not that of principal/agent or employer/employee.

Executed this _____ day of _____ , 19 _____ .

_____   _____
        Florist   Client

By: _____   By: _____
      Authorized Signature   Authorized Signature

Contract Inclusions

Additions of Goods or Services:

Additional floral decorations, rental items, etc., may be added no later than _____ days prior to the function date. All additions after this date will incur an additional expense of _____ percent over the agreed amount.

Extension of Services:

Any extension of services to the outlined schedule of services will be considered as overtime and will be billed at a rate of $ _____ per hour, or any part hour thereof.

Payments:

A deposit representing _____ percent of the anticipated total cost will be due thirty (30) days in advance of the function. The remaining balance will be due two (2) weeks prior to the date of the event. Any final adjustments or additional expenses will be invoiced after the event and due no later than _____ days after receipt. Unpaid invoices will be charged interest at a rate of _____ percent per month after that time.

Taxes:

Local laws and state laws require sales tax be charged on all items and services provided. If client is tax exempt, a tax presentation letter must be returned with this Contract.

Indemnity:

_____ (client) agrees to indemnity and holds _____ (florist), its agents and employees harmless against any claims, demands, actions, judgements, settlements, damages, cost or expenses including, but not limited to, reasonable attorney's fees and disbursements for injury to or death of persons or damage to property arising out of or resulting from negligence or failure to comply with the other provisions as stated in this agreement. Additionally, it is understood that _____ (florist) has no responsibility for products or services as provided by others as noted in this Contract, or otherwise contracted by _____ (client) directly.

Cancellation:

It is understood that in the event of cancellation, client recognizes that _____ (florist) will be entitled to incur damages as a result. The following liquidated damage schedule shall apply: If _____ (client), for any reason whatsoever and at any time, cancels the event, deposit as enclosed with Contract will be retained by _____ (florist) as payment in full. However, full payment will be due and payable by _____ (client) for cancellation for any reason whatsoever, within twenty-four (24) hours of the event.

RENTAL CONTRACT

This Contract is made and entered into by and between _____,
hereinafter called "Florist" and _____, hereinafter called "Customer" for the rental of
certain equipment as listed on Exhibit "A" attached hereto and made a part hereof. Said equipment shall
be

(√) _____ picked up by Customer on _____,

(√) _____ delivered by Florist on _____,

and shall be

(√) _____ returned by Customer on _____.

(√) _____ retrieved by Florist on _____.

In the event the equipment is not returned on the date stated above, Customer shall pay an additional
rental charge of $ _____ per day to Florist. A deposit of $ _____ is required and must be paid before
pickup or delivery. This deposit is refundable in full upon the return in good condition of each piece of
equipment and upon payment in full of all rental charges. At the time of pickup or delivery, the equipment
has been inspected by Customer and is in the following condition: _____
_____
_____
_____.

A cleaning fee of $ _____ per item of equipment will be charged if the equipment is returned without
having been properly cleaned.

Customer shall pay the value of any missing equipment as listed on Exhibit "A." If any equipment
is damaged, Customer shall pay the cost of repair or the difference in value of the equipment in its
damaged condition, whichever is a lesser amount.

Executed this _____ day of _____, 19 ___.

Florist _____   Customer Signature _____

By: _____

Date: _____   Customer
                                              Address: _____
                                              Phone: (_____) _____
                                              Date: _____

Exhibit A to Rental Contract

Equipment/Supplies: **Value:**

_____ $ _____

_____ $ _____

_____ $ _____

_____ $ _____

_____ $ _____

_____ $ _____

_____ $ _____

_____ $ _____

_____ $ _____

_____ $ _____

_____ $ _____

_____ $ _____

_____ $ _____

_____ $ _____

_____ $ _____

_____ $ _____

_____ $ _____

_____ $ _____

_____   _____
          Florist   Customer

By: _____   By: _____
      Authorized Signature   Authorized Signature

Date: _____   Date: _____

Appendix C

INVITATIONS

Come celebrate with us
the 50th Birthday of
Barbara Baker
Saturday, November 20th
at 7:30 in the evening at
Southgate Country Club
1010 North Southgate
Little Rock, Ark

Gifts optional

ENVELOPE SEALS AND LINED ENVELOPES

2540 Anytown
Your City, State 01234

Response Cards and Map Cards

Please respond on or before

August 22, 1992

M _____

Number of persons _____

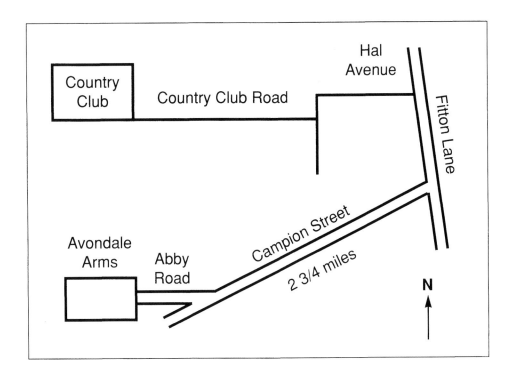

Thank You Notes and Place Cards

Menu or Program

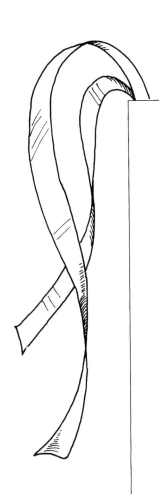

President's Dinner

May 4, 1990

Grand Plaza

Ball Room

Matches, Coasters, and Napkins

Appendix D

Patterns for Foam Board Figures

Patterns for Foam Board Figures

Patterns for Foam Board Figures

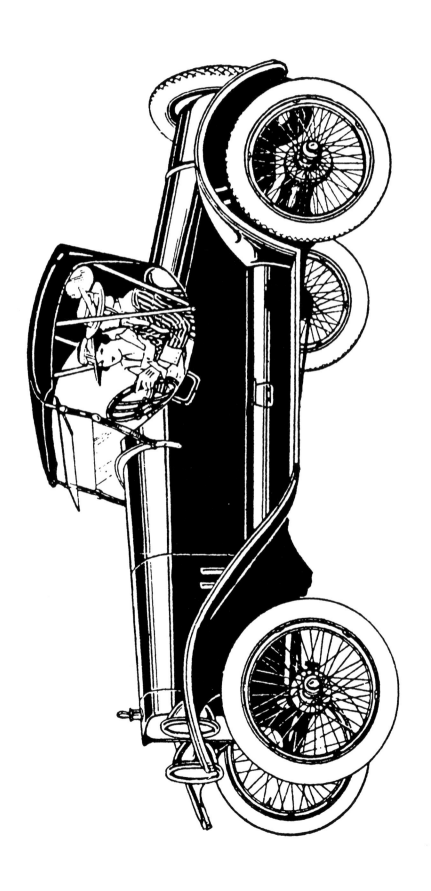

Patterns for Foam Board Figures

Patterns for Foam Board Figures

Patterns for Foam Board Figures

Patterns for Foam Board Figures

Patterns for Foam Board Figures

Patterns for Foam Board Figures

Patterns for Foam Board Figures

Patterns for Foam Board Figures

Patterns for Foam Board Figures

Patterns for Foam Board Figures

Appendix E

Buffet Table Serving Patterns

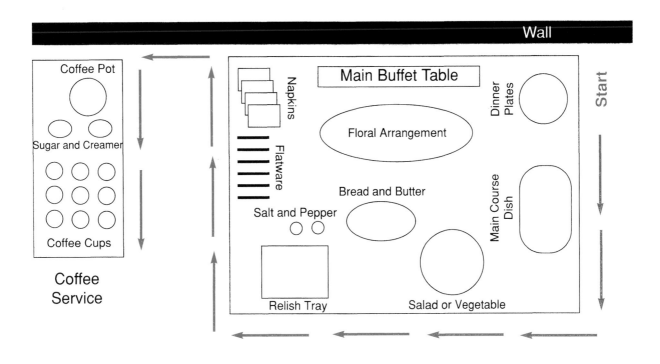

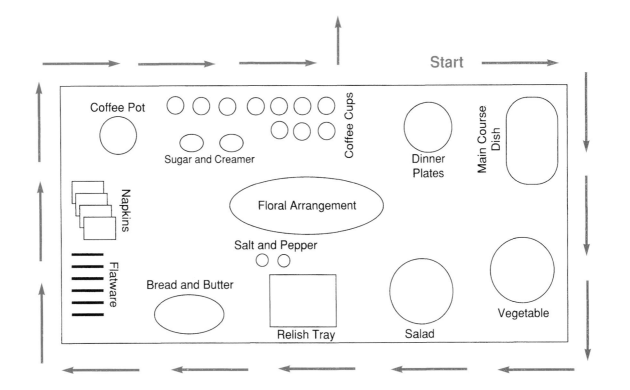

Flatware

Top Row - Left to Right:

Knife for fruit or cheese

Luncheon Knives

Dinner Knife

2 Teaspoons

Soup Spoon

Dessert Fork

Salad Fork

2 Dinner Forks

Iced Tea Spoon

Second Row:

2 Serving Spoons for Vegetables

Ladle for Gravy or Sauces

Nut Spoon

Jelly Spoon

Third Row:

Cake Knife

Two Types of Salt Spoons

2 Butter Knives for Serving Plate

2 Butter Knives for Place Settings

Small Dinner Fork for Children

Small Knife for Children

Small Teaspoon for Children

Sugar Cube Tongs

Fourth Row:

Fork for Condiments

2 Types of Jelly Spoons

Fork and Spoon for a Small Child

Iced Tea Spoon

Pickle and Relish Forks

PLACE SETTINGS

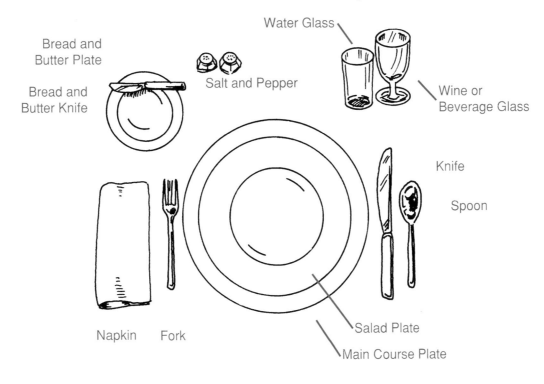

Casual Place Setting

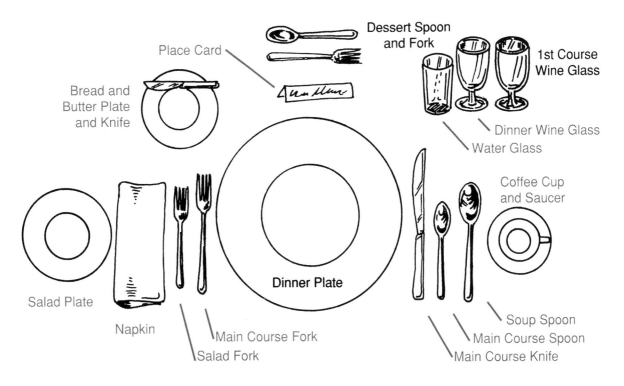

Formal Place Setting

Tableware, Glasses, and Stemware

Tableware - Left to Right:

Dinner Plate

Salad Plate

Bread and Butter Plate

Cup and Saucer

Stemware - Left to Right:

Champagne Flute

Wine Goblet

Water Goblet

American Wedding Champagne Glass

Second Row:

After Dinner Cordial Glass

Tumbler

Candle Types

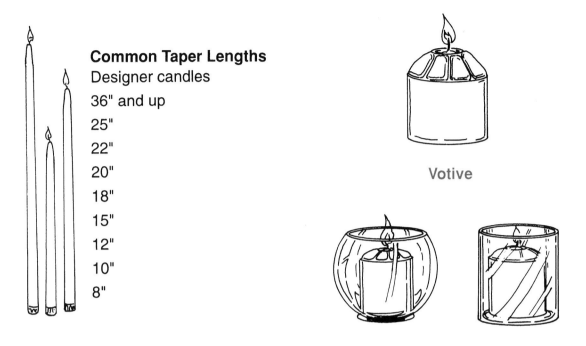

Common Taper Lengths
Designer candles
36" and up
25"
22"
20"
18"
15"
12"
10"
8"

Tapers

Votive

Examples of Common Votive Holders

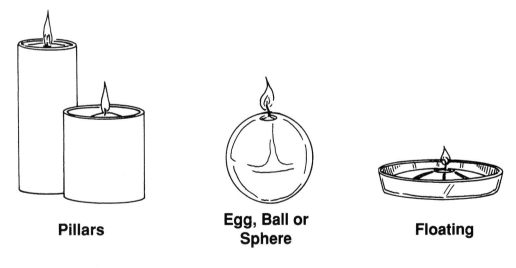

Pillars

Egg, Ball or Sphere

Floating

Decorative Variations

Bibliography

Calvert, Catherine. <u>Having Tea</u>. New York, New York: Clarkson N. Potter, Inc., Crown Publishers, Inc., 1986.

Church, Beverly Reese and Bethany Ewald Bultman. <u>The Joys of Entertaining</u>. New York, New York: Abbeville Press, 1987.

Cornell, Jane. <u>The Art of Table Decoration</u>. New York, New York: Warner Books, Inc., 1980.

Decorator Series booklets, Wichita, Kansas: Pioneer Balloon Company.

Galatte, Nick. Interview, June, 1991. The Flower Cart, Chicago, Illinois.

"Jane Packer Method of Arrangement." <u>Florists' Review</u>, June, 1991, 27-35.

Kemp, Jim. <u>Dining in Style</u>. New York, New York: Sterling Publishing Co., Inc., 1986.

Loring, John. <u>Tiffany Parties</u>. New York, New York: Doubleday, a division of Bantam Doubleday Dell Publishing Group, Inc., 1989.

Moretz, Jim. "Table Guide." <u>Florists' Review</u>, March, 1991, 67-68.

Neff, Rena. <u>Napkin Magic</u>. Gaitherburg, Maryland: The American Cooking Guild, 1990.

Paine, Melanie. <u>Fabric Magic</u>. New York, New York: Pantheon Books, 1987.

Porterfield, Frances. Hot Display. Lansing, Michigan: John Henry Company, 1986.

Porterfield, Frances. "Poolside Parties." Flowers &, September, 1981, 18-19, 95-97.

Stewart, Martha. Entertaining. New York, New York: Clarkson N. Potter, Inc. Crown Publishers, Inc., 1982.

Stewart, Martha. Hors d'Oeuvres. New York, New York: Clarkson N. Potter, Inc. Crown Publishers, Inc., 1984.

Stewart, Martha. Weddings. New York, New York: Clarkson N. Potter, Inc. Crown Publishers, Inc., 1987.

"Summer Projects." Florists' Review, Volume 179, No. 6, 44-46.

Thoma, Migg. Advent Wreath. Augsburger Straße 82, D-8870 Gunzburg: Appel-Druck Donau-Verlag GmbH, 1987.

Turner, Kenneth. Flower Style. New York, New York: Weidenfeld and Nicolson, 1989.

Index

Index